IS THAT ALL THERE IS?

An American Story

Donn Wallace

ISBN: 0692296751
ISBN 13: 9780692296752
Library of Congress Control Number: 2014916856
CreateSpace Independent Publishing Platform
North Charleston, South Carolina

PRAISE FOR IS THAT ALL THERE IS

"I finished the book at four in the AM... found the writing voice very enjoyable and was very interested in the information on what was going on in the world when Hank was living 'his' life... also, a nice job of providing a historical armature for the protagonist's life to play out on. I was sorry to have it stop where it did."
— Susan, Published Mystery Novel Author, Florida

"This book may be controversial and provocative, but it challenges conventional wisdom and could be useful to the reader in doing so. We should all step back from our usual sources of information and opinions from time to time and question whether there are alternative ways of viewing the world around us that could give us different insights and help us understand better the perspectives of others."
— Ron, Finance Executive, Massachusetts

"An intriguing story about a bright, inquisitive, small town boy venturing out to find his American Dream. Ride with Hank, the main character, on Route 66 and during the fun, experience Hollywood's most memorable places. This book is a thought provoking, provocative collection of real life prejudice, family issues, and corruption. It questions the moral fabric of a power seeking American political system utilizing media to influence public opinion. A must read for anyone interested in removing indoctrinated political blinders and as a result, develop insight and a new voice in an ever-changing world."

- Dennis, Real Estate Broker, California

"An enjoyable read for the story, as well as for the thought provoking content of political and economic history. It is a refreshing break from the traditional talking points commonly used to explain our current situation, giving the reader a new perspective to view history. Using a small town guy from "fly over" America makes it easy for people to relate to and grasp concepts which are often dry, particularly to my generation."

- Brett, "Millennial" Doctor of Chiropractic. North Carolina

"Is That All There Is? brilliantly illustrates what makes success in spite of what hampers it. This book will inspire you to revisit the crossroads of your own life and draw useful insights for what's to come. Don't miss it!"

-Steve, Certified Public Accountant, Colorado

IS THAT ALL THERE IS?

For Linda
without whom this book
could not have been written

PREFACE

In 1969, soulful sounding blues singer Peggy Lee recorded a song based on the 1898 short story *"Disillusionment"* by Nobel Prize winning German author Thomas Mann. The story is an existentialist examination of experiencing and overcoming events of despair and disillusionment to achieve fulfillment and meaning in life.

The essence of existentialism is that mere existence – make of it what you might – takes precedence over everything else; that life is what it is, and that is reality. The freedom of the individual to act, and to be responsible for his actions, is the primary source of whatever events and results thereof encompass him in the course of his life.

In the story, the narrator is unburdened with life's tribulations when he sees the ocean for the first time and envisages an unobstructed future for himself. In the song, the singer's solution to her disappointments is to, seemingly reluctantly, *"keep on dancing,"* a euphemism for continuing with life, rather than giving up on it.

Different solutions in different times by different individuals with different culturally imbued views, but in each the individual does what each of us must do to be successful: accept what life hands to us, deal with it the best we can and move on.

The name of the song *"Is That All There Is?"* connotes something is missing from each life experience and, surely, there should have been more to it, for if that is all there is, disappointment and disillusionment will be the end result of experiences... of life.

Although it is truth that achievement of fulfillment in life is solely the responsibility of the individual, and he is responsible for his actions, it is not true he "is the primary source of whatever events and results thereof may encompass him in the course of his life."

This essence of existentialism overlooks much that affects individual lives. Although some have privileged backgrounds affording a view of life likely always "unobstructed," for most "the reality" is quite different. Other factors are "the primary source" of "events and results" that encompass us during our lives.

Time and circumstance are key determinants of the course of our lives over which we have no control. We are but foundlings of both. They determine when, where and to whom we are born, and thus are important cultural factors weighing heavily upon our lives.

The majority of us are small, inconsequential beings fighting each day to stay afloat in a world increasingly less friendly and more difficult to cope with.

The Vietnam War, officially in its fifth year at the time of the recording, was sufficient cause for feelings of "despair and disillusionment" among those of military draft age, their families and others, and set the mental stage for the success of *"Is That All There Is?"*

Now, over four decades later, our circumstances are worse. We are at war for no discernible reasons, economy is in decline, government out of control, taking our rights away and diminishing our future. "The reality" is; we have lost ground... economically, ethically and morally as a nation, and that has adversely affected us individually.

As a result, we must ask; when... under what circumstances... did our outlook change from Ronald Reagan's *"shining city on a hill"* and our implicitly bright future to wondering where did it go, who took it away, how did they do it and what can, or will, *"we the people"* do to recoup it? Is that even possible, or Is That All There Is?

The following story is the recounting of one individual's experiences that provide perspective to the changes "America" has experienced from 1940 to the present.

PART I
THE YEARS
JANUARY 1940 THRU MAY 1964

CHAPTER 1

PARADISE FOUND AND LOST

Winston S. Churchill in *The Second World War* Vol. I Preface stated he *"hangs the chronicle and discussion... upon the thread of the personal experiences of an individual."*

Thus, that being good enough for Winston Churchill and seemingly a good method for recounting our story, we begin with our individual *"thread,"* Hank, twenty-three years and three months after his unspooling under less than auspicious circumstances on a cold dark Colorado morning in January 1940 when clouds of war were looming on two continents.

We have named our *"thread"* Hank in tribute to the prescience of Ayn Rand who foretold in her 1957 novel *Atlas Shrugged*, through its hero Hank Rearden, much of what would happen in America's future that our Hank, only one generation removed from Ms. Rand's hero, has been witness to and personally affected by.

⟫⟪

1963. Hollywood, California, Good Friday morning, April 12, early in the first decade of the nascent "Sexual Revolution" that commenced after government approval of "the Pill" oral contraception for women in 1960, giving them sexual freedom equality with men and thus, the freedom to pursue their desires without physical or life altering consequences.

We open this book at this time because it seemed, at the time, to be the apex, a major turning point from perceived unobstructed future to disillusionment in the short life of our Hank, a member of the "*common herd*" population of "*fly over*" Middle America.

Having overcome, in less than four years, dire financial and personally created, pre "Sexual Revolution" adversity with little perceptible opportunity, and "experiencing and overcoming events of despair and disillusionment," he reached a point where, like Mann in his short story, he was beginning to "envisage an unobstructed future" for himself wherein he could "achieve fulfillment and meaning in life" when that future was suddenly taken away and his mental state reduced to "despair and disillusionment" again through actions by forces beyond his control, thus proving the assertion "the freedom of the individual to act, and to be responsible for his actions, is the primary source of whatever events and results thereof encompass him in the course of his life" is manifestly untrue.

Ironically, this morning was also a short seven months and ten days before the event that would also be the apex of the relatively short life of America… an event that would eventually be recognized as the turning point when its bright future was suddenly clouded, and although unknown to its people at the time, their mental state would eventually be reduced to "despair and disillusionment" by these same forces, further disproving the theory that the individual is the primary source of whatever encompasses him in the course of his life, as well as having significant import upon the life of our "*thread.*"

"*Hello*"

"*I'm ready. When are you going to come get me?*"

Heidi was her name, and *"God! She is beautiful,"* Hank thought. Without makeup, she looked as if she just stepped off the cover of Vogue. Tall, at least five seven, with svelte model's body, long, straight, brown hair. No editing required, at least not to his young, somewhat deprived eyes and experience. Then there was the German accent.

He wasn't dreaming. It really was Hollywood. Really! Sun, palm trees, beautiful people, decent job, small studio apartment – one room that served as living and bedroom, plus a kitchen and bathroom, in an inappropriately named "garden"... because it had a few plants in the entry courtyard... apartment building at 7323 Willoughby Avenue. A couple of blocks west of La Brea, it was conveniently located close to almost everything a young man could desire.

There was even Poinsettia Park with tennis courts and other amenities for exercise and games in the rear, and one apartment building removed to the west. The good life, the much better life Hank was seeking when he left home. A relative paradise... *"best of all possible worlds,"* as Voltaire stated in his *"Candide"* in 1759. And, now this, or more appropriately; her, the woman of every young man's dreams in the place of dreams where one would expect to find her. But it was all about to end.

"A relative paradise"? Yes!

We would need to have been there, where he was just over a year before, to fully comprehend why he would think this.

⇥⇤

His first view of Grand Prairie was not actually of the place, itself, but of where it was supposed to be located on the vast, flat, seemingly interminable plain that stretched westward into the sunset.

About ten miles west of downtown Dallas, Texas on old U.S. Highway 80 is a place called Chalk Hill. It is at this point where the road begins a rather precipitous, at least to a six year old, descent that it is possible to look out over the beginning of the West Texas plains that stretch to El Paso about six hundred miles to the west.

The press is that Fort Worth is where the "West begins," but the cultural wasteland that is West Texas actually begins at the west bank, or we should say, as it is called locally, dike of the Trinity River just west of downtown Dallas, and is interrupted only by the small area west of downtown Fort Worth known as the museum district. Other than that small area in Fort Worth, there is nothing, even to this day, for anyone to make a trip to West Texas for unless they are in either the cattle or oil "*bidness.*"

Grand Prairie could have easily been a capital of part of this wasteland if any of the denizens of the place possessed enough knowledge to have recognized it as a wasteland, not just because of geographic location, but also because of the cultural aridness of the place. But one funny, peculiar thing about people is they know only what they know.

Whereas today, because of the availability of information, it is necessary to indoctrinate people to have them believe what is desired, rather than what is true, back then, plus or minus sixty-five years ago, information depravation accomplished much the same result.

The people did not know much about what was available or happening elsewhere, or what they were missing out on they would have been either happy to be missing, or would have felt deprived of if they had known about it.

The local newspapers, the Grand Prairie Banner and two Dallas papers, the Dallas Morning News and the Dallas Times Herald, were what most people read, as opposed to the Wall Street Journal or The New York Times.

They got all the information they needed, and more, from these, and few had any extra money to invest or really cared much about what was going on in the rest of the world because, as far as they knew, it had very little effect on them. They not only had little interest, they had little need for information about anything that had little perceived effect on their lives.

Television was not available until 1949, and besides Howdy Doody and Roller Derby, the only offering other than the test pattern occupying the screen twenty hours of each day was college football. Of these, only college football had any influence, and that was in the form of group gatherings in front of the televisions of those lucky enough, or "rich" enough to own one.

New York! Where the Hell was that other than in the movies?

It would be ten years post his Grand Prairie life before Hank would learn the extent of a somewhat mutual lack of knowledge and concern between those in Grand Prairie, other places like it, and those who reside in the stone canyons of New York City.

At that time he was assigned accommodations with a stranger, a 'born and bred' New Yorker who expressed disdain, without apology, for anyone unfortunate enough not to share his heritage.

This roommate, astonishingly, adamantly stated he had no interest in, or anything *"in common"* with anyone from *"west of the Hudson River,"* including the attractive gentile blond from Kansas with whom he had a date one evening, but said he was intending to cancel for his afore stated reasons of perceived geographic and heritage incompatibility.

Given the knowledge the one he was speaking to was also from *"west of the Hudson River,"* this statement rather arrogantly established a disdainful attitude his new roommate would subsequently learn is shared by many New Yorkers.

However, most people residing *"west of the Hudson River,"* especially west of the Mississippi River, because of so much media exposure to the real New York and its denizens… not the movie version, probably have much less interest in all things New York and its residents than this roommate still has in the rest of America.

In fact, years later, based on actions and further comments on the subject, some directed toward him personally, Hank was provided a better understanding of what his roommate really meant, which had very little to do with geography. Without doubt, *"west of the Hudson*

River" referred to the vast majority of Americans who did not share his heritage.

Having subsequently become a member of the Council on Foreign Relations and thus, by definition, a supporter of One World Government and other such un-American New York centered ideas, the roommate, in addition to having little interest in the great geographic middle of America and its residents referred to in New York as *"fly over country,"* may also be among those desiring to disenfranchise those they only *"fly over."*

But are demographics so vastly different as those between Grand Prairie and New York important? Yes, by definition. Hank was "raised" in Grand Prairie. His roommate grew up in New York. Amazing how the imbuing of us in our formative years affects us, isn't it?

Given the state of world affairs, influenced by many residing in the environs of New York, and their demonstrated political proclivities, wouldn't we all, most of the world, be much better off had more of us been "raised" in Grand Prairie or one of the other places in the vast expanse of middle America, or at least *"west of the Hudson River"* where we were culturally deprived, but received a good grounding in solid conservative, democratic American values of the kind that made America great, like working, and taking care of our own business, rather than interfering in that of everyone else on the planet?

Possibly being "raised," as is corn, is better than just "growing up." Being "raised" suggests some nurturing and direction during the important growing season, whereas just "growing up" is what weeds do. You know. Weeds just go wherever they want, without any order or direction, and they intrude upon the turf of all of the other non-weed plants as well as fighting other weeds for space. But corn, like the other "raised" plants, grows in neat, orderly rows with the weeds kept out until the time the one "raising" it determines it is time to harvest.

This concept would seem to the organized mind to be a better process than what the weeds have. At least it produces a better, more viable product.

However, Grand Prairie, this little place where Hank was raised and spent sixteen of the most recently passed seventeen years of his young, barely twenty-three years of life was a whole basket of sandwiches short of being a picnic in paradise.

Grand Prairie, Texas, just a couple of miles short of midway between Dallas and Fort Worth had no claim to fame, unless the whistle stop of Harry S. Truman's train in 1948 would count. But, scratch that. He didn't stop; although he did wave.

Hank was standing outside his father's grocery store at the intersection of 10th Street and Jefferson Boulevard, across the highway from the east to west tracks that divide the town when the train came through that afternoon. Harry was standing on the rear platform with a few people. It was just like in the movies.

Harry was facing toward him, waving. He had to be waving to Hank, unless he was waving to those he could not see, all three of them, inside the store. There was no one else in his direction for Harry to be waving to, and other than the store, there wasn't much for him to see except the field of weeds and the rows of little eight hundred square foot, box-like houses behind the store that were built… or more appropriately, "thrown up" quickly, during WWII to house the workers for the North American Aviation "defense" plant that resided about a half mile to the east of where he was standing.

In fact, not only did Grand Prairie not have a claim to fame, it had no discernible reason to exist except provide shade and shelter in the form of the little houses, many within walking distance of the plant, for the thousands of workers who labored producing airplanes needed for the war that ended just three years before, and were still working there producing planes for the next war they were not then aware would be upon them in the short time of a couple of years.

But maybe these comments are not entirely fair to Grand Prairie. It did have, still does, a main street, sensibly named "Main Street," consisting of about two blocks of buildings that obviously predate WWII by at least two decades; and for three or four blocks to the

north are some houses of the same era. There were none immediately to the south because the businesses on the south side of Main
Street back up to the railroad, or railroads.

There were two tracks, one for west bound and one for east bound
trains, eliminating the need to stop, indicating people where the
trains were going, or coming from, had no need for whatever Grand
Prairie had. Also, there were not a sufficient number of people residing in Grand Prairie for the trains to need to stop to deliver anything.

Two tracks enabled trains to speed through town without having
to stop to let another train pass should two of them have the misfortune of getting there at the same time.

Still most obviously concurred with the assessment of lack of reason for existence from the beginning. If not, there would have been
more people residing there before the war generated jobs brought
them there.

It was not like the benefits of Grand Prairie were hidden. As previously described, it was about halfway between Fort Worth and Dallas,
right there on the railroad tracks about midway between the East and
West Coasts of the whole damn country. And Main Street was actually
the afore mentioned Hwy 80 that was the main vehicle thoroughfare
of the time, east to west, coast to coast, across the southern United
States. Everyone could see it!

There were a few more old houses, dating from the beginning of
the century, to the south of the railroad(s). Actually, they were to the
south of the highway that was south of the railroads, the one Harry
looked across to wave.

This highway was also Highway 80, Jefferson Boulevard, the 80
bypass, or was it Main Street that was the 80 bypass? Don't know, but
it is interesting there were two four lane highways and two railroads,
side by side, passing through the middle of town – a swath of land
wider than an Interstate Freeway right of way. So, obviously, even the
original plan was for fast transit through the town - not for taking in
the non-extant scenery.

In fact, these two highways and the railroads were the most prominent man-made features of the town, which is pretty important, giv-
en there were not any non-man-made features on the prairie upon
which Grand Prairie was, seemingly, surreptitiously placed.

To get to Grand Prairie from Dallas via Highway 80, after de-
scending Chalk Hill one must pass through a couple of miles of
bottom lands. This is an area that is low and swampy, and frequently floods when the Trinity River overflows its flood control
dikes.

The water makes the land spongy and virtually unbuildable. It
was what most considered waste land, until self-made and self-pro-
moting, Dallas millionaire O.L. Nelms, determined in the middle of
the 20th century it should not go to waste… completely.

The nature of the land that made it cheap and its proximity to a
predominately blue collar population combined to make it a desirable location for some types of businesses.

Mr. Nelms correctly determined businesses not requiring a lot
of start-up costs, and almost immune to damage from the flood-
ing, could provide attractions to the surrounding, predominately
blue-collar population, and turn a few bucks of profit. Things like
a quarter mile of asphalt and a metal roof covered boardwalk.

Therefore, after Mr. Nelms "development" of this previously barren area in 1954, those approaching the eastern entrance to Grand
Prairie had the pleasure of passing the Yellow Belly Drag Strip on the
right, so named because of the unique, sharp left hand curve at the
end of the strip necessitated by a lack of sufficient land for a real drag
strip that dictated less than NHRA quarter mile speeds or very quick
deceleration, across the highway, the Farmers Market and farther to
the west; the occasional, lack of mud permitting, religious tent revival
meetings where some enterprising minister would "coattail" Nelms'
success by holding a "healing" revival.

There were also, always, at least two of Nelms' ubiquitous, forty
foot freight trailers painted bright white and emblazoned in bright

red on each side with "Thanks to All of You for Helping O.L. Nelms Make Another Million."

After passing through this "scenic" development, it was necessary to make a decision that was really of very little consequence. There was a fork in the road. The left went to the south version of Highway 80 and the right to the Main Street thoroughfare. The left was open, inviting road, except for the junk yard. The right required passing under that dominant "architectural" feature of the town, the railroad.

Both took the unwary traveler through the middle of Grand Prairie and on to the flat, straight sections of asphalt on the west side of town, toward Fort Worth. So, the decision did not matter unless, rather than passing through town, one desired to access a business on the road not taken.

Again the railroad. After making the right or left choice there was not a railroad crossing for at least two miles or more. In fact, places to cross the tracks in Grand Prairie were about as limited as everything else.

The first one the traveler would encounter after making the right or left decision was in front of the north end of the runway of the Dallas Naval Air Station, conveniently almost right against the southernmost highway, less than a couple hundred feet south of the tracks.

That's right; the Navy at least two hundred miles from the nearest ocean. Don't ask. It is a government facility resulting from the decisions of government employees.

To the west side of the air strip was the North American Aviation plant that employed most of the residents of Grand Prairie and was a half mile east of Hank's father's store.

The next crossing was at Fourteenth Street that was the western boundary of the plant. The next was at Eighth Street, less than a half mile to the west. Then, there was one at Fifth Street, one in the middle of town and one to the west of downtown.

For some reason the railroad was elevated above the surrounding land for several miles from the decision bridge, where it was elevated to permit the highway to pass beneath it, to the west side of down-town where it came back down to the level ground, or the ground rose up to meet it. Hank could never understand why, given the flat-ness of the land.

He considered maybe the land's eastward down slope was greater than perceptible to the eye, requiring filling the road bed to make it easier for westward bound trains to maintain their speed through town. But the elevation of the railroad made the tracks more prom-inent than they would have otherwise been, and made navigating them more difficult.

If one were unlucky enough to be desirous of crossing the tracks from south to north when a train was passing through, and be stuck between the south highway and the tracks on the upgrade to the tracks, hopefully, that person would not be an inexperienced driver or a beginner driving a stick shift. The clutch is tricky on a slope.

Trains passing through town caused a traffic problem. Northbound traffic, other than the two cars that would fit on the upgrade between the south highway and the tracks, was stuck on the south side of the highway, causing a traffic pile up until the train passed. Ditto; on the north side, except since Main Street was a few yards farther to the north of the tracks than the southern highway was to the south, the situation was not as bad.

Frequently two trains did meet in town. And several times, over the years, drivers unaware of the double tracks, or not paying atten-tion, met their demise attempting to cross the tracks after the train they were aware of passed, only to be nailed by the train going the other direction, something RR crossing gates at every crossing could have prevented.

Thus, the tracks did much more than divide the town. The real problem of the tracks other than their negative aesthetic prominence and dominance was safety. Whether one was from the "right" or the "wrong" side was not nearly as important.

At the intersection of Highway 80 and... are you ready?... "Center Street," which bisected Main Street's two "main" blocks containing the old buildings and providing access across the railroad in the center of town, there was an old, two-story, red brick building on the southeast corner.

This building had a faded logo on it indicating it was the "Interurban" building that was once the headquarters of that long before failed enterprise.

The Interurban was the mass transit, really a street car system, in the early part of the twentieth century that provided transportation between Dallas and Fort Worth to those who did not have auto transportation. Ergo, inter urban, or between the urban areas.

Given the railroads running smack through the middle of the town, why the Interurban rail based transportation system?

As previously stated, the trains didn't have any reason to stop in Grand Prairie.

Still, one would think demand for rail transportation between Dallas and Fort Worth, especially the downtown areas where both the main Interurban and railroad terminals were located, would have been satisfied by the railroad.

People could get on the train and go from one city to the other really fast, judging from the speed at which the trains whizzed through the town.

That would, however, have overlooked the small number of people who actually chose to live in Grand Prairie and those other two or three small towns and suburbs between Dallas and Fort Worth who did not possess an auto and desired to go into one of the cities to work, or at night where they could hear something other than the trains, or the crickets.

The Interurban tracks were in the center of the southern section of Highway 80 just like the tracks of the streetcars, or trams, in cities until they were removed years before. This probably explained the homes on the south side of the railroad tracks in Grand Prairie.

Those living there desired to be suburban Grand Prairie residents, but did not want to have to cross the tracks of the fast moving trains that killed several residents of the town during Hank's time there just to go to Dallas or Fort Worth.

The Interurban proved, even before WWII, there were some people who desired to reside outside the hustle and bustle of the cities. On the other hand, its short life proved there were not sufficient numbers of them to make catering to their transportation needs a long term economically viable proposition.

There just were not sufficient numbers of people desiring to live in Grand Prairie or the other places on the cultural desert of a prairie between Dallas and Fort Worth who needed or desired public transportation.

<hr />

Clearly, Grand Prairie had very little, if any, reason to exist before the North American Aviation Plant needed bodies that needed work to build the planes needed in the war.

Need. That was it. Not desire, but need. Few people desired to live in Grand Prairie, but because of the war provided jobs, thousands needed to. Thus, the thousands of little, "shade and shelter" box houses located to the east, southeast and southwest of the town's old core of two blocks and the few blocks of old houses surrounding it.

Again, not to be unfair to Grand Prairie, most people in most small towns across America although probably not cognizant of the fact and rationalizations aside, are where they are because they need to be there... not because they desire to be where they are.

They are there for security and safety; to obtain the basic needs of shelter, health and well-being, and financial and personal security provided by the jobs available in places like Grand Prairie. They are not there to reach higher, to achieve or substantially better themselves. For that, people have to be dissatisfied with the status quo of their lives, to dream, to desire to reach for higher goals, to satisfy something more than their basic needs ... and for that, they must leave places like Grand Prairie behind.

Most of the people in Grand Prairie needed to live there and were probably circumstantially destined to continue doing so, but surely, many, or at least a few, desired to live elsewhere where their dreams and desires could be satisfied... if they could just make the break.

Nearby Dallas or Fort Worth would satisfy these goals for many, but both were too close, too familiar, to provide the psychological and physical break needed for the perceived independence and freedom to permit the desired full self-actualization required by many... Hank included.

Places more distant, less familiar, like "Hollywood" or other places they "read" about in the glossy print magazines, or saw in the movies where they would be able to realize whatever potential they believed they possessed, but was stifled by the lack of opportunities in the small towns were more beckoning.

Thus he didn't need to live in Hollywood, but he needed to get out of Grand Prairie.

He was not willing to accept what he experienced there and the limited upside potential he could see was all there was for him. He was certain there was much more out there for him...somewhere, and Hollywood was just fine. He had more knowledge of it than anywhere else he had not been, thanks to the movies and the glossy magazines, and thank god for the right side of the coin, there he was.

CHAPTER 2

"THE END OF THE BEGINNING"

Hank had known for years, at least since he was sixteen, he wanted...desired to leave. No! "Get out." That's so much more appropriate.

People don't say they are going to "leave" prison. They say they are going to "get out.".... get out of confinement, not leave it. So, "get out" is a much more appropriate term for describing his departing the confines of Grand Prairie. "Leave" did not do the act justice. Besides, as they say in Texas, "leave" has a *"whole nother"* meaning.

In the military, "leave" means a short term respite from the drudgery of military life. To be gone, or away, is to be on "leave" from what you are involved in for a while. But it is understood you will be returning after a short period of reprieve from what amounted to, at least before the all-volunteer mercenary military, involuntary confinement.

Therefore, since he never considered the idea of returning to Grand Prairie, or even to Texas, once he left, "leave" was an absolutely, grossly inappropriate term for what he desired to do to Grand Prairie... and Texas.

He did not, however, have what most would consider a justifiable need to get out. His needs were well satisfied all his life, thanks to his father. It was just that he was dissatisfied with life there to the extent he was needy... "needy" in terms of being psychologically and intellectually unsatisfied by the environment of Grand Prairie, the Dallas/Fort Worth area and the whole Texas scene. He did not see any upside for him there.

Unlike most, he was not constrained by cultural inertia; the fear of leaving one's cultural comfort zone of familiar religion, speech... even geography that has held most of his classmates within fifty miles of where they grew up, will probably continue to do so for the rest of their lives, and causes them to desire to return whenever they are away for any length of time. As one friend once said to him, *"We don't know how good we have it here until we go to someplace like New York or London."*

Well, New York and London would not have been at the top of his list of most desirable places to reside, but... the thought of returning to Grand Prairie, Dallas, or Texas never played a role in his thoughts about what the future might hold for him. He was just interested in getting out and doing something with his life. He was absolutely certain there was much more out there for him, somewhere. Maybe even in New York or London. He was not willing to impose any geographical or cultural limitations on his future.

After a year in Los Angeles, he had definitely broken free of any little bit of cultural inertia that could have, very unlikely, been hiding deep within his relatively unused grey matter, and was certain he had found that "much more" in a place that offered a bright, seemingly unlimited future over which he could exercise some control, and for the first time in a long time, if ever, he was enjoying life and optimistic about his future.

But now all of that was about to be taken away. He was no longer going to be responsible for, or in control of, his own destiny, to the extent any of us are.

⇥⇤

In 1944, prior to the Allied invasion of France, Churchill is reported to have broadcast to the British people "*Now, this is not the end. It is not even the beginning of the end, but it is, perhaps the end of the beginning.*"

Churchill was speaking optimistically because he knew what was about to happen that he thought would provide a brighter future for him and his people. He was not in control of his destiny or that of the British people, not of the outcome, but at least he was in control of what he and they were about to do. He knew.

But Hank was not in control of his destiny, nor did he have any idea what was about to happen to him. He did not know. All he could do at that time was hope that in spite of what was about to happen, which was a great, frightening unknown, there would still be a long, bright future for him, somewhere.....somehow, sometime.

Hopefully, this was not about to be the end of the beginning of what seemed would be a great life, nor the beginning of the end. That was difficult to contemplate.

That Good Friday morning 1963, just three months past his twenty-third birthday, he was in bed unusually late. He did not have to go to work because it was Good Friday. He was just lying there contemplating what was about to happen, or could happen to him.

He was about to experience the fourth major change in his young life, and it was frightening.

The other changes he experienced were not as frightening because, although they resulted in lifestyle changes, they were not unknowns. He knew what was going to happen. He was familiar with the results of the changes and they would not have taken him into unknown circumstances or to some unknown place. Although he had not experienced all of them himself, everything about them was familiar to him.

But in this case, he was not sure what was in store for him. He knew it was the end of what he thought was the beginning of a desirable life, or the *"end of the beginning,"* as Churchill stated almost two decades earlier, and the beginning of something, but what? Where?

The only real knowledge he had of this change was he was about to lose his freedom.

It was definitely going to be the end of the beginning of his new life away from his beginnings in Texas, and the end of his short sojourn in paradise. But it was also to be the beginning of something else. It was the end of something he was very happy with, which did not make him happy, but it was also the beginning of something else. He knew not what, and it was the not knowing... the uncertainty of what was to come... that was troubling him.

At least Churchill knew what he was talking about. He knew what was next: the invasion of the European continent by the Allies he rightfully assumed would be the end of *"the beginning"* of the war for his country, which included the bombing of Britain by the Germans and the resultant death and destruction that would, hopefully, be stopped by the massive allied invasion of the continent.

Churchill knew or, at least, was hopeful what he was talking about would be the end of the recent bad times for the British people, even if not necessarily the beginning of good times.

Don't take this comparison wrongly. Hank was not thinking the impact of what was about to happen to him, whatever it was to be, could compare to major events and loss of life in WWII... the loss of his good life to the cessation of the destruction and loss of life in Britain, or what was to happen to him to the invasion of Normandy. He was just contemplating the conceptual difference between knowing and being in control of one's future, versus not knowing and having zero control over it, or for that matter his life in what had been for the last year or so shaping up to look like another time of war.

What happened to the British people was beyond their control. It was wrought by decisions of those in a government hundreds of miles to the east and their own, and as a result of those decisions and actions they were being forced to take actions for which, at least ostensibly, there seemed to be no possible alternative.

For half a decade, their lives and their future were under the control of others, first indirectly the German Government and then directly, their own government.

Now, Hank's life, literally the greatest part of which was under the control of others... parents and teachers, was about to revert from what he thought was the beginning of a life under his own direction to being directly under the control of the U.S Government.

⟞⟝ ⟞⟝

It is amazing how much our lives are subject to the whims of those able to gain control of the tiller of the ship of state and, as a result, over the lives of everyone in the country and possibly millions of lives in other countries. Yet, most never give as much thought to this important subject as they should, especially when they vote, considering the nature of the kind of people who seek the power control of government brings with it.

The U.S. government previously directly interfered in Hank's life when his father was drafted after the U.S. unnecessarily entered WWII.

That incursion completely disrupted his family's lives and changed the course of their future. But, thankfully, his father and mother and he were lucky. The war ended before his father was shipped out to the South Pacific.

The decision of Harry Truman probably saved his father's life and resulted in different lives for him, Hank and his mother than they would have experienced if not for that.

But could he also be so lucky as to have the also unnecessary incursion of the U.S. military into Southeast Asia end before someone in a position with the power to do so could send him to die in a rice paddy or jungle in Vietnam for no benefit to anyone?

He did not know. Was it the end of his life as he had contemplated it? Could it actually be the beginning of the end of his short life? He did not know which it might be. But Churchill's ambiguity aside, there was a much simpler old adage about "ends" that he most definitely thought applied to what was imminently about to happen in his life that seems to have been a theme of it and the lives of many others since prior to this event to the present: *"Every time I get both ends to meet, somebody moves one of the ends."*

✦✦

By April 1963 Hank was certain his life was in such a good state he could truthfully say his opinion was; he had gotten *"both ends to meet."* But, like his father eighteen years before, with his pretty wife, young son, thriving little business and new little house in Oak Cliff, just as he reached that state, the U.S. Government stepped in to unnecessarily *"move one of the ends,"* and that was the end of his good life and what could have been.

He was so engrossed in thoughts about all this while listening to the symphony of his stomach he completely forgot about Heidi. That is how serious the subject matter was.

He had gone to lunch with her the day before. Somehow, during their somewhat strained conversation... she had not been in the states long, her English was less than fluent and his understanding of German was nil... making meaningless small talk just to be talking with her, he broached the subject of what she was going to do the Easter weekend.

In response, because it was now obvious she did not have any plans for the weekend, rather than answering the question, she asked what he planned to do.

He had not even thought about it. Thus, he did not have any plans. But for some reason said he was thinking about going to Las Vegas, he had never been, and as a throw- away line, uttered the words, *"Would you like to go?"* Then he dropped the subject.

He never thought, in his wildest dreams, she would take him seriously or would even consider going, but there she was calling... asking when he was going to come get her. *"Jesus!"* he said to himself, *"Never...in my wildest dreams."*

CHAPTER 3
FAST TRACK IN SLOW LANE TO NOWHERE

E aster weekend 1963 was just about twelve months after Hank's arrival in Los Angeles, settling in "Hollywood," getting a job and beginning his new life.

Before arriving…. even before leaving Grand Prairie… he had no expectations about what he would find "out there"… also no reservations, or fears.

He had the self-confidence provided by a decent education and his father's oft stated confidence in him, as well as life experiences in excess of those of most twenty-two year olds that caused him to feel confident he would be just fine almost anywhere. Thus he was not concerned about not "making it" anywhere. Nor was he concerned about being alone, not having companionship or friends. But what he was not contemplating was any kind of serious relationship, especially one he would consider a long term possibility.

Until Heidi that was not part of his getting out of Grand Prairie plans that were exacerbated as a result of a relationship he thought only a couple of years before would be long term. But everything about Los Angeles in 1962 was like nothing he could have expected... even if he had expectations.

Before beginning the trip that landed him in Los Angeles, he had been as far east as the great metropolis of Longview, Texas about 150 miles to the east of where he spent the prior 16 years, to the south as far as Galveston, about 260 miles, to El Paso 600 miles to the west, and to Tacoma, Washington. Let's face it: his geographic and cultural experience was not particularly broad or diverse.

None of these "travels" were anything to prepare him for Los Angeles. For that matter, neither was Dallas or Fort Worth. He wanted change. Boy! Did he get it?

Except for the Dallas/Fort Worth Turnpike that had spanned the plus or minus thirty miles between the two cities for less than five years, he had never seen the likes of the interstate highway system and freeways that would span the nation, divide and encircle the cities of America a couple of decades later, until he arrived at the outskirts of Los Angeles.

Thanks to President Ike Eisenhower and his plans for a vast interstate highway system to facilitate the movement of military equipment and materiel that was begun during his first term in the presidency in the mid-1950s to protect the nation in the event of war, the ease, safety and speed of traversing the country has been greatly enhanced.

Ike's WWII logistical problems in the 1944/45 European winter were responsible for his facilitating travel throughout most of the U.S. But in 1962 and for at least a decade after that, traversing the country relatively easily, fast and safely was, at best, problematic, as it was without much improvement for the prior four decades.

To travel any distance meant traveling on the meager two lanes of asphalt that connected towns and cities, and going slowly thru traffic and stop lights of every town or city encountered because the highway it was necessary to travel was usually the main business street of every small town and city encountered on the trip.

Thus, traveling was not fast, easy, or safe. Nor was it very pleasurable for most, since they did not possess autos with air conditioning to relieve the summer heat or provide well circulated warm air during winter trips.

Heaters under the dashboard did little to warm whoever might be in the rear seat, and air conditioned autos were not commonplace until the mid-1960s or later, depending on whether one could afford that extra luxury.

Presumably it was the discomfort and general unpleasantness of traveling the highways that could be blamed, at least in part, for his lack of having been very far from home.

Those having never experienced the "pleasure" of driving a couple of hundred miles during the Texas summer heat at sixty miles per hour with the windows down and the hot air blowing through the car because to attempt to do so with the windows up would have resulted in death from suffocation, cannot fully understand why we risked our lives to the possibility of head on collisions or encountering a deer or cow at fifty-five or sixty miles per hour by traveling at night. But that was the way it was.

Not to belabor the point, but traveling at night was really, truly dangerous. The fact of less traffic and more pleasant temperatures providing more pleasurable travel was accompanied by the equivalent of highway Russian Roulette.

Much of the country, especially in large parts of eastern Texas, was "open range," a seemingly stupid holdover from times past wherein ranchers had the right to let their cattle roam anywhere – eliminating the restrictions on grazing and the cost of fences. Thus, the critters were frequently encountered on the highways.

The real danger of this was proven by the fact of the parents of one of Hank's classmates in the eleventh grade hitting a cow in their big Cadillac, and the parents of a friend of his father doing the same thing on the way back home from one of his high school's out of town football games. In both cases, both parents were killed.

There were rarely ever four lane highways outside towns and cities. Therefore, passing lanes were a rarity and when they were provided, it was frequently as a third lane. So, whether they were provided, or not, since they were shared by traffic going in both directions, did not ameliorate the risk of encountering an oncoming vehicle in your lane.

Occasionally there were slowly moving vehicles to be passed by those impatient to get where they were going more quickly. Since the highways were built with cost savings in mind, minimal cutting out of earth was done to reduce hills. The result was a lot of passing on hills by those less astute. This resulted in each hill being a guessing game of whether someone with insufficient intellect and judgment to decide when to safely "pull the trigger" of passing on a hill was going to be coming over a hill in your lane.

This was a frightening consideration if one considered the intellect evidenced by the observable conduct of the average person driving vehicles.

Surely, limiting the issuance of driver's licenses via I.Q. tests being included in the requisites would have reduced the carnage. But that is another matter, as is, thankfully, the fact that the poor highways were not as conducive to moving freight on them as is our subsequently enhanced interstate highway system.

Had we to contend with the large number of trucks taking advantage of Ike's system as are doing so today, we would have traveled even less than we did. But given Hank's lack of "travel" experience it is doubtful any of these enhancements could have served to broaden his experience.

The reason this is true is most of his travel "experiences" prior to his trip to Los Angeles, if we should call them that, took place when he was five years old, or younger.

He was in Cheyenne, Wyoming when he was three. But that was while he was living in Fort Collins, CO, less than fifty miles from

Cheyenne. So it wasn't much of a journey. And he did not even get to see the rodeo his father took him there to see because he fell on a broken Coke bottle when he was getting out of the car. Thus, his only remembrance of that trip is the faint scar on his left knee.

He was born in Greeley, Colorado that cold January morning, and that is less than 20 miles from Fort Collins from which he was moved to Houston, Texas when he was three. But he does have fond memories of the vacation trip to Greely and Fort Collins from Grand Prairie his father took him on when he was thirteen to show him where he was born, where they lived and introduce him to the doctor who delivered him. This was his first memorable "travel" experience

He lived in Houston for a year after leaving Colorado. After that, he probably went to Houston only a couple of times in sixteen years to visit relatives, and visited the beach at Galveston only once, but that was it.

His memories of Houston are of the garage apartment where he lived, its floor plan, triple garages below, vacant corner lot next door, the house on the other side, a terrible storm one night, the evening blackouts because it was during World War II and, most importantly, going downstairs with his father after dinner to sit in front of the garage and talk with him while he had his after dinner cigarette. However, these are also little memories of a three year old that did not provide experience to compare with new times and places nineteen years later.

Thus, given his age during most of this travel and the different places visited or lived, he obviously did not have many memories of it that could provide any comparative "travel experience." There are not many memories for a three or four year old traveling in a car, but the trips to Tacoma, El Paso and Longview... well, those were memorable.

The Tacoma experience could not be compared to Los Angeles, since he was only five at the time, and the trip was not via highway, thus not comparable to his travel in 1962. But it was memorable for him, anyway.

In 1945 his father was stationed at Fort Hood, Texas for Basic Training and for a while after that training. It was just another of those things, those variations that are so different from our everyday lives that seem to stick with us no matter what our age at the time of the occurrence.

Fort Hood is near San Antonio, only a six hour drive from Greenville, Texas where his mother and he were living with her mother on a dead end gravel road, inappropriately named Speedway Street, since his father was drafted.

Due to its proximity, they were able to drive there to visit him. Nothing interesting on that trip... then or today, and he has only a couple of memories of Fort Hood.

But unlike their visit to Tacoma, Washington later in the year, they were able to stay in on-base "housing," which was a small trailer of which there were many comprising a whole village.

These trailers were so close to where the soldiers trained it was possible to see and hear them marching and calling cadence. But he probably would not have remembered this part if not for the new experience of it.

The army picked up the trash from the trailer park, and everything was close together, so it was possible to hear almost everything, including the trash men talking.

He had never heard anything like it. They were speaking German. His father told him they were German prisoners of war captured in Europe and brought to the U.S. to be useful. (Presumably everyone used prisoners of war for work, even the U.S.)

Those were the first non-English speakers he encountered, except for Mexicans, prior to arriving in Los Angeles. But since, he encountered more Germans in California than any nationality other than Mexicans, causing him to wonder if prisoners were permitted to stay after the war. German scientists were brought to the U.S. for its missile program, so, why not?

After Fort Hood, his father was transferred to Fort Lewis Washington, a big military base near Tacoma that was a departure point for soldiers being sent to the Pacific war against Japan.

It was believed he was there to be shipped out to the South Pacific, and Hank's mother wanted to see him before he left for a long period, if not forever, given what was going on in the war in the Pacific.

The trip to Tacoma was traveled via train. It was a more than two thousand mile trip without a compartment, sitting in a padded bench-like seat for three days with a view out the window on the left side of the train, facing toward the front.

The train was long, and Hank and his mother were far enough back that there was a lot of train in front of them. So when it went around a curve to the left, he could see the long line of olive drab colored cars curving in front of him and the big black steam engine pouring a huge cloud of thick black smoke out of its stack that was still fairly thick when it reached where they were seated.

⊨ ⊨

While in Tacoma he had a highway experience unlike any other he experienced before, or after, until Los Angeles. And one he could never forget.

It was night time in a car of someone his father knew. His father was in the front passenger seat, and he and his mother were in the back with him in the seat on the right, behind his father.

Suddenly, as these things always happen, a big motorcycle pulled onto the highway from the right side, his side of the car, right in front of them.

There was no time to stop. The car hit the motorcycle hard, broadside without even time to decrease its speed very much. The driver's head went through the windshield and he was seriously injured. The two guys on the motorcycle were killed instantly. His father, having seen the motorcycle, was apparently able to brace himself. He was not injured. He just had a piece of glass in his shoe. Hank and his mother were tossed around but also not injured.

He would say many years later that his being only five years old at the time, most would say he could not remember this. But given his ability to remember his dog and the stream behind his house when he was three, and other memories between the ages of three and five, he could assure them had they been in an accident like that one, the impact and aftermath with the police and ambulances, the flashing lights, the injured guy in the car and the rest of it, even if not in possession of great recall abilities, this would be indelibly imprinted in their memory because they survived it.

This and his other memory of Tacoma in 1945, although not contributive to the reason for this little side trip there, is meaningful in some way to every other American over the age of seventy, no matter where they were that day.

He and his mother were staying in a hotel in downtown Tacoma close enough to Fort Lewis for his father to visit on his weekend passes. Thus, they were there, on the streets, on August 14, 1945, VJ Day, Victory over Japan Day, when the cessation of hostilities with Japan was announced by President Truman.

This was a very big deal manifest in a lot of people in the streets, a lot of noise; horns honking and sirens, people hugging and kissing, and crying with joy. His father came to visit, and it was only then they knew he was not going to be sent to the war in the Pacific.

Years later his father told him just how big the day was for him, personally. He was already assigned his departure day, was packed and ready to get on the ship, and was not informed until earlier that day he would not be going to the war in the Pacific.

That day and the news were also very big for the entire country. Happiness and change of attitudes about the future were prevalent

31

everywhere. The despair and disillusionment of the previous four years of war were swept away immediately.

A burden was lifted off the people, permitting them to feel, as Mann described; unburdened when he saw the ocean for the first time and envisaged an unobstructed future for himself.

It was as though the people no longer burdened by war and its consequences could again take control of their lives and endeavor to achieve whatever they desired to bring fulfillment and meaning to them.

The travel back to Texas was boring for Hank. Having done the three day train trip previously, fairly recently, and most likely, like all children, able to sleep through almost anything that does not interest them, he slept most of the return trip.

⊷⊱⊰⊶

His next travel recollection was about six months later, in 1946. Like many memories, it is the different or change events, places or people meaningful in our lives we remember. This memory is meaningful because it was his first sight of where he would spend the next sixteen years of his life. Well, not really.

It was just his first view from Chalk Hill of that "interminable plain" upon which his father assured him; Grand Prairie was just a short distance *"out there"*... somewhere... as he pointed directly ahead, through the glare of the afternoon sun on the windshield of the little Ford pickup for Hank who was squeezed between his father and his pregnant mother in its tight quarters with the long, floor mounted gear shift lever between his legs.

Then, eight years later, after he was fourteen, he began to drive that same Highway 80 back up Chalk Hill to Dallas by himself, and his father and he occasionally drove the seventy miles east of Dallas to his father's old family farm at Shirley, Texas near Sulphur Springs that he purchased in 1949.

Other than that there was not much travel after the 1953 trip north to Colorado except for very few trips to visit family in east Texas or Houston until 1961 when he drove 'all the way' to Longview in east Texas on business for a job working for a patio construction and home improvement company where he was, amazingly, quickly promoted to be in charge of the shop and field crews at the age of barely twenty-one.

One of the salesmen sold a large redwood and fiberglass, multi-curved patio cover to be built across the back of the large home of a retired oilman in Longview, and although he normally took care of project inspection and planning, because of its size and cost, his boss, the owner of the company, decided to go with him to check it out.

He preferred the comfort of his big new Oldsmobile convertible to Hank's little Ford Falcon station wagon, so they went in his car.

Apparently he was out late the night before because he did not want to drive. But he failed to ask about Hank's previous night. He should have. Before they got to Longview he fell asleep at over sixty miles per hour.

The rumbling of the gravel on the shoulder of the road woke both of them... fortunately, Hank first. His boss was not happy with the situation he awoke to, but no problem. No damage to the new Olds. They made it safely to Longview, and took care of their business. But the boss drove back to the Dallas office where they began that morning.

This initial trip to Longview was, seemingly, a bad omen: Hank went back to spend a couple of days with the crew to ensure the job got going properly.

He had a cheap hotel room with one of the ubiquitous oil wells pumping outside his window that prevented his getting much sleep. So after a couple of days into the job he left, and, *"as luck would have it,"* especially after his initial bad omen, all did not go well.

The day after he left he got a call from the crew in Longview. A big windstorm hit that day before the workmen secured the posts supporting the roof of the patio to the foundation and it was virtually destroyed. He had to return.

He spent more days than planned to ensure the damage was properly repaired, but they were long days that did not leave any time to explore Longview… as if there was anything to explore.

There were no buildings over two stories, a large number of wrecking yards, of course the oil wells, and there seemed to be a competition between the builders of burlesque joints and churches to see which could build the most of their particular edifices to satisfy these seemingly equal but diverse interests of the town's blue collar population, which he thought strange, given Longview's location smack in the middle of the "Bible Belt."

Longview was about as far away from Los Angeles, demographically, topographically, meteorologically, architecturally, culturally, to use these last two terms loosely, religiously and any other possible comparison of the two places, as one could get… just no comparison except, maybe, the vast abyss between beauty, style, intelligence and overall desirability of the two.

Longview's existence was, again, the result of "need," not desire.

It was the discovery of oil that provided its *raison d'etre*… to provide shade and shelter, and places to care for and entertain the roughnecks and others engaged in pulling the "black gold" out of the ground.

For Hank, the thought of living in Longview, or other places like it, compared to Los Angeles or other places of culture, entertainment, good climate, education…..civilization, is sufficient to cause one not to desire to *"keep on dancing."*

Even Grand Prairie was a "relative paradise," to also use this term loosely. It was close to two cities and what they offered, whereas Longview was in the middle of nowhere with nothing to do except work, honky-tonk, drink, and go to the strip joints and churches.

Sometime in late 1960 before he ceased working for his father to take the position with the patio company he made his longest sort of solo road trip to that date, driving six hundred miles to El Paso on old coast to coast Highway 80 that was the main drag through Grand Prairie.

This was his first trip across that "seemingly interminable plain" of nothingness that "stretched westward into the sunset" beyond Fort Worth to El Paso. Boring, unenlightening, non-scenic wasteland are all fairly descriptive of the geography that must be traversed to get to El Paso that, quite frankly, he did not think worth getting to.

It struck him as one of those places wherein the only benefit it provides is a place to go to the restroom and get something to drink, as proven by the fact its principal reason for existing is the government chose it for another of its big military installations, which is one interesting disclosure of traveling the highways and byways of America: there are so damned many military installations.

Within the six hundred miles between Dallas and El Paso are installations in Grand Prairie, Fort Worth, Sweetwater and El Paso. Then, in addition to Fort Hood, there is Fort Sam Houston in San Antonio, Bergstrom Air Force Base near Austin, and a dozen more… just in Texas.

It is doubtful most people are aware how much military is in America relative to the rest of the economy, how much geographic space it occupies, how much of an unnecessary economic burden it is on each of us, or how much it affects the lives of all of us who are not involved in its activities, but doubly doubtful; not a state, or American citizen, is unscathed by it, which should not be overlooked because comparison of other places with Los Angeles is our purpose here.

Los Angeles and Southern California probably have more than their share of the military. It is just that due to the geographic size, huge economy and the large population of the area, its military content is not nearly as obvious as it is in wastelands wherein the military is the foundation for the local economy and the military, parasitic populations.

It is obvious that without the military, El Paso would either not exist or would be nothing but another wide spot on the highway between Dallas/Fort Worth and Los Angeles, which is a fair assessment given the lack of anything other than desolation between the two.

The places in between, such as Midland/Odessa and Abilene, existed initially only because watering holes were needed in times past by those unlucky enough to travel across this expanse of nothingness. Thus again, it was "need," not desire.

Then they also got lucky with the discovery of oil. Still most even if in the oil "bidness," except for those who are there for the oil field jobs, choose to live to the East in the cities of Dallas or Fort Worth.

But even though the terrain and everything about travel between Dallas and El Paso is really boring, Hank's trip was not.

It was not for pleasure. It was, as was most of his travel during the last couple of years, for business, or to be honest; "work," not business.

His father had gotten a contract doing the excavation work on several of the new AT&T microwave telecommunications towers between East and West Texas, and he enlisted Hank to transport some equipment needed at these jobsites.

This trip he was driving a big old Ford truck tractor pulling a forty foot, flat bed, tandem axle trailer on which there was a tractor with a backhoe, buckets for this machine and several small but heavy, related construction equipment items.

Somewhere along the way, unmemorable as it was... it all looked the same, so it doesn't make any difference where... there was, surprise, a small hill. Fortunately it was "small." But given the table top flatness of most of the terrain, it was just luck there was a hill he had zero difficulty getting up by gearing down, as necessary.

Although it was small, it was fortunate it did require some down shifting into lower gears because as he crested the hill and began the descent down the west side, when he tapped the brakes, nothing! The brake pedal rapidly went to the floor. No brakes!

He was going down-hill with tens of thousands of pounds of steel on a trailer behind him with nothing between it and him except the thin sheet metal back of the truck cab. Although chained down, there was no way the load would not come loose and in his direction if he hit anything.

He didn't panic. Because of low gear required for climbing the hill, he was not going very fast. But because of the potential force of weight and gravity, there was no way to prevent the rig from picking up speed, and the possibility of resulting in a deadly crash. But there was nothing to do but analyze the situation and try to figure how to stop the damned thing without hitting something and causing the load to crash through the back of the cab, killing him.

Not panicking and keeping a cool head, as he was later told in the military was one of his few favorable attributes, saved the day and Hank. But that would be more than stretching the truth. Luck! It was just plain old luck that saved him that day.

While he was trying to keep a cool head, analyzing the situation, there, maybe a hundred yards ahead, on the right side of the road was one of those road side "parks" provided by the Texas Highway Department for travelers to stop to rest and relieve themselves. And fortunately for him, the Department did everything within its capability to make the experience as pleasurable as possible for those availing themselves of the opportunities afforded by this "park."

Endeavoring to make it more park-like, so as to obscure the reality of the topography of the surrounding sandy "landscape," the Department planted a row of large shrubs and small trees parallel to the highway to separate it from the "park" to further enhance the ambiance in which travelers would find themselves upon leaving the highway.

That this landscaping survived there was amazing. Maybe they also sprang for the expense of a water-well. However, survive, it did. Not just survive. It thrived, and grew big and strong.

This row of shrubbery and trees stretched from the entrance to the exit of the "park," a distance he was too busy to gauge, but it was long enough.

He took out most of the hard work of the Department employees. When he stopped there was not much of the trees and shrubbery remaining. But he stopped, which was his only concern.

That shrubbery functioned much like the runaway truck ramps filled with deep gravel provided in the mountains to enable truck drivers to stop their trucks that have gotten out of control or lost their braking. Hank says, even today, every time he sees one of those he feels a little empathy with whoever has been fortunate for it to be there to save his life.

Also, fortunately he was not traveling solo that day. Robert, the operator of the tractor and backhoe he was transporting, was traveling with him in a pickup carrying small tools and parts.

Robert was somewhere in his late forties, if not early fifties, and had been working for Hank's father for a few years. He was one of those guys who could operate and repair anything, which is the reason he was the one chosen to operate and take care of the equipment that was going to be somewhere in the middle of nowhere, on top of the highest elevation available, far away from any resources or help should anything go wrong as is frequently the case when dealing with equipment, as just happened.

He really was in possession of a cool head… never rattled by anything, always in a good mood and happy, always mellow.

Anyone who was ever close enough to Robert to see the whites of his eyes, as was stated somewhere in history about when to fire at the advancing enemy, would understand he would have been in trouble if he was lying in wait and Robert was the advancing enemy because

Robert didn't have any "whites" in his eyes. Where his whites should have been, there was only red.

It is doubtful he could have functioned without alcohol in his veins. He was never "sober." But he was one of the best tracked, or crawler, front end loader and backhoe operators, anywhere. And since all anyone wanted when they hired equipment to do an earth moving job was proficiency and timeliness. He was in demand.

No one cared how much or what he had in his veins, except the few times he encountered the law while driving on public streets. Then there was a little different attitude toward Robert and the equipment he was operating there.

Traditionally blood alcohol level is used to determine pass or fail with regard to whether one is under the influence, but surely that would not have worked in Robert's case. He could have amazed everyone by failing this test, but still passing the physical coordination and speech part of the test because he had been under the influence for so long that was who he was.

If Robert were able to avoid the blood alcohol content test, he would have passed as sober with flying colors. In fact, it is possible it would have been a lot less safe for Robert to have been driving without sufficient alcohol content.

Anyway, Hank was fortunate old Robert, whatever his condition, was along with him that day because he very quickly ascertained the problem with the air brake system was a leak permitting it to lose pressure, rather than a more serious problem of the system compressor malfunctioning that he could not have repaired on the side of the road. So he repaired the leak quickly and they were on their way again before a Highway Patrol Trooper happened by.

Had that happened, they likely could have been assessed hundreds, if not thousands of dollars for damage to the "park" landscape.

Thus this episode left him a little shaken... actually a lot, so they were not on their way quite as rapidly as they were prior to the incident. He drove very carefully and deliberately the rest of the trip.

During the balance of the drive to El Paso, and while he was at the roadside while the truck was being repaired, one of the reasons this incident rendered him shaken was the memory of a family tragedy a few years earlier, and how lucky he had just been.

In 1953, his uncle I.T., his father's youngest brother, was killed in a truck accident while he was driving his GMC truck, pulling a "reefer" trailer, which is an enclosed refrigerated trailer used to haul perishable food items on long hauls.

He delivered his load and was driving with the trailer empty, "dead heading," to the location somewhere in California where he was to pick up his next load.

He fell asleep around 3:00 A.M. when he should not have been driving, ran off the road and hit an embankment. The impact caused the trailer to do what Hank was afraid could have happened in his little incident. It crashed into the back of the truck tractor cab, squeezing his uncle between the front of the trailer and the dashboard of the truck.

It took four hours to extricate him. The rescuers said he was alive and talking with them all the time until they freed him. Then he died instantly.

This was another one of those heart rending stories where a young man goes off to war for his country, survives years of being shot at and other near death situations, then returns home to die in a freak accident while going about his normal activities of supporting himself and his family.

Hank's uncle I.T., Junior, named for his father Ira Thomas, served on the battleship USS Missouri in the Pacific and was on board during the celebrating in Tacoma on August 14, as well as on September 2, 1945 when the formal ceremony of the surrender of Japan was signed on that ship in Tokyo Harbor.

He used to think it was amazing how many times during the early years of his life of auto travel in the U.S., before the development of multi-lane, controlled access, much improved highway system was mostly completed, he witnessed serious accidents in which people were killed or injured, the injury or death of people he knew, or came close himself.

He could remember his two high school classmates being killed at a Grand Prairie railway crossing, his barber dying in a head on collision three blocks from his home, the father of one classmate dying in an accident, a good friend barely surviving an accident, his helping pull a guy out of a car involved in an accident on the highway between O.L. Nelms' market and drag strip, another lady dying while he and others were awaiting the ambulance after she was hit broadside, a car hitting the brick wall at the Overhead Door factory across from his father's little market in Oak Cliff on what was called the Fort Worth Cutoff part of Highway 80 in 1945 just before he was inducted into the army, and another serious accident two miles west of there in front of the golf driving range that was there in the 1950s.

There were probably more, but these are the only ones he could remember, and didn't desire trying to remember more. It was too depressing.

⤙ ⤚

When his father was informed of his truck brake and roadside park incident, he told Hank not to drive the truck back home. He said he was to stay away from trucks from that date on because trucks and he were not a safe combination. This was his position because this was not Hank's first truck incident within the prior two years. And this third near miss played a role in his decision to go to work for the home improvement company.

The first was the summer he graduated from high school, June 1958. He was driving one of his father's dump trucks, a green Ford with a long wheel base with more space between the dump bed and the cab of the truck than usual. He was driving it on a job where they were excavating foundations for three new buildings at East Texas State Teacher's College in Commerce, Texas a few miles from his father's family farm near Sulphur Springs.

There were half a dozen dump trucks being loaded with the dirt excavated. They were hauling the loads a couple of miles down a two lane farm to market asphalt road to dump it on land owned by the college, then returning for another load.

It was eight hours of repetitious tedium on a road with next to zero traffic and open land with no obstacles. He had been doing it for a few days. What could go wrong?

The round trip was simple. After he drove the couple of miles down the road, he made a right turn off the highway onto the gravel entrance road to the farm then a left turn off that road into the pasture. After a hundred yards, or so, a right turn through an open gate into another pasture where he dumped the loads.

Since he was driving a loaded dump truck across a grass covered pasture, and he had to make a turn through a gate about twelve feet wide, he was going only, maybe ten miles per hour. Thankfully!

When driving down the farm to market, whether empty or loaded, he drove about fifty miles per hour, which was a safe speed unless there was some problem. Loaded dump trucks do not stop on a dime, and they have a tendency to tip over, possibly more than once, should there be any sudden turning right or left at that speed.

So, the boring routine was; get loaded, then down the road into the farm, across the pasture, through the gate and dump. Then retrace back to the campus to get loaded and do it again... several times a day for a few days. No problem. The kind of repetition you could perform in your sleep if moving vehicles were not involved.

Early one afternoon, after several loads, he did it again, looking forward with great anticipation to the joy of doing it several more times before the day was over, then for a few more days after that.

So it went; get loaded, down the road, into the farm, across the pasture, right turn through……… *"Right turn! Right turn! Damn it! Jesus!"* he literally screamed as he turned right, and the steering wheel was spinning right, but the truck was still going straight ahead across the pasture. It did not make the turn through the gate.

The key to what happened was the spinning steering wheel. The steering linkage had broken. Something he never heard of happening before, or since. It was just another of those freak happenings that cause people to die. And "die" is precisely what would have happened to Hank on that bright sunny summer day in lovely east Texas in June of 1958 at the age of eighteen if that linkage had broken a few minutes before, or after, when he would have been driving down the Farm to Market road at fifty miles per hour.

Had that happened, he obviously would not have been around to have his second truck experience that, although not as unusual as the steering linkage breaking was uncommon.

It was sometime in 1960 a few months before the El Paso trip when he was driving another of his father's dump trucks on a job in Grand Prairie.

He was hauling dirt to a site on the edge of the city park in a big, red F7 Ford that had a huge, powerful flathead V8 Lincoln engine in it. It had tremendous torque – apparently too much.

As he geared down going uphill next to a small lake there was a loud, metallic "bang." The rear of the truck dropped to the right side and it stopped almost instantly. It scared the Hell out of him. This time uphill; next time downhill. His father was right. Trucks were not his "thing."

He got out of the cab, which was raised up high on the driver's side to the extent the left front tire was so high off the pavement he had to jump down from the running board that was normally just a step down. It was immediately obvious with the front tire being raised off the ground like that and the loaded bed of the truck leaning so precariously to the right the truck was on the verge of tipping over.

As he walked toward the back of the truck to see what happened, he placed the heel of his left hand under the front corner of the dump bed that was normally less than shoulder height, but was now at the elevation of his head, and gently pushed up. He quickly took his hand away because his gentle push moved the bed upward.

Considering there was over twenty thousand pounds of dirt in the bed, this was either an amazing feat of strength or the truck was on the verge of tipping over.

Walking around the back of the truck he was able to see what happened. The solid steel axel twisted into two parts from the strain of the combination of the torque of the engine in a low gear and the weight it was pulling up the hill. The right rear set of dual wheels was partially down the hill with the brake drum and a small part of the axel attached. The rest of the axle was protruding out of the axle housing with its broken end on the pavement.

All that was keeping the truck from turning over and rolling into the water below was that one and one-half inch thick axel that was wedged between the rear end housing and the pavement. Had the end of the axel not remained in the rear end housing, the truck would have turned over immediately and rolled down the hill into the water. Close call!

When his father saw this he seemed to be more upset than Hank. He commented on how he was saved by the axle then sent him home, got equipment and a crew to clean up the mess, and get the truck back to his equipment yard.

⊷⊰⊹⊱⊷

Over years of driving long distances alone before satellite radio, tapes or CDs, Hank learned those hours of solitude, in addition to being relished, are great times for thinking, reminiscing, contemplating, planning and introspection.

This is what he did during the remaining hours of his trip to El Paso. He thought. He thought about the past and the future. Thought about what happened to him during the prior year. Thought about what he was doing and why was he doing it? Thought about how he was on a fast track in the slow lane to nowhere, and had to get off.

Just shy of twenty-one years old, and except for nine months in college he spent the past two and one-half years since high school in construction related work... six months doing ordinary labor – lifting and loading and a year working for his father operating a backhoe, driving trucks and supervising earthmoving jobs.

Although he earned almost four thousand dollars in 1960, not bad compensation during that time, he did not think this, when he should have been finishing his degree in architecture and planning his career in that, his chosen field, was a good use of his time.

But, there it is – the key word: "think."

He was, as are most young people without proper guidance; too busy acting to do the proper amount of thinking for their own benefit.

He garnered some experience and some education during those two and one-half years, but very little of the work part of it was the result of thinking and planning. It was the result of that dirty little word that keeps popping up in most lives: "need."

He put himself into a situation where he needed to go to work after his first year of college. That, as luck would have it, was the summer of 1959 when the country was beginning to experience the worst recession since the end of WWII. Jobs were difficult to find. He had to take what he could find. That was a laborer job at one dollar per hour for sixty hours per week.

His 1959 tax return showed only $1,514.65 of taxable income. Fortunately, he was able to move from that to a union wage equipment operator's job in 1960 that yielded two and one-half that at $3,936.65, not even working full time. So, his lack of thinking and planning resulted in hardship for only about six months... which was more than enough.

In addition to this work, he used his architectural training to generate additional income.

He designed a large home for a wealthy business owner, regularly converted architectural drawings to detailed shop fabrication drawings for a large architectural steel manufacturer, designed and provided architectural drawings for strip shopping centers for an investor and added to his income by doing some sub-contracting. So, financially, he was doing about as well as young college graduates; able to buy a nice car and a home and live reasonably well before the age of twenty-one.

He gained a lot of work and life experience, but life was not as he planned when he was going to school or when he began studying architecture. He planned from the age of fifteen to be an architect. Maybe if he had been able to finish college and begin his architectural career, he would have been less dissatisfied with life and circumstances where he was, as are most Americans who spend their lives within fifty miles of where they grew up. But he doubted it. There was always a little gnawing somewhere in the back of his head saying *"This can't be all there is."*

⊷⊱⊰⊶

El Paso was not much. As they say, *"nothing to write home about"* which must have presented a dilemma to those thousands of military personnel stationed there, but maybe not.

Maybe their problem was what not to write home about.

Ciudad Juarez, Mexico is very few miles away. Maybe the desire for contented soldiers was the reason the U.S. Government situated Fort Bliss there.

But his only memories of El Paso were a few buildings taller than any others since Fort Worth, some evidence of the beginnings of the interstate highway system, thanks to the proximity of the military and Ike's grand scheme, that it was winter and cold as hell at night due to the desert environment, and the Green Frog lounge downtown with the young Latino lady in a tight gold lamé dress who thought he was a young soldier who might want to go back to Juarez with her for some fun. Wrong! He was young, but not stupid.

Other than for military R & R, like this young lady, and a legal entry point from Mexico, El Paso is just the point on the map where the vast cultural desert of nothingness extending from the Trinity River to a few miles east of California's Pacific beaches is handed off to New Mexico he was not unhappy to depart.

So, two days after arriving, getting Robert squared away at the jobsite about twenty-five miles northeast of the city in the Hueco "Mountains," and ensconced in a cheesy little motel that was the only option close to the job, he gladly followed his father's orders not to drive the truck back, boarded a Continental Trailways bus… another "experience" not recommended… for the six hundred mile, twelve hour retreat from his trials on the western frontier.

Although the accommodations and traveling companions on this bus ride and the one other taken since were not a recipe for enjoyable travel, at least he did not have to look at a repeat of the scenic wonders of West Texas for six more hours and drive a truck in the dark for another six. He found thinking himself to sleep easily accomplished even though his thoughts were not all that pleasant.

On the westward part of the excursion he dwelt on his experiences, some not so pleasant, but mostly beneficial, due to the experience gained from them. But what became very clear to him from his hours long retracing of his personal history was that experience was not what he was lacking. It was exposure.

It is possible to gain experience while sitting in one spot doing the same thing over and over. He had quite a lot of experience operating a backhoe while sitting in the seat pulling the levers. Ditto driving a truck, and even bent over a drafting table drawing plans. But unless these tasks are performed in different environments, or different places, among different people, there is no exposure to anything different. A tremendous increase in experience can be gained without exposure to, or learning about, anything else.

At twenty-one years old, other than time prior to his sixth year, he spent no more than a few days – not even a month – outside a small, few hundred square mile area around Grand Prairie, Texas, and even a year later at the age of twenty-two, after a year with the patio company, he had rarely been more than one hundred miles in any direction away from Grand Prairie.

He had zero exposure to different people, religions, topography, architecture or culture… nothing except what he read or saw in movies, on television, and on a vacation trip to Colorado.

He had nothing to compare with Los Angeles except a few hundred square mile area of Texas and the occasional visitor to the area that he met.

North Central Texas, primarily Dallas/Fort Worth was it. "It" being the sum total of his exposure to the same place and same culture those years… a boring, limiting, very small world that even the last year of 1961 with the patio company did not change.

Even though it was a good year in which he earned $4,475.33, and gained added, different experience, he was still stuck in a small dissatisfying and disappointing little world and life. But that was now changed. He had gotten out.

When he decided to go, and set the date to do so, it did not matter whether he headed east or west. His only objectives were to "get out" and go as far away as possible via automobile. Distance and change were all that mattered. The only two limiting factors were the Pacific or Atlantic oceans… nothing else.

When it was determined he was headed west, he decided he was not going via the same route he traveled to El Paso and had been traversing back and forth through Grand Prairie, and to and from Dallas for the last sixteen years. No. His objective was change, and traveling the same old road was not change. Therefore, he decided if he was going to satisfy his desire for change, he would do it right out of the starting gate of the road to his new life.

"If you ever plan to motor west
Travel my way, the highway that's the best.
Get your kicks on Route 66."

He never heard a song, or saw a television show about Highway 80, and having traveled it half the twelve hundred mile distance to the Pacific Coast, he could understand why.

It is really difficult to write and sing about nothing but boredom, and as consideration for a television show; it was proven a few years later that a show about some guys roving in the desert for the best part of twenty-six weeks was not likely to be a hit.

No choice. From Fort Worth, rather than west on 80, he headed northwest to Amarillo and a road that offered some *"kicks,"* rather than interminable nothingness, unless the song was a fraud, and Route 66 was like Highway 80.

Also, he was influenced by the escapism of movies and television, especially the television series "Route 66."

He had been watching it for two years, and had he never experienced the nothingness of Highway 80 would still have chosen Route 66 anyway because of the adventures of the two young guys, actors Martin Milner and George Maharis, in Milner's character, Todd's 1960 Corvette for those two seasons while dreaming, like so many young men, about doing that and leaving the drudgery and boredom of their lives far behind.

He didn't have a Corvette, but he had the next best thing: a new 1962 Anniversary Gold Edition 327 cubic inch 350 horse-power Chevrolet Impala Super Sport in which he was betting he could get some *"kicks,"* as well as find freedom and adventure on those two lanes of asphalt.

He would experience some of the escapism provided by the movies and TV, as had so many before on the highway John Steinbeck called the *"Mother Road."*

Look out, "Albuquerque, Gallup, Flagstaff, Kingman, Barstow" and Los Angeles.

CHAPTER 4
BOB'S RULE

After seeing Los Angeles, it was obvious to Hank his lack of travel and exposure had nothing to do with being unable to compare Los Angeles to anything. It would have been incomparable, even for those widely traveled and having seen many cities.

Anyone could have visited almost any other city in the world, and surely in the U.S., and not have found anything to compare to it.

"Los Angeles" was not just the city. It was a huge, sprawling, growing metropolis of many incorporated cities, which combined are referred to as "Los Angeles."

Anyone living in any one of the cities that make up the greater metropolitan area when traveling to Dallas, if asked *"Where are you from?"* would have answered *"Los Angeles."*

However, it was not just size to which its uniqueness or incomparability were attributable, nor was it "Hollywood" or the movie industry. There were, and still are, many other large industries that provide the economic base for the metropolitan area.

The aircraft and "defense" industries are a large part of the economy, as is much other manufacturing. Also, because of the attraction of the economic might of all this industry, combined with the favorable climate, the city was a human magnet for people from all over the country desiring to participate in its well-known economic growth. This also made the housing and home building industries a large part of the area's economic base.

But what made the area unique were two salient features, one topographical and the other manmade. The combination of the two is unique to Los Angeles.

Anyone could go to almost any American city and see several pretty tall buildings they could go into and up several floors to have a view of the surrounding area and other buildings, but not in Los Angeles. There was a dearth of tall buildings. In fact, the tallest building in the area was the Los Angeles City Hall that was only thirty-two stories and 454 feet tall.

Due to potential earthquakes, a building height limitation of 150 feet was imposed in Los Angeles until 1960, except, obviously, for the government, which even then, at that level could do whatever it wanted. So architecture and tall buildings were definitely not salient features. They did not exist. Even Dallas had more tall buildings than Los Angeles.

But the lack of tall buildings did not take Los Angeles out of the view business. One feature of its topography provides the opportunity for spectacular views.

The Hollywood Hills provide miles of streets and thousands, probably hundreds of thousands, of acres of land from which there are outstanding views of the San Fernando Valley to the north and the Los Angeles Basin to the south. Thus, it is fair to call the Hollywood Hills, a topographical feature located smack in the middle of the metropolitan area, a salient feature of some note.

Who hasn't heard of them, even if they haven't seen them? And no one could be there without seeing them from everywhere in the area.

The other salient feature is not thus because of its uniqueness, but because of its magnitude and effect on the area. In this one way, this manmade feature of Los Angeles is comparable, not in size, but in relative dominance, to the city in which it is located, much as it is in Grand Prairie.

In Grand Prairie the dominant man-made features are two widths of Highway 80 that pass through the center of the entire length of the town and the railway that parallels them.

Although Los Angeles is missing the railway part of this combination feature, the freeways were, as they still are today, even with the addition of the previously missing tall buildings, definitely the dominant man-made feature of the entire metropolitan area.

The highway and railway are negative dominant features in Grand Prairie. They divide the town, adversely affecting maneuverability. But this is not the case in Los Angeles.

Although the "Hills" divide the L.A. Basin from the "Valley" and adversely affect access between the two, they make up for this inconvenience in the topographical benefits they provide, and the freeways increase maneuverability within and between both areas.

It is the combination of these two features, the topography of the Hollywood Hills and the man-made freeways that provides Los Angeles its uniqueness.

Nowhere else in the country is it possible to have a view over such a large, populated area while having one's feet planted firmly on the ground, as is possible from the Hollywood Hills. At night it is truly spectacular.

The sound of the freeways… the rushing sound of rubber on pavement of thousands and thousands of vehicles, especially from anywhere in the Hollywood Hills at night, is something that cannot be found in any other city, anywhere. It is ubiquitous throughout the entire area. It is unique to Los Angeles, and is one of Hank's most pleasant memories of it.

Frequently, at night, during his time in L.A. he would drive up to his favorite spot on Mulholland Drive, lie back on the hood and windshield of his car and listen to the mesmerizing, soothing sound of the rush of rubber of what was probably millions of tires on pavement while marveling at the sight of the millions of twinkling lights representing the presence of millions of others who were there not because they needed to be, but because they desired to be there.

Los Angeles, unlike the place he spent the previous sixteen years, and most other places, was a city of desire, not need.

What he found in Los Angeles was, at least for him, like a bright new day in America.

His past, twelve hundred miles to the east, was like a darkness from which he emerged Rip Van Winkle-like after a twenty year sleep.

Even Route 66 he chose for the trip was a big disappointment in the *"kicks"* department. It was much like more of what he was accustomed for years in Texas with some different topography, scenery and a lot of tourist oriented kitsch thrown in. But upon his arrival in Los Angeles everything was turned around, maybe upside down. He didn't know which, but it was positive. It was as though his sun set in the east and there was a new dawn for him in the west.

This "new dawn" was like the beginning of a new life for him. He could envision an unobstructed future for the first time in his life. It was almost as though he was like a human rocket set to take off on a long voyage of exploration and discovery.

Although he could not have perceived this at the time, Los Angeles was his launch pad. He was just placed upon it, and the next twelve months were going to be his time of preparation for what was to follow.

He could never have begun to imagine that what he thought to be the disillusioning end of his short time in Los Angeles where we began this story was not the apex of his short life, or that rather than being a major negative turning point, it was blast off time for him.

Though he did not have any way of knowing it at the time, receiving his notice, Heidi and departure were the equivalent of "countdown, ignition, and launch" to his future.

By the time he is brought back down to earth over three decades and several "lives" later, he will have experienced a vast array of experiences and discoveries…beyond what any person of his limited background, or probably anyone else, could ever have begun to imagine or dream: experiences and discoveries of pleasure, achievement, success, satisfaction, enjoyment, "fulfillment and meaning," as well as "despair and disillusionment" that, taken in concert will leave him in a perpetually unsated state, continuing to ponder the perennial question of a successful life: "Is That All There Is?"

Although approaching a mental state of euphoria, relative to his past state of mind, engendered by the perception of promise Los Angeles offered to him, and not giving any consideration to the decades beyond, he still had his head properly screwed on with regard to priorities: shelter and income to protect and sustain him. Everything else would have to be worked in around those two priorities, or later.

Shelter in the form of the studio apartment on Willoughby Avenue was not a problem. His aunt "Sis" arranged it for him right away.

He stopped in to stay with her for a couple of days, and being on her sofa probably elicited her assistance in this that might otherwise not have been provided with the same alacrity.

Income was another matter. He was strictly on his own on this one, which he found a "tad" more challenging.

He spent at least a month perusing the help wanted ads in the newspaper, which was his only source because he did not know anyone in Los Angeles except his aunt and uncle and their two daughters, neither of whom were, shall we say, "connected."

During this time he did a little exploring of the area – Hollywood, Beverly Hills, Bel Air – getting the lay of the land and what was available in the way of relatively inexpensive entertainment and ways to spend time when not working… assuming he could find a job.

He had an interest in architecture and building as well as the history and ambiance of "Hollywood." So he took advantage of being able to view the many different types of architecture and locations of homes in the area.

He saw some decent, even fairly nice homes in the Hollywood Hills for twenty to twenty-five thousand dollars that, although seems really inexpensive compared to the hundreds of thousands and even millions of dollars those homes go for today, from his point of view was really expensive.

He sold his little "box" house in Grand Prairie the year before for five thousand dollars, and it was possible to buy a really nice, large, brick home, on a large lot, in a good neighborhood there, or even in Dallas, for less than twenty-five thousand dollars. That compared with these small stucco structures on postage stamp size lots seemed a deal. But, of course, the difference was in the old saying, "location, location, location."

Whereas Dallas was only a draw for young people desiring to depart the small towns of Texas, Louisiana, Oklahoma and Arkansas, Los Angeles, being a magnet for the entire country... even the world, the demand, quality, and demographics, versus supply and location in proximity to much more desirable...everything, including climate, beauty, the ocean and beaches, "Hollywood," excitement and more highly paying jobs would naturally make real estate on the west side of L.A. significantly more expensive.

This was a different world. He was fully aware of that. That was the reason he was there, and, anyway, he wasn't really pricing, just exploring, endeavoring to satisfy his curiosity about his new home and the differences between it and where he came from.

Beverly Hills and Bel Air? Forget about it. The best areas of Dallas, Highland Park and University Park were nothing in comparison.

There are nice homes there, but not a tremendous diversity of styles, and most are just lined up the same distance from the curbs on streets that are mostly more of the same. Of course there are exceptions, but not many.

Beverly Hills and Bel Air had neighborhoods, streets and homes like he had never seen. There was a multiplicity of styles, sizes and shapes at different angles and distances from streets on different size plots of land, some small and some huge with big walls and gates.

They were on hillsides, on flat parcels, and some were tucked up on hillsides among the trees, but all visually broadcast wealth and sophistication. Everything about Beverly Hills and Bel Air said, *"If you live here, you have made it…you have arrived."*

He even acted like a normal, yahoo tourist, which in one way he was. Although he was not a tourist, per se, because he moved to the area, as opposed to just passing through, he was just as curious as the average tourist to see where some of the people he had been watching in the movies and on TV for several years lived.

He almost shamefully bought one of those "Maps to the Star's Homes" street vendors have been "hawking" with their yellow lettered, blue signs along Sunset Boulevard for years. Then he went in search of some of the stars' homes.

The only one he can remember to the extent he can still sort of visualize its size, style, shape and location set back from the street in the trees was the home of Dean Martin, the singer, movie star and TV personality. He can still remember it because he really liked the guy and watched his musical variety TV show primarily because he was so entertaining.

Martin was a good looking Italian guy with a great voice and a casual, personable style, great to listen to and watch, compared to most of his contemporaries like Frank Sinatra who did not seem to be a pleasant person.

Dean Martin was an all-round talent and good guy, as well… a rare combination who in Hank's opinion, deserved his estate with the mansion, and more.

He really was more like a tourist when it came to visiting and viewing homes in the ritzy residential areas of Los Angeles. He was as curious as anyone else to see how the other half, really more like the other one percent, lived. But that was it. He had no dreams or aspirations about living in places like those. It was so far above anything he ever experienced the thought of having a home like any of those never entered his mind. They really were more like a dream world, or even beyond that.

Even though this visit to "Hollywood" real estate dream land was almost a year before he was to meet Heidi, his reaction to any thought of ever living at this level of residential splendor and quality would have been the same as his stated expectation of being with her: *"Never...in my wildest dreams."*

But, if nothing else, the next twelve months would begin to hammer a dent into those dismal thoughts of limited potential, as would his last month in L.A. remove any similar thoughts regarding women. Subsequent experiences in later years would serve to eliminate any further thoughts of limitation about anything possibly remaining in the back of his predominately blue-collar Grand Prairie nurtured little mass of grey matter.

Also, Bob, his roommate for a month, gifted him with a rule for success: *"If you don't ask, you aren't going to get any,"* which Hank, mostly successfully, has followed since. In fact, he applied it when endeavoring to satisfy his immediate need for income.

He left Grand Prairie with five hundred dollars cash and a few possessions, mostly clothing, in the trunk of his car. After the trip out, renting an apartment and over a month of living expenses, with the next month's rent due shortly, the need for income was on the verge of becoming critical. He even began eating street vendor tacos to conserve cash.

Fortunately, his clothing stash included some pretty decent duds; white shirts and ties, nice slacks and sport coats, including three Botany 500 sport coats that cost fifty dollars each that, today, anyone would immediately think: fifty dollars are pretty cheap sport coats. But that would ignore the fact fifty dollars in 1962 was equal to over four hundred dollars in 2013 when a $400 sport coat was pretty nice.

One might also think it strange a twenty-two year old who was doing construction related work and supervision would be wearing the equivalent of $400 sport coats. But that would also overlook a couple of significant differences between 1962 and 2013.

Remember: he was making about four hundred dollars per month, almost five thousand dollars per year, a company car and the gas to fuel it, plus the proceeds of his architectural work and subcontracting, and five thousand dollars in 1962 was the equivalent of over forty thousand dollars in purchasing power, or almost the median family income in 2013.

Also, there were societal norms almost five decades ago that have been lost. Unlike today, people were expected to be appropriately attired for various occasions.

When they went out in the evening, especially Friday and Saturday, to clubs or nice places for dinner, men usually wore ties. Not to have done so would have attracted attention of the wrong kind.

When on a date, even for the movies, they usually wore a sport coat. It was important to be well dressed. What one did for a living was not a reason to be inappropriately attired when going out to dinner, to a function or a night club. But Hank probably dressed better than most because his clothes were more expensive than average.

That had been the case for as long as he could remember because his mother always bought more expensive clothing for him and his brother than most kids in Grand Prairie wore. She liked nice things and did not deprive him or his brother in that way. So, when he was buying for himself, he shopped the same stores he grew up with.

Anyway, the point is he was prepared for employment that was a step up from what he was accustomed to. After all, that was the reasoning for leaving Grand Prairie behind.

He did not even take any blue collar type "work" clothes with him. That type of employment was not part of his plans. He was sartorially prepared for only white collar work, and that was all he was going to look for.

His first hook in the water caught a potential golden opportunity. He responded to an advertisement for a trainee stockbroker at Merrill

Lynch on Wilshire Boulevard in Beverly Hills just a block from Rodeo Drive. Damned good thing he had the proper attire for this type of employment in a neighborhood like that because without it; no deal.

However, he was well and properly attired. The guy liked him. He gave the pitch about how much money a nice looking young man who looked the part could make being a stockbroker in Beverly Hills. Having already toured the neighborhoods in the area, Hank could envisage the potential he was talking about.

The problem was it was not a position providing the immediate income he was desperately in need of. He signed on anyway, and began going to the Merrill Lynch office at night with a couple of others the Merrill Lynch guy determined were worth spending time to train.

He went for several nights while continuing to peruse the want ads, looking for something that would satisfy his employment and income objectives...with emphasis on the latter.

After a few days he found a help wanted ad for someone with architectural and construction experience desired for a company in the business of selling and erecting steel buildings and factory built housing.

It sounded as though they were looking for someone older, but in his opinion, he had experience beyond his years in these areas because of work in his father's business and the summer jobs with plumbing and electrical contractors since he was fifteen, plus the last two years in construction supervisory positions... seven years of experience and education.

How much more could they want? He thought he was as well qualified as they would find.

Any "thoughts of limitation" regarding this position were non-existent in his little grey matter. This position was for him... assuming it paid well enough and that pay would begin rolling in immediately.

He made an appointment for later that day, put on coat and tie and went to find the address of the appointment sufficiently in advance of the scheduled time to ensure he would not be late.

It was at an employment agency. He had to wait a few minutes to see the lady responsible for screening applicants for the position. She was a tough sell.

Middle aged lady who had obviously been at her job for a while, asked a lot of questions he answered knowledgeably. Told her his experience and why he was perfect for the position.

Resume? *"No. I just got to Los Angeles and am looking for a position with compensation and potential commensurate with my experience, which I thought it better to articulate in person than for someone to read it without seeing me"*

Further, he said, *"I could go write a resume and get it typed, but why? You wouldn't know any more about me than what I have told you, and by that time someone less qualified might be hired for the position."*

He could tell she was about to try to get rid of him when she said, *"Do you know how many young men your age there are in L.A. looking for jobs who, like you, are 1-A, first on the list to be drafted, which does not make them desirable employees?"*

Without blinking, as he reached for his leather western wallet, Hank said, *"No. But how many of them are ready to pay you in advance for a chance at this position."*

By the time the word "position" exited his mouth, he slapped his last $100 bill on her desk, at which point she looked at him and said, *"Just a minute,"* picked up the phone and began speaking with someone about an appointment an hour later.

It appeared Bob's rule just came through for him, big time.

He asked fairly adamantly and was about to get the appointment he asked for. That caused him to think *"Bob's rule"* was THE ticket to a seat in the fast lane, as he would many times in the future. No more slow lane for Hank! But the incident caused him to rethink that wallet.

He hoped the employment lady did not notice it. He had it since he was barely out of puberty. Brown with the white horse head on it outlined in little brass studs... definitely passé, not executive accoutrement. It had to go before anyone else could see it.

But even of more immediate concern, not to be over-looked, was the fact the lady addressed about the power of the federal government to interfere in the average insignificant person's life without consideration for it.

Just the specter of what the government could do to a small, in a demographic sense, insignificant being such as Hank by interfering in something as simple as his getting an innocuous, little job is, in retrospect, frightening.

If the tentacles of those within and behind the government can reach down to each individual through rules that frighten people away from giving a job to a person, even to destroying families' lives and sending individuals to their death for no reason of any benefit to the country or anyone except a few in the government and those who put them there, what rights or future do we have? It is the answer to that question that is frightening.

The draft status issue being raised by the lady was disconcerting because it was something that had been bouncing around in his head in a dysfunctional manner for the last few months, since July 1961 when President Kennedy requested an increase in the size of the U.S. Army, Navy and Air Force, the draft call to be doubled and for some of the reserves to be placed on active duty. This put all young American males on notice their lives belonged not to them, but to the Government to do with what it desired.

The ostensible reason for Kennedy's action was the Berlin Crisis of the previous month of June 1961. This was caused when Soviet President Khrushchev proposed a change in the agreement under which the U.S. and other allied countries had access to West Berlin, in essence, possibly denying them access. This resulted in a significant escalation in the Cold War between the U.S.S.R. and the U.S.

To demonstrate the reality of concern about the possible results of increased tensions, Kennedy proposed the designation of "fall out" shelters and stocking them with food, water and other essentials.

On the other side of this "war," in August the Soviets began construction of the Berlin Wall to divide West and East Berlin, eliminating movement between these two sections of the city that was divided between the Soviets and Allies at the end of World War II.

The reinforced masonry Wall was completed only two months later, in October 1961.

But the really frightening aspect of this entire episode, putting the world on the brink of nuclear holocaust, is it was the unnecessary creation of dolts and geopolitical neophytes in the White House risking the country...if not the entire world...for their own stupid ideas of right and wrong, and endeavoring to impose them on the rest of the world.

In April 1961 two months prior to Khrushchev's verbal belligerence over Berlin, the misadventure hatched under Eisenhower, the Bay of Pigs invasion of Cuba, which was the genesis of this confrontation, was undertaken by the Kennedy Administration.

This was a U.S. Government backed attempt to invade Cuba to remove Fidel Castro from power in which a small, U.S. trained "army," to use the term loosely, of Florida based Cuban expatriates was launched from U.S. soil. It failed within three days.

This misadventure was, again, the result of inconceivably stupid thinking: Castro was a communist. The U.S. was capitalistic. Communism was wrong. Capitalism was right. The Cuban expatriates were capitalists. From this brilliance was born the Bay of Pigs invasion. Never mind Castro was able to launch a revolution and take control in Cuba was the direct result of the nature of the government he was able to overthrow, seemingly with the support of most Cubans.

U.S. "capitalist" puppet dictator, Batista, being a crook and impoverishing the Cuban people while being personally rewarded very handsomely by U.S. business interests and the U.S. Mafia whose

Cuban gambling interests were big beneficiaries of Batista's government was the real source of the unrest that enabled Castro to come to power.

Cubans who expatriated to the U.S. were members of the class who were beneficiaries of the Batista regime and were sore losers because his being removed by Castro cost them dearly.

It was not about ideology for the Florida based expatriates. It was about money. Pure and simple: billions of dollars. Power and ideology were important only because they were the source of the money.

It was also, in fact, the biggest reason for the business interests controlled U.S. Government. But money (or oil) can never be revealed to the American public as the reason for sending their sons to die in foreign lands even though that has proven to be the case... over and over.

Khrushchev and the Soviets were communists. Their ideologically consistent, communist "brothers" were just invaded by the U.S. For whatever reason did not matter. Khrushchev had millions of communist followers to whom the U.S. invasion of communist Cuba was a big deal.

Did it ever enter the minds of the "brilliant" ones in the U.S. Government that Khrushchev and other communists might take umbrage at Cuba being invaded by their ideological enemy, the U.S., and retaliate in some way? That they might be getting into something bigger than just restoring a group to power in a small country to recoup their lost financial interests? Guess not.

Thus, because a hand-full of financially driven ideological, hubristic, not so smart nuts in the U.S. Government and their U.S. business masters were seemingly incapable of adequately considering the consequences of their actions, Hank and several hundred thousand... maybe millions... other young Americans were finding it difficult to get jobs, and were subject to being put into harm's way to protect the financial interests of a few fat cats in the U.S. military/ industrial war based economy.

Of course Khrushchev and the Soviets were blamed for increased Cold War tensions because the dots of the Bay of Pigs and the Berlin Crisis were never connected for the masses. But Hank knew it was not Khrushchev's, but Kennedy's fault he was a draft risk.

CHAPTER 5

FIRST SUCCESS OF BOB'S RULE

The appointment was on the second floor of a New York Life insurance building at the corner of West 6th Street and South Lafayette Park Place, at the edge of Hancock Park, a very nice residential neighborhood. There was a big park, Lafayette Park, across 6th Street, and Wilshire Boulevard across the park to the south.

Getting there from his apartment on Willoughby Avenue was only a fifteen minute drive down La Brea then east on 6th Street, a pleasant drive through the nice residential area of Hancock Park, avoiding traffic on the busy main thoroughfare, Wilshire Boulevard.

The location was perfect. No traffic hassle, not a long commute and it was close to restaurants, entertainment and shopping on Wilshire Boulevard.

Hank was so happy about the appointment he overlooked that his elation might be a little premature. He had the appointment, but not the job. The fact of his last one hundred dollar bill last seen lying on the desk of the employment agency lady was almost forgotten. But he was now fully cognizant if he did not get the job, he was screwed financially.

⊷ ⊶

The office was small, not more than five hundred square feet, not fifty percent larger than the average two car garage. Directly in front of the door, across the room by the bank of windows that spanned the room overlooking 6th Street and the park, at a desk perpendicular to the windows and the door, sat a mid-fiftyish elegant looking gentleman with slicked back silver hair in a nice grey suit with white shirt and tie. Immediately to the right of the door was a desk at which sat a smallish girl, about Hank's age, with short black hair. He immediately turned right in front of her and quietly *announced "I have an appointment to see Mr. Benz."*

She said they were expecting him, as Mr. Benz simultaneously invited him over to his desk.

He was very nice, engaged in a little get acquainted conversation, asked a few questions...not many, and explained some of what his business was about.

In the course of the conversation he asked Hank if he would like to join them, to which he obviously... given his need for income... responded in the affirmative and somehow, sometime in the conversation, was hired at four hundred dollars per month (equivalent to almost $4,000 in 2013) on a probationary basis, to see how it would work out, or something like that.

That settled, Mr. Benz... that's what he called him from that day on, as did Sandra, the secretary... then formally introduced him to the expatriate Cuban lady in her early forties who was partially hidden behind a large drafting table that was behind the one column in the room and the bank of filing cabinets for which it served as sort of an anchor.

In the introduction he explained she was an architect in Cuba, but was now his *"architect."*

Then he motioned toward the desk behind Sandra that would be his, shook hands and said in his fairly heavy German accent, *"See you in the morning."*

To say Hank departed happily would be a bit of an understatement.

He experienced his first success with Bob's rule and learned that being a little aggressive in pursuing what he wanted was not a bad thing. He thought; had he only applied Bob's rule, and not gotten aggressive when the lady was about to dismiss him due to his draft status, he would not have gotten the interview that resulted in the job.

Sandra affirmed this the next day at lunch when she told him, *"Because of what the lady at the employment agency told Mr. Benz about you, he decided to hire you before he met you."*

He didn't realize it at the time, but his next move was, in retrospect, not very astute.

That night, after getting the job, he went to Merrill Lynch and told the guy there he had gotten a job and would not be coming back. The guy tried his best to encourage him not to quit, again pointing out the opportunity.

He could have, should have continued with the Merrill Lynch program. It would not have cost him anything but time in the evenings after work, and it would have been a great learning experience that could have paid off in the future had the new job not worked out, or if he decided it a better opportunity. But he didn't.

He, not too intelligently, decided to stay with what was comfortable... what he grew up with, rather than expanding his breadth of knowledge and opportunities.

It even seems inconsistent with the Hank who only recently made a decision to change his life, and acted on it by moving to a distant, strange place.

He thought about this and decided he acted as he did in this situation because of his upbringing, and lack of contact with anyone in the professions or the financial industry other than his doctor and local banker.

He had no idea of the opportunity even though he could see the evidence of money and financial success in Beverly Hills and the residential areas surrounding it. He had not quite completely shaken off the nurturing aspects of blue collar Grand Prairie.

But that is probably not entirely fair to Grand Prairie, either. He was certain there were some there who were familiar with the financial industry and investing in the stock market.

In fact, he was aware of one girl in his class from the seventh to twelfth grades whose father did not work per se, but owned an oil distribution business and lived in one of the nicest homes in town. Surely, he was one who could have provided the necessary guidance that would have set him on the potentially more financially productive course.

⟞⟝ ⟞⟝

Parental guidance is extremely important to how we fare in life. The nurturing by parents during the formative years is almost indelibly embedded and more difficult to overcome than the inertia of culture because of the intimacy.

Thus, it could be argued the surest guarantee of success would be to pick one's parents, but that wouldn't work very well because we would not have the necessary knowledge to know who to pick. Therefore, we are stuck with the luck of the draw and have to do our best to deal with what life handed to us in the womb, just as we must with what we encounter once free of it.

Most are probably happy or at least reasonably satisfied with the hand life dealt them in the form of where they are, who they are and the life course initially set for them by their parents, and the nurturing they provided, but some are not.

Then there are some who may not have a very well defined map for their course in life due to dysfunctional parenting. That is to say; parenting that is abnormal or incomplete.

Hank was certain he was member of the group with the ill-defined course due to dysfunctional parenting because his parents had divergent views on almost everything.

In that sense he did not have what could be called a matched or complete set. They disagreed on everything from religion to bill paying.

His father was a laid back, happy-go-lucky *"give-a-shit"* who was happy most of the time and conveyed that through his attitude and conduct. He was quick witted and very good with numbers.

His mother was a rarely happy, concerned about everything, for want of a better term, *"pain- in-the-ass"* to everyone around her. She was quick tempered, musical and creative.

Where his father was what we would call *"solid."* She was, shall we say, *"out there."*

Given this dysfunctional upbringing wherein his father spent a lot time teaching, nurturing, providing guidance, moral support and reassurance, even via mail at least once a month after he was in Los Angeles, his mother spent a little time telling him what was wrong with him and how or what he could, or should be, or do, including to *"come back home to stay,"* no wonder he chose the wrong fork in the road occasionally.

Being a product of this "parenting" and "nurturing," he could understand why his actions regarding the jobs were inconsistent with those that got him to Los Angeles.

He also understood why he followed the course his father would have counseled, which given his financial situation would have been solid advice. But his mother's genetic input got him to L.A., and caused that little gnawing in the back of his mind that he also *"could have, should have"* done more, been more and also pursued the other opportunity.

This time he chose only one road in the fork, making his life easier and less demanding. Whether it was the correct road would be determined later. But for the moment, he was happy with the decision. If it was the right decision, he would still be happy later. If it was not, he would have solved his pressing financial problem, making any future decision less dependent upon need. Then he would be free financially to let the other side rule and "take a flier" on whatever would seem to offer the greatest long term potential.

"Whatever?" This could have been his first big career mistake. But if it was, it would only be one of several over the next five decades. It was not going to be his last.

But he was adamant… to himself… that no matter how many mistakes he made he would not end up like his parents who never had a life. They never went anywhere, did anything or knew much to pass on to the two children who were really their only life.

Fortunately, his father who grew up in a fairly normal way insofar as he went to school, worked, interfaced with others and the world, provided guidance, whereas his mother who had almost zero interface with the world and was thus steeped in ignorance about it, took his brother under her wing… to his detriment. However, Hank knew he must give credit to both for their shared demonstrated concern for him after he left home.

Although his father supported and encouraged success in California, his mother wanted him to come back to all she knew or desired, the home and faux hearth she did her damnedest to ensure his brother did not leave, both constantly asked if he needed money, ensuring him if he did to not fail to ask, and insisted he call home frequently, *"collect."*

Each in their own way really did care and wanted him to succeed. It was just that neither really knew what success was, or how to assist in its achievement. But he had at least a small idea of what he thought would be considered success.

To him Mr. Benz seemed to be a pretty successful guy…successful beyond what the office conveyed. He had the franchise for the Los

Angeles area and more for StranSteel buildings, which was a big rigid frame steel building manufacturer. He also either owned or was part owner of a factory east of L.A., in Redlands, California, that produced factory built residential structures with an emphasis on unique A-frame structures that were popular second homes in the mountains east of Los Angeles. in places like Crestline.

His office gave no indication of all that was going on. With no employees outside the Redlands factory except two, now three, in the little office, he was a smart guy with little overhead, equipment, or permanent field employees, but maximum flexibility and profits.

The two businesses, rigid frame steel buildings and factory built housing, were separate except for the fact one guy controlled them. The rigid frame steel building business was commercial and the other, obviously residential.

Rigid frame steel buildings have been ubiquitous throughout the country for decades. They usually house factory or warehouse operations, but many have been disguised, by changing their exterior finish and building false fronts on them, and used for commercial purposes.

Their appeal is cost and speed of construction. They are constructed using steel I-beams for wall and roof structural members. The side supports and roof beams are manufactured in a factory and delivered to the job site with one side and one-half of the roof structure, or rafter, in one big piece. Then large cranes are utilized to lift the two sides and hold them until the two pieces are bolted to the foundation on either side and to one another in the middle, at the top.

When all these pieces are in place they are connected with small steel "runners" that extend from one end of the building to the other along the side walls and the roof. After these are in place, the metal sides and roof panels are screwed to these "runners," creating a structurally, very solid building at a fraction of the cost and time of construction for a conventionally constructed building. And, because of the nature and light weight of the structure, it is possible to have a much larger, clear span space without interior columns, thus providing a larger unobstructed space at lower cost.

Factory built housing is housing wherein large sections of houses are completely finished indoors, in a factory, and the sections are hauled to the job site where the house is assembled by bolting these sections together and to the foundation. The fact that weather does not interfere with the construction process, all components are purchased on a large, wholesale basis, the workers do not have to be highly paid "tradesmen" and finishing is required only where the connections are made, results in cost and time savings relative to site built structures similar to those in the steel buildings.

The benefits of both types of construction are known to those desiring either. Thus, when desirous of building in 1962, potential customers looked in the telephone book Yellow Pages wherein companies like StranSteel that was a nationally recognized vendor and Benz Fabricated Buildings advertised. It was thus, potential customers were generated.

Potential customers telephoned the Benz office. The secretary, Sandra, answered the phone, gathered the information, including whether they were interested in commercial or residential structures, contact information, etc. and that was given to Hank. Then he was the company representative with the responsibility of converting them to customers.

Because of his construction and architectural experience and knowledge, it was easy for him to step into this position immediately without any extensive training required.

After almost seven years of work in both residential and commercial/industrial design and construction, architectural training and having designed and built both types, he was professionally conversant about all aspects of the design and construction of both. That is why Mr. Benz hired him.

The only "training" he needed was to become familiar with the specifics of the StranSteel buildings, the catalogues with design specifications and prices, and the various floor plans and pricing of the factory built houses. Everything he needed to learn about the steel building business was at his desk.

To be completely familiar with the factory built housing beyond the plans and pricing that were also available at his desk Mr. Benz took him on a tour of the housing plant.

After that he was off and running, contacting those who called about one of the products, and doing his best to convert them to customers.

If, after a phone conversation, sufficient interest was demonstrated, he would go meet with them, possibly visit the site of the planned construction, and discuss design and pricing. Then, if conversations merited it, he would work with the "architect" to develop a plan and rendering, and with Mr. Benz to develop a bid for the project, which he would then present to the client.

This new job was definitely white collar construction related work, involving a lot of conversing and planning with people who were not construction people, but business executives.

Rather than dealing with equipment operators, construction foremen, superintendents and homeowners, he was dealing with business owners and executives of companies. It was exactly the step up he wanted. Thus, after less than a month in a new, large city, he was, if only a little bit, successful.

The position, not "job,"...let's forget that term...required a lot of running around, traversing the freeways around Los Angeles and the San Fernando Valley. Thus, in addition to his background and hands on experience in the business of Benz Fabricated Buildings, there was one other "thing" he had that was essential to being able to adequately fulfill the demands of the position: the new Chevy. Without it, he would have been at a disadvantage on what his father termed, years earlier after a visit to L.A, the *"race track"* where the traffic flowed fast.

Also, if his car had not been a nice looking, late model, he would have been at a disadvantage because he would not have presented a proper image to clients who were considering spending hundreds of thousands of dollars.

He was perceived pretty young to be doing what he was doing. So, had he not appeared successful, he would have been at a disadvantage "right out of the box"...or the car.

But he wasn't. He was successful with clients on the phone and in the field, and seemed to be successful in his new, rather diverse office environment, which had he not been, would have prevented him from being able to fulfill the requirements of the position.

There he was, a 22 year old Texan who had never been anywhere, or interfaced with anyone other than people of the same limited, religious and cultural background, in a rather small, confined space with a boss who was German, a secretary who was a nice Jewish girl and a Catholic, Cuban refugee from Castro whose English was not great, all three of whom he had to work with to fulfill the requirements of the position.

He was not only responsible for initial contacts with prospective clients and selling to them, which required him to coordinate closely with Sandra, he was also involved in development of plans, requiring a lot of give and take with the "architect," and pricing, construction and coordination requiring precise communication between him and Mr. Benz. Amazingly, they all worked well together.

During his time with Benz he dealt with many prospective clients, several they did projects with. One was large, and there were also some small ones. But one prospect he was not successful in converting to a client became a serious disappointment.

Of the small projects, one was residential and one was commercial. The residential project was a house on a high point in Malibu overlooking the ocean. The site was phenomenal. That building site alone would be worth millions today.

The other small project was not even a building. He designed and built a new façade for an old retail building on Van Nuys Boulevard in the Valley using steel building components. It was built using the steel building "runners" for a framework to which he attached bright red sheets of the steel building panels in a vertical position.

The one large project while he was with Benz was really very large. They designed and built a freight handling and distribution center at Los Angeles International Airport for Yellow Transit, a nationwide freight transportation company.

The building was long with, at least, two dozen overhead doors on either side opening onto long loading docks. At one end was a two story office facility. The project was not yet completed when he was forced to leave Benz.

But the one potential client he was unsuccessful in converting into a client was very disappointing because the potential was huge.

It was in January 1963, and he was amazed as he drove north through the Caheunga Pass to the Valley there was a light dusting of snow on the ground on the north side of the Hollywood Hills. He never expected that in Southern California

The potential client was a new restaurant chain with an office out Lankershim Boulevard in North Hollywood beyond Universal Studios that, after several conversations with them about their desires for uniqueness, size and other considerations, he and the "architect" designed a prototype using the residential factory A-frame design, but using steel components that could be manufactured by the steel building company, easily transported and assembled on site.

They listened to his presentation, seemed interested and asked to keep the presentation materials for discussion with others who would be party to the final decision about what they were going to do. He followed up, but never heard from them again. That was too bad. This could have been a multi-year, multi-million dollar deal.

Over two years later, in 1965, on Lemmon Avenue just north of Oak Lawn in Dallas, Texas, he saw his first International House of Pancakes A-frame restaurant.

But this is getting ahead of the story. North Dallas, 1965 was almost another lifetime after Los Angeles, or so it seemed, after the drastic life style and life altering changes he experienced in the intervening two years.

Having settled into his work at Benz, which was strictly nine to five Monday thru Friday with weekends free, and not having burdened himself by continuing the Merrill Lynch training, he had week nights and weekends free. He had income, no worries and time to explore, meet people, and have a social life. He really was "happy later."

CHAPTER 6

"HOLLYWOOD"

The residents at 7323 Willoughby were like the cast of a TV situation comedy. First, there was the resident manager who was a short, mid fortyish, red head, freckled, heavy-set, Jewish lady from New Jersey who sounded as though she just left Camden.

She spent a couple of hours every evening perched on the steps outside her second floor apartment, located at the right rear corner of the courtyard, a position that provided her an almost security system motion detector-like scan of the entire courtyard and out to the street, ensuring nothing, absolutely nothing, took place at 7323 Willoughby she was not intimately familiar with. She was, in fact, a sort of apartment security system.

She had been in her position as manager...and probably on her perch...for several years. And although she sounded as though she just arrived from New Jersey, she had been in L.A. most of her life.

This made her a good source for Hank for just about anything he needed to know about the area. So he usually spent a few minutes chatting with her each evening after he came home from work or from his workout in the park. She didn't seem to have much of a life outside the apartment and was always happy for the attention.

She attended Hollywood High School, that was not far from the apartment, with some notables, and she liked to tell the yokel kid from Texas about her experiences growing up in "Hollywood." Some were good stories of which her favorite was about Doris Day's costar in many movies, Rock Hudson, who was a classmate.

Hank enjoyed the light formula, semi-musical movies the two made. Doris Day was the cute, blonde, freckled girl next door, semi-comedic singer and Rock Hudson was THE good looking leading man of his day… a hunk, which Ms. Manager thought was humorous because, according to her, Rock was really a *"flaming fag."* The word back then was not "gay."

This was years before groups began adopting euphuisms to avoid stating the truth or to misdirect people from what they are about for reasons known only to them. But Hank has never cared what anyone is, does, or how he refers to himself.

He has known and worked with many gay people over the years. In fact, he usually gets along better with "gay" than with "straight" men because many are creative enjoy good food, clothes and beauty in all things.

The sexual orientation of Rock was not news to him. Almost everyone knew he was, even in Grand Prairie, but this was the first, first hand confirmation of it he had heard, which was meaningless in itself because, after all, the movies are "Hollywood" make believe. So what's the problem with a guy making money entertaining people pretending to prefer something he really doesn't, as long as he does a good job of it?

It was only her story and take on it that made it interesting, and it was his first up close and personal Hollywood story that, ironically, he would have a tangential experience with twenty-five years later when he and his wife bought a home in Beverly Hills in what is locally referred to there as *"gay gulch."*

Although Rock passed away a year or so before they moved in, his home was about a hundred yards from theirs, and they would frequently encounter another famous leading man who shared a lot with Rock other than choice of neighborhood.

Both were big, tall masculine leading men. Frequently when they encountered him on the street in the neighborhood George Peppard would greet them with his booming baritone voice that would echo through their little end of the canyon.

Peppard was also a favorite of Hank's. He was a different, more serious leading man than Hudson, who played soldiers, pilots and other masculine action roles of which his favorite was in *"The Carpet Baggers"* wherein there was one of those memorable movie lines of the time.

When he asked his costar Elizabeth Ashley what she would like to see on their honeymoon, her response, *"Lots and lots of beautiful ceilings,"* was racy for the time.

Peppard passed away a few years after Hudson. But the departure of both seems to have been the beginning of a void in "Hollywood" for big good looking masculine men.

Ms. Manager had a friend who also lived in the complex she had over for coffee and conversation occasionally. This lady was also Jewish, in her early forties, slender and not unattractive, although she was twenty years Hank's senior.

One evening when he was coming home, Ms. Manager was on her perch. After a couple minutes of chat, she asked if he would like to stop by her apartment an hour or so later for some coffee and sweet roll she got from the Helms Bakery truck that morning.

The truck came by the apartment on a regular schedule. The driver blew a whistle and anyone who wanted bread or great pastries could go out to the street and buy them. Since he had become a fan of Helms' sweets, not to miss a good pastry, he agreed.

When he went to her apartment he was surprised Ms. Manager's lady friend was also there. She failed to mention she was going to be there. It was a set up.

While they were having coffee and pastries, they engaged in the usual, meaningless, conversation one would expect between casual acquaintances. But then it shifted to what they were going to be doing the rest of that evening. The lady friend said something unmemorable, but Ms. Manager became almost mother-like with something like *"Why don't you kids?"*

The lady friend had also become pretty friendly the last few minutes, so she and Hank left together and went to his apartment.

He couldn't remember whether it was her suggestion, but it doesn't make any difference. It was obvious that was her intention from the beginning, as it was the intention of Ms. Manager. So, that evening, he was seduced by a woman twenty years older than he. But it took two of them to do it, and it took a bit of planning and preparation on their part. He thought he should have been flattered.

This was the first time he had an apartment manager take sufficient interest in him to endeavor to assist in his sexual life, really just get him laid, but it was not the last.

This time, he was certain Ms. Manager thought she was doing her friend a favor by "fixing her-up" with a much younger, reasonably attractive guy. But more importantly, because they were like coconspirators in the deed, her friend would be obligated to provide Ms. Manager all the details.

Thus, it was a certainty her interest in the deed was more vicarious participation than gifting her friend with Hank. The next time it would be well intended match making by a manager who thought her friend needed a boyfriend.

Another of the 7323 characters was an Italian guy about forty years old who was a waiter at Diamond Jim's steak house in Hollywood. He was a straight, married, nice guy who worked as much as he could. Hank never saw him without his black slacks, white shirt and black tie, either coming from, or going to work. He also wore black garters on his biceps. That was the uniform because Diamond Jim's décor and ambiance was late nineteenth century brothel. It had flocked red wall paper and lots of brass.

He was like a characterization of the typical movies' Italian waiter, short dark Italian with black hair and moustache, mannerisms and all. He was always chatty and friendly.

One day he asked Hank if he had ever been to Diamond Jim's. When he told him no, he thought it was expensive, he said *"You must come."*

A few days later he arranged for Hank to go on a certain night when he was working, and confirmed a reservation.

He had a great steak dinner. His waiter friend stopped to chat as much as possible. Ensured he was happy with the meal. Then, when he was finished and asked for the check, his waiter friend refused to give it to him. He said he shouldn't worry about it. It was on him. And he hoped he enjoyed it.

It was beginning to seem like he had a family looking out for him; free coffee and pastries, free unsolicited sex, free dinners in nice restaurants. What could be next?

There was a tall, attractive, well-built, well-coiffed blonde who lived on the second floor at the front, across the courtyard from him.

She was late twenties, maybe thirty years old. He could ascertain she was well built because she could be found sunning in her bikini on a canvas beach chair in back of the complex on weekends.

Early one Saturday afternoon there was a knock at his door. It was she, minus bikini, dressed. She asked if he danced. He answered in the affirmative. Then she asked if he would like to go to a dance with her that evening. How could he refuse? She said where they were going he should wear coat and tie.

He now had five people to be grateful to for enhancing his California experience in a fairly short period of time. Thanks to his father for spending a lot of time teaching him to dance, his manager and her friend for the older woman experience, his waiter friend for great, free food, and, now, his new blonde friend for what was yet to be determined, but one thing was certain: No *"California Dreamin"* for Hank. It was reality...all the way.

They went to the Ambassador Hotel on Wilshire Boulevard in the area that was part of old, nostalgic "Hollywood," across from the second Brown Derby, not far from Perino's famous Italian restaurant and the apartment building where William Randolph Hearst kept his mistress, Marion Davies, in the 1920s.

Thanks to his mother's glossy movie magazines like "Photoplay," he was aware of all of this. Too bad he was "out there" where she always dreamed of being... and she was still in Grand Prairie.

The Coconut Grove! The Coconut Grove in the Ambassador Hotel; it could not get any more old "Hollywood" than that. Hank in coat and tie and his date in her full length cream colored, clingy, satin gown... maybe it was silk. That was where they were going dancing.

He drove up to the front of the Ambassador Hotel in his shiny, gold, Impala Super Sport. No embarrassment in that. Nor was there any when his new blonde friend stepped out in her shiny, clingy cream colored gown, assisted by the doorman, under all the little lights in the ceiling of the *porte-cochère.* Hell! They even looked like they were part of old "Hollywood." Well she did, anyway. He wondered what Marion Davies looked like. He doubted she was more impressive looking than his hot, blonde date for the evening.

That was just about where the "Hollywood" nostalgia ended. Into the hotel and thru the lobby they went. O.K., the lobby was appropriately decorated. Looked like what one would expect a piece of old "Hollywood" glamour to look like. But the Coconut Grove, THE Coconut Grove?

It was an embarrassment. Not for Hank or his date, but for the Coconut Grove. It reminded him of a high school gym decorated for a beach theme dance with some impressively large, faux palm trees.

There was live music by a small orchestra, like from the "big band era." The members were appropriately attired to represent that era. The music was good. The other people there were properly attired and reasonably attractive. Service was O.K. They danced and had a good time, he thought.

There was plenty of room for a large number of people to dance, as there would have been on any basketball court. But he could not get over the disappointment of the Coconut Grove he heard about for years.

He had been to many school dances in the gym. Even proms were in the school gym. But since graduating high school, he had been dancing many nights in clubs and hotel ballrooms around Dallas and Fort Worth. Some of them were nice; some not so. But he did not remember being as disappointed with the ambiance anywhere as he was that evening.

The hotel ballrooms in Dallas and Fort Worth were better and more completely decorated than the Coconut Grove that was, after all, just a hotel ballroom that did not seem appropriately decorated for what was expected to be happening there. Given its reputation, it was far short of his expectations. It was not as nice as other ballrooms he had been to in, God help us, Texas.

Thus, his first big night in Los Angeles, was a great disappointment. He was too much a romantic. Expectations were too high. But the Coconut Grove was definitely one of those disappointing times he would call, in retrospect, a "Peggy Lee Moment."

The moment he walked into the Coconut Grove his thoughts were commensurate with the question: "Is That All There Is?" And that tempered the enjoyment of the evening.

He knew "Hollywood" is not a real place. Not a physical place. "Hollywood" describes an imaginary realm of fantasy and make-believe – not of reality, but of perception.

It exists only in the mind. It is an amorphous concept of joy and pleasure. That is the reason it is placed it in quotes herein.

As a big time movie producer would tell him years later, *"Dammit, Hank. This is not the real world. All we are trying to do here is make goddamn movies."*

The only real Hollywood is the sign in the hills. But the realm of the concept of "Hollywood" is defined by those many places of fact and nostalgia that are real.

The many bars, restaurants, hotels, studios, streets, apartment buildings and residential areas that have been popular eating and drinking establishments, residences, places of work and play, and entertainment for those who have populated, expanded and exploited the concept of "Hollywood" are real. They are the physical manifestation, the foundation, of the perception of "Hollywood" extant in the minds of millions of people, including Hank's… 'til that night'

They are found throughout an area of over three hundred square miles, encompassing a large part of the city of Los Angeles, and parts, if not all, of the cities of Beverly Hills, Santa Monica, Culver City, Burbank and other parts of the San Fernando Valley, stretching from the east end of Wilshire Boulevard to the Pacific Ocean at Santa Monica and Malibu in the west and from Burbank in the north to Culver City in the south.

The entire area is not considered "Hollywood." It is only those many places scattered throughout it that comprise what we know as "Hollywood." Still, "romantic" or not, when Hank and many others of us encounter a place or a product that does not live up to, or survive an objective evaluation of the reality of it versus its hype or its reputation, and is therefore disappointing, some find it difficult to suppress the expression of that opinion.

He did that at some point after departing the Coconut Grove. It was not well received, and that was that, but no problem.

It was like Christmas morning. Sometimes the contents of a pretty package are disappointing, and a sad fact of life is the greatest disappointments in life are people. The two disappointments of the evening were not his first, nor his last.

However, he did get to dance at the Coconut Grove before it was closed down. In the future, he would also lunch at the Brown Derby and dine at Perino's before they were torn down, eat chili at Chasen's before it was turned into a market, and lunch in movie studio commissaries.

He would also stay at the Ambassador Hotel, before it was demolished, live in a Beverly Hills home built for an international performing star and shower frequently in the shower used by Darryl F. Zanuck. Life was good and going to get even better.

CHAPTER 7

THE CALIFORNIANS

Russ was a guy about Hank's age who lived on the first floor about forty feet from the door to his apartment who was the source of his brief relationship with Bob of "*Bob's rule,*" and whose apartment was a scene of almost constant activity...of the comings and goings of a variety of people who were so frequently there that if 7323 Willoughby were a TV program, they would have to be included as members of the cast... probably along with Russ as the main characters, after Ms. Manager.

Bob was a roommate of Russ who was planning to return home to New Jersey for stay of unknown duration. Not desiring to foot more than half the rent, Russ sought a new roommate.

He found one. Only problem was timing. The roommate had to move in before Bob's planned departure, or no deal. Solution: Hank.

He agreed to let Bob stay with him for a while... not very long... between the date the new roommate moved in and his planned departure.

It was O.K. with him because Bob was a good guy who had been in L.A. for a while, so he was a benefit to the new arrival. He knew places to go, so he and Hank went out together some.

He was humorous and sociable in terms of being friendly and providing companionship, at least to Hank, but maybe not to everyone. In the strictest sense of the term "sociable" he may have been too ready to offer companionship from the point of view of some.

One night they were in a little Lebanese restaurant, Shakers at 6756 Hollywood Boulevard, he introduced Hank to. He liked it. It was nice. Not expensive. The food was good. The owner and his wife were accommodating and solicitous toward customers, and as a result, as he watched his father do in his business years before, they developed a following of regulars, some of whom were interesting.

It was a comfortable neighborhood bar he liked and frequented for the duration of his time in Los Angeles. It was so comfortable that maybe Bob became a little too comfortable there.

One night when he and Hank were sitting in a booth he got up and went to the bar. Hank didn't understand why. Since they had a waiter, he wondered where Bob was going. So he watched as he went directly to an attractive young lady sitting at the bar. He spoke with her for a few minutes. Then she slapped him.

He came back to the table acting normal, as though nothing happened. Intrigued by his nonchalance after what he just witnessed, Hank asked him, *"What happened?"*

He said, *"After talking with her a couple of minutes, I asked her if she wanted to fuck."*

Surprised, Hank said, *"You what!"*

Bob responded, *"Yeah. I ask every one of them I meet, if I have an opportunity."*

Still somewhat amazed, Hank said, *"You do?"*

Bob's response was, *"If you don't ask, you aren't going to get any,"* which he followed up with, *"you'd be surprised how often it works."*

That is the source of *"Bob's rule."*

Shortly afterward Bob returned to New Jersey, and Hank never saw him again, but received a letter later that he was alive and well in New Jersey.

He has been grateful to him ever since for the gift of *"Bob's rule"* for which he has greatly expanded the field of use and determined, *"You know what? Bob was right. You'd be surprised how often... and well... it works."*

⊷⊱⊰⊶

Also among the "friends" of Russ who continued to be regulars in his new little world at 7323 was Russ' mother, his sometime girl-friend Judy, an Iranian girl, also a sometime girlfriend, and a male friend whose names are forgotten. There were many others who came and went, but these were the only regulars of any note... the main cast.

Russ' mother was a kick. She was a mid-forties peroxide blonde who drove one of those Ford Skyliner retractable hard top convert-ibles Ford built for only three years. Hers was the latest, a turquoise and cream '59. She was always dressed as though she was going some-where important and she always called Russ *"darling"* as she kissed, really pecked at him Continental fashion, on each cheek, both in greeting and when departing.

All these others were also about the same age as Hank. Judy was a nice Jewish girl. Pretty. Blonde hair cut short and fashionable. From a wealthy family in Beverly Hills, she drove her own new, gray Cadillac Coupe de Ville. He went with her and others for a day at the beach one weekend. She was very nice, pleasant and educated.

The Iranian girl was attractive, but a little fleshy. She was olive skinned with black hair, had been in the country quite a while, but wasn't born in the U.S. She was nice and seemed well educated. She was from an affluent family and drove a new Thunderbird.

The male friend seemed more immature than the others. His family owned a chain, or a big interest in a chain of grocery stores. He drove his own little red Porsche. He was also a nice guy.

Russ, Hank guessed, based on his mother, his friends and his attitude, also did not have to worry about where his next meal would be coming from if he were out of work. He drove one of those newer, more streamlined MGs, a MG A, which he drove because he was more of a sport car guy than a comfort seeker.

He was less settled... a little wilder than the others. For example: he liked to drive his MG on the sidewalks of Hollywood Boulevard late at night and race MGs up on Mulholland Drive after midnight. He was a native of Los Angeles, as were Judy and the male friend.

The group was different from the people Hank grew up with and those he had been associating with since he graduated from high school. They were, for want of a better term, a step up in sophistication, in the worldly wise sense, better educated, more open, self-assured and, he thought; definitely more enjoyable to associate with.

However, before he became very well acquainted with Russ and friends, he toured the area around the apartments on foot to become acquainted with it. This included the park behind the apartments that consisted of tennis courts, a playing field large enough to play half field football, and a workout, gymnastics area well equipped with parallel bars, high bar and rings.

One of the first observations he made was the large number of fairly young people with nice cars and good tennis gear playing tennis during the day on week days he assumed must be members of the wealthier strata that did not have to work or had positions that gave them the flexibility to get away for a few sets whenever they desired.

He was amazed when he heard some of them talking. Many were out of work, or between jobs in the entertainment industry. They talked as though their drawing unemployment benefit was just a benefit of the type of work they did that was not stable.

He had never heard people talking openly, shamelessly, about drawing unemployment money, rather than working full time jobs if they could.

Although the courts had lights with coin boxes you could deposit quarters in to play at night, there was rarely ever anyone playing at night. But the pop...pop...pop of tennis balls began so early every morning he didn't need an alarm clock to awaken when he needed to go to work.

He could have generously assumed they could not afford to pay for the lights, but their gear and their autos dispelled any notion of that possibility.

He learned many of them were working at night, off the books, as waiters and bartenders where they made as much as they did in their day jobs when they were working. Thus, in essence they were crooks, by any definition, illegally taking money they did not earn, or deserve.

He hoped this was not the norm in California because this would be indicative of a culture different from what he was accustomed to, and did not desire to become a part of.

But the gymnastics and playing field areas were different. They were vacant during weekdays, but busy after work hours during the week and during the day only on weekends. These were people he was more interested in getting to know for that reason and because they were working on being physically fit, and developing their bodies.

He began going to the gymnastics area and talking with the guys who were regulars. They were friendly and willing to help him get started trying to get his less than buff body in better condition.

In this endeavor he found they were really like unpaid coaches, eager to help someone better himself physically because they thought it was important. Why else would they have been spending all the time and exertion had they not thought it important? They also could have been working evenings and making more money.

His recent choice of employment and nights free, rather than continuing with the Merrill Lynch program, gave him something in common with these guys in addition to working out.

They had similar work, moral and ethical values he found comforting. It meant these guys were among the more trustworthy Californians in the neighborhood.

Actually, most of them did live in the neighborhood, whereas it seemed the tennis bums drove to the courts. They lived elsewhere.

He began going to the park and working out every other night, religiously. Some nights he would play touch football after his workout, until one night he slipped on the damp evening grass and tore a groin muscle.

That was the worst pain he ever experienced until that time. He did not know it was just a mild precursor to real pain he would experience in later years. But still, it was six weeks after the tear before he was able to walk without pain. So after that night he stuck to his workout routine and a little jogging around the park afterward.

It took less than a month after he began working out before he began to show noticeable results, which was really pretty fast. In fact, one of the older guys who began helping him, and was in outstanding physical condition came across the park to where he was working out one evening to complement him on his progress.. He said he could see the difference in his body from halfway across the park, and congratulated him on his diligence and fast results, which Hank learned would be something he could depend on even when he was much older.

Within six months he gained twenty pounds and added two inches to his chest, while retaining his waist size. His stomach was hard and arms were much larger. He was "buff."

This was accomplished through a simple routine of pushups, dips and sit ups on the parallel bars, chins, pull ups and pull ups with presses on the high bar, and climbing up one side of the pipe A-frame that supported the rings, about twenty feet to the top, down the other and back up and down again in three repetitions using only his arms... no legs.

It was routine and diligence that paid off. The physical conditioning made him feel better and adherence to a set routine...neither was
previously a part of his life...did not just pay off in short term results.
Both became part of his life he has adhered to religiously ever since
with, according to his doctors and lack of most of the usual age related ailments, positive long term health enhancement.

Also, his sudden interest in developing his body was fortuitous.

When he began doing this he had no idea what lay before him
in terms of lifestyle changes that, as a result of his new found like of
physical conditioning and adherence to routine, would be easier for
him.

Much like the purchase of the new Chevrolet, it would be just
dumb luck that would benefit him in ways he could never have
foreseen.

⊱⊰

It was not just the guys in the park who were friendly. All the guys he
met were much friendlier than he was accustomed to in Texas.

Whereas in Texas males tended to be belligerent and not terribly
friendly, in Los Angeles they were more self-assured. They did not act
as though their manliness was on trial all the time.

If he happened to sit down at a bar next to a female who was with
a male companion, rather than acting like he was irritated if Hank
said something to the female, he was as likely to ask him to keep her
company if he went to the men's room. He found this refreshing.

This also, at least once, worked out well. At the Lebanese restaurant and bar on Hollywood Boulevard there was a young couple who
became regulars. The female, Priscilla, was a reasonably attractive
red head from Poughkeepsie... how could he forget that... New York.

One night when her boyfriend went to the men's room she slipped
her phone number to him and asked him to phone her, which he did,
and she invited him to her place for dinner, and for the evening.

He, naturally, accepted. He was beginning to appreciate Los Angeles more and more every day… especially at night.

There were, however, a couple of times when "guys" were a little friendlier than he liked. He felt like the young lady at the bar with Bob that night but he restrained himself.

Down the street from the Lebanese restaurant was the Hollywood Roosevelt Hotel that had a lively bar he liked, the Cinegrill. It was not a "gay" bar. The clientele always consisted of couples and singles of both sexes of all ages. There were after theater, after dinner and hotel guests. But twice he had older "guys" at the bar offer to buy drinks for him. One time it was a line he had heard before in different surroundings, *"My, what a cute accent. Where are you from, Texas or Oklahoma?"* That was enough!

But this was a positive "Hollywood" experience. He decided he had to get rid of either his buff body or the Texas accent to avoid these advances. The body won. He began to work as diligently to get rid of the accent as he was doing to condition his body. He has benefited from that decision, ever since, also.

⇥⇤

When he wasn't out and about by himself, Russ and one of his entourage or other friends were usually available to go out or do something in the evenings and he also joined them on excursions to the beach on some weekends, although he has never been much of a beach person… maybe because of a night on one in Texas.

The sun and sand never were an attractive combination for him although he did enjoy running in the sand fifteen years later when he had an apartment on Coronado Island near San Diego. In fact, it was Russ' girlfriend Judy with whom he first ran on a beach, in 1962 at Malibu.

Most of the time, he liked to go out alone to see what might develop. Another place he found interesting was a large club on Santa Monica Boulevard in Hollywood close to Beverly Hills.

P. J.'s had live music and a nice long bar at which the actress Stella Stevens could occasionally be found sitting at the far end, away from the front door. He heard she was the lady friend of the owner.

It was there one night he had the first of his many "small world" experiences.

Treni Lopez the popular Latino musician and singer, recording artist from Texas was performing with his band. After watching and listening for a while with the standing audience in the room set aside for live performances, as the group was beginning to take a break, he was leaving to go to the bar when he heard a male voice from behind call his name.

He turned around just in time for the guy who called his name to grab his hand and shoulder. It was Mickey Jones from Grand Prairie who lived in his neighborhood when they were growing up. He had not seen Mickey since they were fifteen years old when Mickey would occasionally give him a ride home from school on the back of his bike.

He left Grand Prairie and moved to the western Dallas suburb of Oak Cliff before high school. There he attended Sunset High, the same school as Lopez, where he began playing drums in Lopez' band.

It was embarrassing. While playing in the band up on the stage, Mickey picked him out of the audience of several dozen after not having seen him for at least seven years, while he had been watching Mickey and the other four or five people on the stage without noticing him. But it was a pleasant experience. He was happy to see Mickey, and hear how well he was doing. (It is always nice to see someone you know who is a normal, nice person achieve a high level of success.) A few years later he saw Mickey in a couple of B biker movies.

⚔️

It was about this same time he had another small world experience.... this one involving a young lady he met as a result of having the phone number of the American Airlines Stewardess College back in Texas.

One day, as he was driving on Sunset Boulevard, he happened to look up at the famous billboard near La Cienega, and there she was. Gay Love... her real name (Her parents had a sense of humor.) who answered the phone one night in late 1961 or early 1962 when he phoned the College was on the billboard with two other American stewardesses.

That night he phoned, Gay and he had a blind date, which was not a problem, since she was an American Airlines stewardess, and he had never seen one that was not attractive.

They spent a pleasant time at the Colonial club on the "Strip" between Grand Prairie and Arlington. She was really attractive. No wonder she was one of those chosen to promote the airline. But he did not see her again. She graduated and left the Dallas/Fort Worth area.

This day, accepting fate, he decided to try to contact her after seeing her on the billboard. He phoned the American Airlines operations center in L.A., told the lady who answered the phone the whole story, asked if Gay was stationed in L.A. The lady confirmed she was. He asked for her number. The lady said that was not possible. It was against company rules, but recognizing another opportunity to apply *"Bob's rule"* and a little assertiveness, as he had so successfully in pursuit of employment, decided to do just that. Success again! Bob was really a lot smarter than he appeared.

Gay lived pretty far down the beach south of LAX, Los Angeles International Airport. She seemed happy to see him. They had a pleasant evening. Bob was right again, but... and probably a mistake... and another he would make again, at least once... no, many more... he decided against all the driving just to be with another lovely young lady, given he was surrounded by them, and he was definitely not interested in "jumping back into bed"... so to speak... for another long term relationship. *"Been there, done that."*

No. Thanks. Life at that time was strictly devoted to the present. So, *c'est le vie!*

☛⬩☚

Another night when he decided to go it alone proved... as he determined for future reference, also... all that driving was not necessary to satisfy his short term lifestyle desires.

He had been out for the evening and was returning home between ten and eleven when, as he was getting out of his car, the Iranian girl was coming from Russ' apartment. Apparently she came to see him unexpectedly, and he was not home.

She asked him if he would like to go with her to have a drink or two. Why not? He had nothing else to do... except go to bed by himself, maybe.

She said they could go in her Thunderbird. She drove. Took him to a popular "Hollywood" hangout in Sunset Plaza on Sunset Boulevard, Cyrano's.

When she entered, it was obvious it was not her first time there. The maître d' happily greeted her by name while hugging her.

They had two expensive drinks. When it was time to leave, he offered to pay, but as with his Italian waiter friend, she would not permit it. Said it was her idea, thus her treat. It was definitely her show, then and later when she took him back to his apartment without asking if that was what he would like. She just assumed, or most likely didn't care.

This was the second time he was the beneficiary of a seductress at 7323 Willoughby. If he had been able to keep his mouth shut about "Hollywood" it would have been the third.

Had he picked the right apartment complex? It certainly seemed that way. Or, maybe, it was just Los Angeles. He did not know, did not care. But this was also not the last time he would experience a similar occurrence in a similar place, under similar circumstances. The only difference being the next time it would have long lasting results.

Everyone seemed to be interested in ensuring he was having a good time in Los Angeles. Even his Aunt Sis' oldest daughter, his cousin Donna, got in on the act.

She phoned one day to tell him she met a really cute girl who just started working with her at the telephone exchange as an operator, and she wanted to set him up on a blind date with her.

He told her he was not interested in a blind date, and a tiny lie that he had never had one... he didn't think American Stewardesses counted... and didn't see any need for them, unless the prospective date was one better not seen before the date.

Donna insisted she would not lie to him; the girl was really nice and good looking. Besides, why would she do something that would cause him to have a bad time and be mad at her after the fact? That made sense, so he relented. Still, he was concerned.

One night during his relationship with him, Bob made a blind date with a telephone operator. Hank remembered telling him that might not be a smart move since you never knew what you were going to get in a blind date... unless she was an American Stewardess. (Heavy emphasis on WAS because it is different over 50 years later.)

He thought blind dating is like pot luck dinner where you can't determine what is in the pot even after you see it. Thus, you don't desire to eat it even after you see it.

He always wondered if people brought only things they would not eat because there was something wrong with them... or worse.

A blind date is the same. Even if she looks good, one still has to wonder why she resorts to this. What is wrong with her to be revealed later, resulting in something analogous to indigestion?

Bob insisted this girl had such a lovely, sexy voice, he had spoken to her several times, liked talking with her etc., etc. How bad could it be?

They went in Hank's car (Bob didn't have one.), picked up his date first, then Bob's. As an editorial note, it should be stated right now: Bob's rule was not in play that night.

The girl seemed nice. She did have a nice voice. She seemed intelligent. He could understand why Bob said what he did about her.

When they got into the car, he got out to permit her to get into the back seat on his side because Bob had gone to the passenger side, and it would have been a bit of a hassle for the young lady to get in on that side and make her way over to the driver's side of the back seat. She weighed north of two hundred pounds... maybe two fifty.

Bob lied. He did not *"ask every one of them"* he met. Apparently *"Bob's rule,"* like wrestling, had a weight limit. It was this he was thinking about on the way to his date.

Bob's solution... unlike *"Bob's rule,"* Hank has never had to resort to... didn't contain any verbalization. After a short drive away from the "baggage"... this was how Bob treated her... pick up point, they stopped at a red light. (This is when he realized why Bob got in on the passenger side. He planned.)

There, in the middle of the street, Bob pushed on the back of Hank's date's passenger seat, asked her to open the door, got out and walked away, leaving Hank to clean up his mess he would not have had Bob listened to him.

Now, there he was, not having listened to himself, going to have to deal with whatever was about to happen, alone. He was hoping he was about to experience an evening wherein he was more likely to apply *"Bob's rule"* than "Bob's solution."

Donna did not lie. She was attractive and well dressed. But he was about to experience a "twofer" of firsts in one evening. A blind date and.............

She had a male cat. Full grown. Little sucker must have thought he was a lion. He came to the door with her, and did not look friendly. He wasn't. She asked Hank if he would like to have something to drink before they went out.

Upscale lady; suggested they have a glass of wine, and he take a seat on the sofa, as she headed for the kitchen. Oops! As he turned toward the sofa, the guard dog, aka cat, leapt upon the sofa and turned to face him off with a hiss that said, *"Don't you dare!"*

She took him off the sofa, apologized, put him on the floor while telling him something like *"Bad cat,"* and continued toward the kitchen.

Yeah. Hank was certain cat paid attention to her warning from the way he stayed in the room, casing him as burglar might do a place he is about to rob, figuring out the best course of attack.

He was right. She returned with two glasses of wine, handed one to him and turned to sit down. As she was beginning to sit a reasonable distance from him so she could turn facing him to permit them to have a get acquainted chat, cat went back into action.

The little sucker jumped up onto the sofa again, back to her, facing Hank. Very close. Ears back, mouth wide open, he let out a loud, very angry hiss that made the previous one sound like a friendly greeting.

Hank was certain had cat been big enough, he would have attacked and killed him. He was in love and was going to ensure he did not have any competition. He... it was not like a dog protecting someone from harm. He was protecting his love like a jealous lover. She would prove later she was aware of this little creature's idea of his place in her life.

Hank took a couple of sips and suggested *"Maybe we should get on the road,"* probably subconsciously picking the word "road" over "going" or leave," or some other, because at that moment he was thinking bad thoughts about his newfound little enemy.

He never had a liking for cats after that. He was always suspicious of them after that experience... even thirty years later, to the year, when his wife, out of the blue one day, suggested she wanted *"to get a cat"* he had an immediate flashback, and not one that brought the pleasure of that evening to mind. Why? Why would she suddenly want to have a cat? Why in Hell would anyone in her right mind want to bring one of those things into her house? (He would learn later.)

He had a pleasant evening. Must have been before midnight when they returned to her place, then the usual sitting in the car for a while after a pleasant date with a friendly, attractive female.

When he thought it was time, he suggested he should go and started to open the car door. As the interior light came on she said *"just a minute."*

She needed to find her keys, and began digging in her purse, as women often do. After a minute or two; Surprise! She said she could not find her keys.

They discussed what they were going to do. Her apartment was on the second floor of a two story house that had only two units – one on each floor. Thus, getting in through a window was not a possibility because he didn't have a ladder in the car.

She didn't want to phone her landlords, the older couple who owned the house, to get a key because it was too late. Since she lived there only a short time she was concerned calling them at that late hour would not look good to them. What to do?

Shortly, she had the solution: she would go home with him and he could bring her back in the morning when she would feel comfortable asking her landlords for a key. So, off they went to Hank's apartment, as he was fairly certain she planned earlier.

The certainty... as, unknown to her; she was the third one to accomplish this feet in less than three months... of this was confirmed in his mind a few years later when he met another young lady in a club with whom he got on pretty well, danced a few times, and when it was time to go, he walked her to her car only to find the parking lot locked.

The next morning he said something to her about the night and the luck of the parking lot being locked, to which she immediately responded, *"Luck had nothing to do with it,"* further elaborating that she *"knew what time the parking lot closed"* because she parked there all the time. Then he remembered the prominent sign with the closing time posted that would have been difficult to miss had he been driving into the lot.

This time, he could not remember a time when her keys could have fallen from his date's purse. Locked gate? Lost keys? Different ploy, same result?

Yes. Similar to the later experience; the problem was resolved in the morning. When she was putting herself together, she miraculously *"found"* her keys. Seems she couldn't see them in the dim light of the car's interior light, and she could not feel them either. But she could find them in the morning light?

He humorously thought, she really was sort of a genuine "blind date."

He appreciated the demonstrated, female deviousness in both these experiences. He benefited from it both times. But, thinking about it, he was certain this is never employed for the benefit of the other party. It is always selfish, one sided. Men are only lucky when it is to their benefit.

However, he thought it flattering to be desired for self-satisfaction… and he was thankful for "the Pill," its liberating effect on women relieving them of any potential burden resulting from their decisions or actions, and the timing of its approval vis-à-vis the date of his birth.

He also considered himself lucky both times because the ladies' deviousness permitted him to avoid having to utilize *"Bob's rule,"* and the potential embarrassment of a *"no."*

Maybe their intent was to forestall his asking to prevent their answering *"yes"* and losing face over it? Who knows? Trying to answer that would be comparable to trying to understand a government decision about a navy base hundreds of miles from the ocean.

But there was one big difference between this blind date experience and the parking lot experience: the lack of honesty about the deviousness. However, he thought there was a reason for which he could excuse her… to give her a face saving out.

She was afraid… No. She knew…her little tiger would have ruined her plans if she took Hank back to her place. Therefore he was grateful she considered that because he was certain the evening would have turned out much differently…"Sexual Revolution," or not.

Cats were not changed by it. They have always been territorial and possessive of the human who takes care of and feeds them, especially if the human is female and sleeps with them. Also, they are very agile, smart, cunning and not afraid of anything… of any size.

But furry feline experiences aside, Hank was beginning to really like Los Angeles women. They were a lot different from what he was accustomed to in Texas; more direct and more enjoyable, seemingly more comfortable in their "Revolution" than his Texas experiences.

⇥ ⇤

He spent more time with Russ and friends. Russ' MG would seat only two, the Porsche also two, his Chevy, five. So, if there were more than two of them going out without one of the girls with the big comfortable cars, they usually ended up in his Chevy.

They went to clubs and restaurants mostly within the area between Beverly Hills and Western Avenue, a distance of about five miles east to west, the Hollywood Hills to the north, and Pico Boulevard to the south. Thus, most of his entertainment activities were within an area of about twenty-five square miles, except when he occasionally went to Santa Monica or the beach.

This was a much smaller geographic area than he traversed for entertainment in Texas, and it had so much more to offer it was incredible.

Having hundreds of thousands of people within this area provided the basis for much more entertainment than could be found in the entire Dallas/Fort Worth metro area. It was also more expensive. He had his first $1.25 coke there… in 1962.

He also found *"Hollywood"* could be dangerous for the uninitiated.

Russ was really a bit of luck for him. Without someone like he, about his age, who knew the area, and with whom he got along well, he would have had to waste a lot of time finding where, and where not, to go. Thus, he was a great asset to Hank's social life except when he got him into trouble or almost killed.

One day he and Judy came to him with a request. Apparently Russ had some kind of problem with her father, or vice versa. They did not tell him what it was, and he did not ask. Didn't think it was any of his business. But whatever it was, as a result of the problem Judy could not go out with Russ. If her parents knew about it, she was grounded for a while and prevented from using her Cadillac.

So, they asked him if he would pose as Judy's date, pick her up and return her later in the evening. He said no problem. Happy to do good friends a favor because they really did like one another a lot and they were both nice to him.

The night of the faux date he dressed nicely in slacks, long sleeve shirt and a sporty vest, all well-coordinated. Or, so he thought, until after he arrived at Judy's big home in Beverly Hills.

The maid met him at the door and showed him into the living room where the grand-mother was waiting. The way she looked at him, he felt as though he needed a mirror to check out his appearance because something must have been wrong with it.

It seemed to go downhill from there. Shortly, her mother and father came into the room. No problem, he had been through this setup before where the daughter is told not to come in until the parents have time to check out the date. But this time it was different. There was almost visible hatred.

He thought he felt as Jew must have being interrogated by Nazis. Based on movies he had seen that was the best comparison he could conceive. He had never been through such an offensive, belligerent, brutal interrogation like that. EVER! Even later in the military when he went through training interrogations, they were never as personal as this one.

Unlike most of the other people he knew during his days in L.A., he remembered Judy's last name as a result of this unforgettable experience, but he considered the experience so bad he never disclosed it when relating the experience to anyone.

Judy was a really nice girl and he did not want to risk embarrassing her. But he will never forget this experience, or the name of the bigoted asses that treated him that way.

There was no excuse for it, especially from people who continually bitch and complain about persecution? Well, since that date, they have not been able to elicit any sympathy from Hank. He really did not appreciate being mistreated by anyone for whatever misguided perception they might have. He was not their problem. His opinion based on what he experienced that night was they are their own biggest problem.

Although he could never have guessed, it got even worse. Absolutely incredible!

The next morning, Judy phoned him. She said, and he swears this is a direct quote, because he will never forget it, *"Hank, I can't go out with you again. My father told me 'if you go out with that goddamned Goy again I will disown you."*

He knew Judy would not call to tell him that because she was in on the fact that he was not really her date for the prior evening. Thus, she had no reason to phone him with that message. The only reason she would have done that was because her father told her to do it and was listening to ensure she delivered the message, as instructed.

It was difficult for him to imagine what kind of "man" would treat his daughter this way. What could possibly have driven him… he who lived in a Beverly Hills mansion and was obviously successful… to treat his daughter, or him he knew nothing about, except he was not Jewish, like that?

A few years later he would quietly recall this incident when his roommate would make denigrating comments about anyone who lives *"west of the Hudson river,"* and think of the irony in the fact that this jerk who shared his roommate's heritage and some of his views of others who did not share their heritage lived *"west of the Hudson river."*

He really didn't care about the views held by either of these two. But he was disturbed by the fact this obviously testicular challenged coward did not have the balls to personally call him, which he is sorry to have to say was the first, but not the last, time he had this experience with people of this same intolerance in Los Angeles who also did not have the testicular fortitude to confront someone, but sent an underling to do his unprovoked dirty work.

He wondered how nice Jewish girls like Judy and Sandra, and other nice Jewish people he knew, live within this kind of "culture." How could they, and be so nice?

Really! How could anyone treat others as these people or the Baptists in Texas treat others whose only "crime" is not sharing the same beliefs that are based on some intangible and meaningless philosophy, religion or whatever drives them?

How can people like either of these start wars over their unreal inconsequential in the real world differences? What the hell is going on in the heads of those for whom their religion is more important than the real world that keeps them from treating the beliefs of others with the respect they expect for themselves?

⊷⊶

To Hank's knowledge, he never knew a Jewish person before. Surely, there must have been some in Grand Prairie, but he couldn't remember any religious edifices other than Christian.

Maybe there were some, but not enough to support a synagogue, and they went to Dallas for their worship. He didn't know, but he was certain had there been any and they conducted themselves like these it very likely would have happened only once because they would have found a whole new meaning for "prejudice and intolerance" and learned the Christian version is worse... likely physical.

He witnessed bigotry in Grand Prairie by Christians. There were two Baptist groups. From what he knew they were all Baptists. There was no discernible difference. But that was not the way they saw it.

There was some narrowly defined difference in what each was devoted to. But what he just experienced he did not consider bigotry. It was persecution. He received horribly ill treatment just because they thought he may have held some views different from theirs.

That experience was intolerable. It was obvious what the problem between Russ and Judy's father was: Russ was not Jewish.

Hank thought he was like himself, neutral – no religious beliefs, which as a result of this incident and Christian conduct he witnessed while growing up in Grand Prairie made him feel vastly superior to people who could let what he thought to be a myth cause them to treat others as they do just because they may have different beliefs.

He was not happy with Russ and Judy for failing to inform him of the reason for the subterfuge of the evening. However, he did not press the matter because he did not think they could have imagined the response elicited from Judy's father. So, he gave them a pass on it, accepting there are always some members of every group that are rabid, and writing this off as just another example of that conduct.

The next memorable experience Russ subjected him to, was not a disturbing or negative reflection on a large portion of the population of Los Angeles, as this one was. It was just one that almost got him killed.

One week Russ told him they were going to a great party Friday night. He said they would be going late, it could last all weekend, and he should get plenty of rest after work Friday and the day before.

O.K., he thought. He wasn't really interested in a multi-day party, but he had a car. So he could leave whenever he desired.

The party was in a "Hollywood" apartment. When he entered he was immediately aware this was not going to be like any party he ever attended.

Lying on the floor perpendicular to the door was a guy flat on his back, out like a stone, fully dressed in a tuxedo. Had he been standing, he would have looked fantastic. They stepped over him and entered. No one else was paying any attention to him, nor did they.

There were quite a few people there. None dressed like our friend at the door. Everyone else was casually dressed; slacks and shirts. No coats. No ties. They were laughing and talking, usual party activity. Everyone was drinking something other than beer. No beer bottles. No baseball caps. No drugs. It was just a nicely dressed gathering of young people, having a Friday night party. He and Russ joined in for a couple of hours.

Then later, after midnight, between one and two A.M., someone suggested they (?) go up to Mulholland to race MGs. From the response, there must have been several MG owners there. Could this have been the reason Russ demanded he drive his car to the party?

That he did, but remembering he thought he might want to leave early, Hank drove his car and followed Russ to the party location.

Still, against his better judgment, he permitted himself to be talked into joining in. He was going with a guy in a new MG Midget. A little car, not very powerful thus no high speed. How dangerous could that be? He was about to find out.

The course chosen to Mulholland was up Laurel Canyon, a winding, fairly steep grade street. It was misting rain sufficiently to cause the street to be slippery. Two or three curves up the hill it happened. He can remember only the two bright lights about the height of his head above the pavement coming straight at him.

It was a large Dodge convertible, a pretty heavy car that lost its traction sliding down the hill as the driver applied the brakes on the curve, coming straight at him, head on.

Much like the accident in Tacoma, he doesn't remember the crash, just the aftermath. But again, the crash put the head of the driver partially through the windshield.

Hank, as seems to be the story of much of his life, smiled on by fortune, braced himself with his right forearm and elbow against the small windshield post he already had his hand holding onto the top of before he saw the lights. When he saw the lights, he reacted by squeezing the top of the windshield, and that held his arm in its position against the post.

His head hit his arm, not the windshield. He broke the aluminum windshield post off at his elbow, which was bruised, but nothing else, no other injuries, just one bruise.

The emergency personnel at the scene were amazed. The MG was totaled, and he just expended the fourth of his nine lives, not including the near miss with the little lion.

Thankfully, he still had five left. At only twenty-two, the way things had been going the last few years he might need them.

Racing on Mulholland just added another to what he was certain must have been a long list of those opposed to such nonsense. He determined his use of Mulholland was a much smarter, better use of its heights. Sitting up there at night listening to that unique freeway sound and watching the twinkling lights was a safe, enjoyable delight.

For over a year, he had a successful, exciting time in Los Angeles, especially compared to his experiences the prior three and one-half years in the place he left behind. But, unfortunately, as seems to be an unofficial, but true, rule of life; *"all good things must end."* And those endings are usually not of our own making. They are most frequently brought about by others interfering in our lives in some way detrimental to us.

CHAPTER 8

"GREETINGS"

A round the first of April 1963, Hank received one of those rare, if ever, phone calls from his mother he knew would be bad news. She rarely conveyed any other kind.

When he left Grand Prairie, he didn't know where he was going. Thus, he did not have a forwarding address, and even after he left home and moved elsewhere in Grand Prairie, he never bothered to notify anyone. No need. A nineteen year old doesn't receive much important mail other than from utility providers that, obviously, have his mailing address. Therefore, most records anyone had of him showed his mailing address as it was four years before, including those at the Selective Service.

Funny name, that. It is anything but a "Service," and it is not "Selective." As will be proven later; it is as much a "Service" as the Internal Revenue of the same misnomer.

Does everyone employed by the government think the rest of the population of this country is stupid? The answer must be *"Yes,"* emphatically! How else could they deliberately apply the euphemism "Service" to what they do to us? Guaranteed: the only "service" anyone should expect when they receive correspondence from any government agency is that a mare receives from a stud.

He was aware of that, since fairly early in his life, thanks to his father. When he was drafted in 1944, his and his family's life was pretty much "serviced" up by the government. They moved into a new home a few months previously, and he had started a new little business that was going well. When he was drafted all of that was lost.

Also, after he got out of the military and started a new business, it seemed the government employees of the Internal Revenue "Service" had in their job description to harass and "service" him frequently, as Hank learned is their *modus operandi* with anyone who has the audacity to start a business and be self-employed.

This was confirmed for him by an IRS agent several years later when he told him *"You must be a crook. Why else would you be filing a return on a personal corporation?"*

But his mother was not calling about the I.R.S. It was worse. She phoned to inform him he just received a *"GREETINGS"* letter from the Selective Service informing him his government was ordering him to report for induction into the United States Army at Dallas, Texas on May 6, 1963, roughly thirty days thence.

It was thus he was informed his government was going to begin "servicing" him in about thirty days. But before he could report to them for "servicing" they were going to be "servicing" up his life for the next thirty days by forcing him to give up his good job, displace him from the place he was enjoying living, and force him to return to Texas.

His life was being completely "serviced" up, possibly ended at the age of twenty-three, by the same government, shall we say; assholes who "brilliantly" pulled off the Bay of Pigs almost exactly two years before, and they were doing it for the same reason behind that failed endeavor.

Their sole purpose was to attempt to further line the pockets of themselves and their puppet masters in the greedy culture of corporate America and its military/industrial complex that has found sustenance in war and the blood of young Americans it has drained in its unnecessary warmongering since WWII, in 1950, and previously in 1898 and 1917.

He was about to become cannon fodder, along with hundreds of thousands of other young Americans as Kennedy requested, but not for his stated Berlin Crisis reason.

It would become obvious later that "our" government planned to use him and hundreds of thousands of other young Americans in its planned, unnecessary expansion of its current incursion into Southeast Asia, which he thought *"This is really great... bullshit!"*

The U.S. deployed "advisors" in Vietnam, since during the Korean War, beginning in 1950, and even before, since WWII, unknown to the American public. Then they began to escalate in the early 1960s by tripling U.S. troop levels there in 1961 and tripling them again in 1962. There was no question about what the government's plans for him and the others were.

⊷⊶

Not to be trite, but there is a saying that goes something like *"Behind every cloud there is a silver lining."* Well, there was no silver lining behind the cloud the government just hung over Hank's head. The forecast for the next thirty days was nothing but cloudy skies with potential rain to dampen the spirit. However, to use an expression misappropriated by his mother, a *"little ray of sunshine"* suddenly appeared thru the clouds that could possibly provide a little respite during the despair of the balance of April, 1963.

Heidi arrived about same the time as the *"GREETINGS."* It was a few days before or after, but in his memory the two events were contemporaneous.

She went to work in the next office past his after leaving the elevator. He got only a brief glimpse of her as she passed his office door

111

when Sandra opened it to return from the ladies' room. He looked up briefly only because he heard a clicking of high heels on the tile floor in the hallway that was not familiar.

Intrigued, he asked Sandra, *"Who was that?"* She replied she was the new girl in the office next door. Pressing for more information, as any young man his age whose interests were moderately influenced by hormones would, he learned from Sandra that she was fairly tall, very pretty, well dressed and German.

She said she could not provide more information because it was difficult to converse with her due to her limited English, compounded by the accent, but since she had been listening to Mr. Benz for so long, Sandra was certain she was German. All this positive information caused Hank's intrigue to quickly evolve into strong interest.

He was determined to meet her. But because of what Sandra told him, it could be difficult to just walk up and start a conversation. Besides, where would he "walk up"? She was only in the hall to come to work, go to the ladies room or lunch, or to leave after work. Of these options, the only logical time to attempt to meet her would be lunch.

But there was no way to just "walk up" to her in the narrow hallway that would not be obvious. Lying in wait downstairs at the front door or in the elevator lobby would be even more obvious. That would look like an attempted "pick up," which he did not consider a viable alternative. And, in either of those situations, it would be necessary to try to engage her in conversation. It would be awkward if they could not communicate. If that happened, what could he do next?

He had probably seen too many movies. He devised a movie-like approach.

The next time he heard her in the hall, he counted the heal clicks on the tile from her door to his. The next day he waited for her to depart for lunch, as she had the day before. Then when she left for lunch, he counted her steps, calculating exactly when to back out of his office door, acting like he was locking it, and bumping into her with his backside.

It worked. He apologized profusely as he accompanied her to the elevator, and even while getting on with her. As the elevator doors closed, he turned to her saying he was sorry, again.

It was a small elevator. She was close. *"God,"* he thought, *"she really is tall and pretty."* She sort of blushed as though she knew what he was thinking. He got weak in the knees, actually physically affected.

They parted in front of the building, she with a little *"bye."* But that was not going to be the end of it. He knew if she was going to lunch she would walk to 6th Street and then westward. There was no place to go to lunch in any other direction. He also planned this.

He walked to his car parked at the curb just north of the driveway entrance to their building and waited until she turned the corner and had enough time to get a hundred feet, or so, on 6th Street. Then he started the car and drove around the corner westward on 6th Street with his passenger side window down in preparation.

He slowed as he pulled up close to the curb next to her and asked if she would like a ride as he simultaneously motioned with his right hand index finger pointed westward.

As she got in the car she said in pretty good English, *"I like your car."* That was a good place to start. The Chevy was looking more and more like a great investment. Without it he would not have the position in the building where she was now working and she would not be sitting next to him in it, nor would he have even been in California without it.

He thanked her. Asked where she was going. She made some comment he did not understand. He asked again. Then he understood she was going to the closest place to their building to have lunch because it was within walking distance, the cafeteria in the big church less than a quarter mile west on 6th Street.

As he pulled up to the curb close to the entrance to the building where she wanted to go he asked if she would like to go to a nice place on Wilshire at least a mile farther to the west. He thought he detected a spark of interest when he said it, but she declined and said she was meeting a friend or some other excuse to stay with her stated plan for lunch. But thinking about sparks and the possibility of some smoldering, he suggested maybe tomorrow. She nodded and, somewhat blushingly, said, *"Yes."*

It was beginning to look like letting Bob stay with him that short time was as good an investment as the Chevy. However, considering the cost of the vehicle versus the cost of Bob's stay, a calculation of the return on investment would definitely go in Bob's favor.

Heidi and he had lunch the next day. Then they had lunch again before the Thursday he popped the question about the possibility of her going to Las Vegas with him. During this time they developed the ability to communicate a little better, and he got the impression her understanding of English was better than she was acknowledging.

He did not know what her job was, but he knew she could not be a receptionist, a secretary or in a position to deal with the public unless the people she worked with were German or she had a better command of English than she was demonstrating.

Mr. Benz was German. Did he have something to do with her job next to his office? Maybe he had other interests next door Hank was unaware of.

He was not happy about Hank being drafted, but he didn't indicate any dissatisfaction with him about his being drafted after being with him less than a year. Possibly because he worked out well, and he desired him to stay, Mr. Benz said he contacted an attorney to determine if anything could be done to prevent his having to leave.

Maybe he never knew about his 1-A status and the possibility, no, probability, of his being drafted unless the employment agency lady phoned him after he left her office and had further discussion about him, which was doubtful. She had no reason, actually a disincentive, to have further conversation about this. She was paid for filling the position. When Benz hired him she had completed her task and earned her commission, plus the $100 Hank laid on her desk. Thus, it was doubtful she would have created more work for herself. Hank's position was; his money would be on Benz not knowing his status.

Anyway, his departure and going into the military within the next thirty days was *fait accompli*. In plain English, it was a done deal. One of his *"ends"* had been moved.

⊷ ⊶

After a five hour drive Heidi and he arrived in Las Vegas. Having been distracted thinking about his fate he was late picking her up. It was late afternoon when they arrived. Since they were to be there two nights, the first order of business was a place to stay.

In 1963, where the road from L.A. entered Vegas is called "The Strip" today. Then, before construction of all the big hotels and casinos, it was where the five main casinos and all the motels were located. He stopped at a nice looking motel and got a room.

He knew Vegas was a late night, or all night, town where little happened before dark. He assumed Heidi was also aware of this. Therefore, without discussing the matter, he suggested they get some sleep to rest up for a late evening, or possibly an "all-nighter."

The room had only one double bed. They got undressed, completely, and into bed… she rather nonchalantly, considering the tenure and nature of their relationship. They did not immediately try to get some rest in preparation for the night out on the town. Neither bothered to pull the covers up.

As soon as they were on the bed Heidi turned to face him, reached over with her left hand and gently ran her fingers through the fine brown hair on his chest as she said, *"I like this. I have never been with a boy before with this."*

He immediately noted her use of the term *"boy"* as opposed to "man," thinking *"She is younger than I am, as I thought. If she were older she would not have said 'boy,' and if she were very experienced she would surely*

115

have been with at least one who had hair on his chest, unless..." But that is where his extraneous thinking stopped.

Her hand did not stop at his chest, and as it moved farther she commented approvingly about his body as she also gently glided it down his firm abdomen.

⤜⤛ ⤜⤛

All he is willing to say about this today is; Los Angeles was a different world from that whence he came. He had some really good times there. More first time experiences in a year than in his entire life, before. But this one was a world apart from all the others.

There was a tremendous dichroism in the facets of this jewel between her softly stated innocence and her worldly wise conduct.

She was impressive from his initial glimpse. Minus the clothing she made look better than it should she looked even better than he imagined. She was really something. It was difficult to fathom. Sweet. Smooth. Slim. Svelte. Silky. Sexy. SSSssssisling all in one.

She had all the appropriate English S-words covered. He didn't know what it was like in German, but he would bet it was the same.

The combination of looks, poise, grace, sophistication and the rest of the package are very difficult to describe in any language, or find in any country. Though the term *"World Class"* is over worked, she was it.

She was also more-worldly than the others. He learned during their lunches she came to Los Angeles from Brazil.

What was a young German lady her age...based on her *"boy"* he was sure she was at least two years younger than he... doing in Brazil, now Los Angeles? If she could afford all the travel, why did she have a job? What was it? How did she get it so quickly?

Also, she had one of those "von" names that in Germany have a probability of linkage to nobility. The success record of *"Bob's rule,"* aside, it seemed it was too easy to get her to bed in Las Vegas.

All this caused him to engage in too much of what he has always been inclined to do too much of; thinking. So he decided to suppress that and enjoy their time in Vegas. He did not desire another Coconut Grove outcome, especially with this one.

He did have a good time. Judging from her attitude, he thought she did also. He liked her very much. She expressed admiration for his physique and there were other indications she seemed to like him as much as he liked her. Maybe she was just a good actress?

Back in L.A. his time was spent preparing to leave; getting work wrapped up, packing and spending as much time as possible with Heidi, making the most of his remaining limited time with her, toward the end of which she suddenly informed him she also decided to leave and return to Germany at about the same time as his departure.

That seemed strange to him, given the short time she was there. Also she decided to make the Atlantic crossing via ship, which was difficult for him to comprehend.

Why would a young lady desire to spend all those days alone on a big ship? But he went with her to buy a steamer trunk even though he could not fathom what she could have accumulated in a month requiring a steamer trunk.

As strange as that was, he just put it with the other unanswered questions and considered himself lucky for his time in Los Angeles, especially the last four weeks with her, ignoring his sixty-two year old Aunt Sis who insisted, seriously, probably influenced by her age and WWII knowledge, and Heidi's nationality, *"She is a spy!"*

Before he departed, as he and Heidi were saying their goodbyes, she suggested...sounding pretty positive or he could have just been wishing it was... she could possibly see him *"in Germany before long because the U.S. Military sends a lot of soldiers there."*

This whole enjoyable episode was puzzling to him.

There were many Germans in Brazil including many Nazis who escaped Germany after WWII, at least 100 of them wanted war criminals, and twenty thousand Germans settled in Brazil between the end of the war and 1959.

After Portuguese, German is the most widely spoken language there.

Also, in the 1930s Nazis spent millions building a compound for Hitler in Los Angeles in the Hollywood Hills in contemplation of his winning the war.

Brazil and other Latin countries were not unfriendly to Fascism. The shared goal of Nazis in Brazil and L.A. was a worldwide Fascist totalitarian government not unlike what those in power in the U.S. and its military/industrial complex seem to have been pursuing since the end of the war, more aggressively since the beginning of the new millennium in 2001, deploying the U.S military in actions in which this seems the not too thinly veiled ultimate objective of the "New World Order" announced by the first president Bush.

That the U.S. Government gave a pass to many in Hitler's regime and subsequently employed them in highly classified U.S. military "defense" positions, or the fact of several high profile Nazi war criminals running around Latin America for over two decades without being caught should not be overlooked. Fascism is not dead today, even in the U.S. where there are indications of a bent in that direction by many holding high positions in the government.

Also, the New York investment bank where Prescott Bush, grandfather of the recent President Bush, was a senior officer had some of its assets seized during WWII under the trading with the enemy act for alleged dealings with Hitler.

Although we surely will never know about actual connections, if any, between the powerful in the U.S. and its stated enemy Fascists in WWII, we should be aware of the foregoing and constantly vigilant of actions by the powerful here indicative of where we are headed.

Also, Hank will never know whether Heidi was only a lovely young German with relatives in Brazil who decided to stop in L.A. for a month where he was lucky to meet her and have some very memorable times, or if she was in L.A. for business with the people next door, and if so, what that business could have been, if she was checking him out on information from Mr. Benz with some future in mind... he is fair with blue eyes... or her family had contacts within the U.S. Government that could have influenced where he would be stationed... oh so many questions.

Ten years later, he was in her hometown of Hamburg, but chose not to make an effort to contact her because he was happily married for three years to the first person he met since her he considered in the same league. Also, he has always had a habit of not going back, not keeping in touch, not returning, that today he recognizes has potentially had an adverse effect, or not, on his life, and left him wondering what could have been... especially when he occasionally sees one of the bevy of beautiful German Brazilian super models flaunted in Victoria's Secret catalogues and its annual "fashion" show.

But, as the French say, *"telle est la vie."* Such is life.

CHAPTER 9

BACK TO THE PAST

Returning to the place he was so desirous of getting out of was not a trip of desire for Hank. It was pure necessity. He had to go back there because "Uncle Sam" ordered it.

Since this was not a trip of adventure, desire, escapism or new experiences, he decided to head back the uninteresting way, Highway 80, thinking he might as well see whether the southern parts of New Mexico and Arizona are as barren and uninteresting as West Texas.

He was not disappointed. They were. It was another 500 miles of interminable nothingness, which although it did not disappoint him, was depressing.

He had seen all of Route 66 between Texas and L.A. and the kitsch it had to offer the year before on his way to L.A. that was, surprisingly, a tad less interesting than the song would lead anyone to believe. Additionally, the TV show was, as is so much in life, a complete fraud.

None of the really interesting places or any of the pretty and different people in the show were to be found anywhere along this highway of "despair and disillusionment," which, with deference to

Steinbeck, struck him as somewhat short of a "Mother" of anything other than disappointment, but it was a little more interesting than Highway 80.

Steinbeck endeavored to convey it was THE "Mother," or the first of the highways in the vast system of two lane strips of asphalt planned to connect the cities of America for its newly emerging automobile culture of the second and third decades of the twentieth century, which in a way it was. Route 66 was specifically created for those desiring to travel via automobile between Chicago and Los Angeles.

It may seem a little out of the way to go almost five hundred miles south through Joplin Missouri, then sixteen hundred miles west to get to Los Angeles from Chicago, but that would be overlooking one of the most prominent topographical features of the United States, the Rocky Mountains, which it would have been much more challenging and expensive, and taken much longer, to build the highway through than around.

So south to Joplin, westward across four hundred miles of the flat nothingness of Oklahoma to Amarillo Hank did not have to travel this time, but would find years later is like West Texas with grass, then onward through more of the same in New Mexico to avoid the mountains, and have all that nice flat land on which to quickly and inexpensively build Route 66 to Los Angeles.

Hank couldn't remember whether Steinbeck was traveling with his dog *"Charlie"* on this trip or if that was a different trip. But he thought if it was the Route 66 trip he was lucky to have Charlie with him as a diversion from the reality of the America through which it passes, and he must have had some distraction to be able to write so favorably about his *"Mother Road."*

His incredulity continued to increase until after Gallup, New Mexico when he seriously wondered: *"Were Steinbeck or the song writer really here, and, if so, what were they drinking... or smoking?"* He thought for there to have been any validity in the lyrics, or Steinbeck's views,

Route 66 must have been vastly different in the decades prior to 1962, but he doubted it.

Not much changed between the time highways like Route 66 were built and development of the Interstate highway system. The towns and the people of America remained little changed until the Interstate highways permitted travelers to pass them by.

This was the death knell for many towns and small cities because so much business dependent upon the highways that passed through them disappeared or moved out to the Interstate. Thus, with the Interstate travelers have been deprived of, or spared, depending upon one's point of view, the experience of the real Middle America of places like Tucumcari and Gallup, and even Grand Prairie.

The thousands of miles of four lanes of sterile concrete that replaced those two lane ribbons of black asphalt have served to homogenize America by forcing people to desert the small towns and cities for need of sustenance, even survival.

Advancement of ease of travel through the vast Interstate highway system has served to deprive America of much of its culture and character. Most of America is now a sterile environment of sameness, void of character and connection with what made it "America"...kitsch and all.

As for the misleading appeal of the TV "Route 66," he later learned most of it was filmed elsewhere, even some of it in Canada. But he understood the reasoning behind this.

The producers were also probably misled by the song and Steinbeck's review and, after traveling some of the highway, decided the program would not be successful unless they lied to America and it was set somewhere more scenic, more attractive, and more appealing to the viewing audience, many of whom, like Hank. would have been watching the program from towns in Middle America, longing for the escapism and adventure of new experiences it offered.

The concept was a good one, especially given the catchy tune and the use of the Corvette – something most could only dream of owning. Thus, to continue with the project, but to film it somewhere else was a successful idea. Somewhere more scenic, more attractive that would leave the viewer favorably impressed, not feeling "despair and disillusionment" that surely that is not "all there is" to America, and would keep viewers desiring to get into their Chevrolets and *"See the U.S.A.,"* as Dina Shore was singing encouragement to them in her Chevrolet sponsored TV show during the same era,.

It sucked him in. He had now *"been there"* and *"seen that"* in his Chevrolet, and he did not need to experience it again, nor did he need anything to divert or distract him from whatever the five hundred miles of Highway 80 he had not traveled had to offer.

This trip was not about new travel experiences or new destinations. It was entirely about getting from point A, Los Angeles, to point B, Dallas, and he was sure the miles of Highway 80 he did not experience were much like the six hundred he had traveled.

He was just going to let his thoughts and memories keep him company. As on his last trip on this road, he was certain there would be nothing to distract him from getting to know himself a little better.

The past year in Los Angeles produced an enhanced mental state as well as a physical metamorphosis for him. He was changed, changed physically for the better. That was obvious, as the guy in the park confirmed, and as had Heidi, more recently. Thankfully, she had not seen the before. But her complementary comment was reassuring because it was the first like that he received from a female. The physical change and the complements it elicited had a positive mental effect. They enhanced confidence.

It was as if his new physique was the manifestation of a new Hank. Well, not really a new one, just a physically enhanced version.

He was obviously not lacking self-confidence before his physical enhancement. Had he been he could not have made the decision to strike out in search of another place… something better. Nor would he have had the chutzpah to so aggressively apply *"Bob's rule"* in endeavoring to get the position with Benz.

No. He had confidence before. But what developed along with his body while he was in Los Angeles was an enhanced ability to demonstrate and apply that confidence. He attained a higher level of confidence.

As addressed before; Los Angeles was a like a launch pad to his future… obviously, metaphorically. But he did feel lighter, like it was easier to rise up, to do more, to experience more; as if it really was a "lift off" from the past. The future was up. In that sense, Los Angeles was a metaphorical launch pad.

But leaving L.A. in the rear view mirror and heading back to his past, he was already beginning to slow mentally, to feel heavier. That wonderful feeling of lightness, of being able to rise above his past was seeping away. It was as if his mind was prematurely adjusting to the speech patterns of the zone he was about to reenter. Those that must, surely, be a result of the functioning speed of the processors from which they emanate.

Rather than looking to the future, he was looking to the past where he was headed; back to the sunset in the east, leaving the brightness of his sunrise at his back.

Still speaking metaphorically, it was as though he was headed back toward the millstone that previously burdened him, held him down for so long. Where, like the speech patterns, everything moved more slowly. Even in his dreams. Maybe that was the reason for his mental commentary about Los Angeles real estate and Heidi: *"never…in my wildest dreams."* Lack of exposure limits even one's dreams.

As a post-pubescent kid Hank frequently had dreams wherein he was floating above all that was familiar. These began after he was beyond the play times, when he was becoming aware of the world beyond school, home and playing. Probably around the age of fourteen, when he began working outside his father's little business world and influence to the extent other adults, outside of school teachers, also had some influence on his life.

He was moving as though he was moving away. Trying to leave behind all he was surveying. But he never did. It was as if something was holding him in place, preventing his leaving. Yet all he could determine was holding him in place like a millstone was that which he was surveying.

Grand Prairie was his millstone. It was a burden. It was the burden that prevented him from floating away in his dreams. For years, it held him there, above the same landscape… night after night. And in the dream, it was always dark. Never light.

Every night he was looking down on his father's little store at 10th and Jefferson, where he first lived in Grand Prairie. On the little duplex in the 500 block of Austin Street where he moved when his father made enough money to rent a house, on David Crockett Elementary and Grand Prairie Junior High School, on the blackness of the dirt of Crockett Park, next to the school where he played softball (and where later, that night on Thanksgiving weekend in 1958, he would do something that changed his future), on the Street where he moved when he was nine and stayed until he was nineteen, on all the little houses around there where most of the others he knew lived and played, on Brother Bill Yeager's little church on 8th where he learned so much about religion and its hypocrisy, on his father's other store next to the old Interurban building that he had to close after only three years because of the hypocrisy of those who professed their goodness and beliefs in Brother Bill's little Church and the others around town, upon so much that seemed like a burden that could never be lifted.

There was no foreseeable way out of this darkness.

CHAPTER 10

THE EARLY YEARS

1946. Hank moved to Grand Prairie not long after his father was discharged from the army on February 25th. Why Grand Prairie? His father could have moved back to Dallas where he had the little business and the home he had to sell because of his being drafted. He could have started over there or anywhere within the limitations of his financial ability. Sure it didn't cost much to get started in Grand Prairie. But what about some other place?

His father was intellectually astute. But like so many others...like most... he never thought about moving up, about going to school, about bettering himself or his lot in life, or that of his family. He was content to be as he was, but do a little better financially than those with whom he associated... was familiar with.

He was kind of like those who never desire to leave the neighborhoods of their youth. Although he worked long and hard every day, he was intellectually lazy. Hank's mother said he was like an old shoe; comfortable as he was. He had no desire to change. He did only what he wanted to do, nothing else.

Hank always thought they were like the peasantry of America. Like the farmers and little local vendors, butchers, blacksmiths and merchants throughout history. Either content to remain at the socio-economic and cultural level into which they came into this world with no desire to be anywhere else when they left it, or forced to accept it, rationalize their lot in life and live with it.

Before he was drafted March 13, 1945 he had the newest Ford sedan it was possible to buy. A 1941 model, because when the war began the production of automobiles for sale to the public ceased. But while he was in the army Hank's mother had a 1940 model.

He downgraded to add to the cash Hank and his mother would have to live on. Then when he got out of the army and went to Grand Prairie he had a 1940 Ford pickup, a further downgrade for practical business reasons. He needed it to haul the stuff he planned to get started making money with.

When Hank, his father and mother arrived at their new home in Grand Prairie, it wasn't one. It was an old, wooden garage building sitting on a vacant corner lot at 10th and Jefferson Boulevard. No plumbing, save one sink. No interior ceiling. No interior wall. No finish. No nothing. It still had overhead garage doors across the front. Concrete floors and exposed two-by-four studs. But a parking lot had been graveled across the entire front of the building. And Hank's mother was pregnant with his brother.

He could have gotten a job and rented a place for them to live, but no. He had other plans. What they were was not immediately obvious, nor were they very soon thereafter.

Who knows how he decided on Grand Prairie, but he obviously did some research that resulted in this decision. Then he spent some time finding the lot, renting it, finding the building, making a deal to purchase it, having a concrete slab of the appropriate size poured on the lot, and the building moved to the lot. All of this required a lot of planning and work. Also, some cash.

When they arrived, all the building contained was a bed, a baby bed in preparation for the fairly imminent event, some chairs, a table, and a counter constructed around the sink.

There may have been a little more. But that was about it, except for a pile of some building materials... more two-by-fours and sheetrock panels.

As soon as they arrived he spent time building a wall separating the back half, "living space," from the front half, and installing a screen door for access between the two. Then it was "finished." At that point he had only three hundred sixty-five dollars left.

No way to know how much he had before he secured the land and the building, but it could not have been a very large amount. Considering that amount was left over from what he left Hank and his mother when he was drafted, after they lived for the year he was in the army, made the round trip to Tacoma and lived in a decent hotel for a month, and there was enough to do what he did and have cash left over was amazing.

It is even more amazing that whatever the amount, it was the result of a small fruit stand literally built of cardboard on a wooden frame on a corner lot at a major traffic light intersection on Highway 80 in the western Dallas suburb of Oak Cliff for just a few months.

With proceeds from this stand he even bought the new home in a nice neighborhood that had to be given up when he was drafted.

Location, location, location. He must have been ahead of his time in the study of demographics, proximity, access, population growth trends and other important factors in successful retailing, such as figuring out what people need and making it convenient.

The fruit stand lot was across the street from a service station on a side street that was a main access street from the subdivisions to the south that were rapidly being enlarged due to the booming war based economy.

That access was to Highway 80, the main thoroughfare for people going to and from work in downtown Dallas, and workplaces in between, as well as to the west.

Thousands of people passed the little stand daily, and it was noticeable because the traffic light that enabled safer and easy access to it made it more noticeable than it would have been elsewhere because of the speed of the traffic flow on the highway. It was easily and safely accessible to the people living in the suburbs to the south on the weekends when they were doing their shopping.

The fact he was drafted and taken away from this little gold mine was another among the many amazing facts about this time.

He moved to Dallas from Houston where he moved from Colorado to increase his income from ten dollars a week working in a grocery store to ninety cents per hour, thirty-six dollars per week, at the Brown Root factory in Houston working as a welder on construction of the LST landing ships the U.S. was employing in the South Pacific. A job he got without any prior welding experience.

While there his foot was badly broken when a steel beam fell on it. As a result, he was unable to work and was laid off. He returned to Dallas, probably because that was where his family was, and his father and older brother were in the produce business. He went back to what he knew.

Doing what he needed to establish the little fruit stand was done while he was on crutches, barely able to get around. He could not lift anything because he could not stand without his crutches. He had only recently laid them aside and was still not fully mobile without them when he was drafted. But that was O.K. Remember: it was the government making the decisions about what he could or would do… not him.

He was not acceptable to work at a good job, but he was good enough to be cannon fodder in a war the U.S. Government, headed by another member of the out of touch, effete "elite," Roosevelt, as is now fairly well known, deliberately got the U.S. into against the will of the vast majority of Americans.

Roosevelt's intent was to endeavor to end the depression by lining the pockets of those of his own kind who were owners of the military/industrial complex companies that would employ America and pocket the profits of the war. (Anyone who doesn't believe this should study the reason the Japanese attacked Pearl Harbor and the deliberate mishandling of the communications regarding the attack that have now been declassified.)

They sent him to Bakers and Cooks School. He was previously helping build the ships to transport thousands of young Americans to their deaths in the South Pacific. Now, he would be feeding them to ensure they would be well fed before they were killed or injured. He was still contributing to the war effort, as every good American was supposed to.

The Brown Root company has since become part of the Halliburton Company that was where the same group of people who are in control of the U.S Government today placed Dick Cheney for a few years to make him rich so he could continue to be a good little servant to their interests.

That is the same Halliburton that has continued to benefit from U.S. military endeavors around the world, including Vietnam and the billions and billions of dollars paid to them in Iraq after Mr. Cheney and his little charge, effete "elite" member, were put into office sixty years later to continue to look after their interests by starting the war in Iraq and giving "no bid" contracts worth billions to Halliburton and other connected companies.

Note Mr. Cheney, when asked about his not being in the military during Vietnam when so many other Americans his age lost their lives and limbs, responded in his own words that he *"had other things to do."*

Hank's father should have sold out, bought in, become a good little servant, *"had other things to do"* and never drafted. But he could not do that because he was only an average working American… not "connected." And like most non connected honest working Americans who died in that conflict, it was not necessary for America to be in, he was too moral and ethical to do what Roosevelts and Cheneys of the world do; spill the blood of innocents for money and power.

Considering his success with his little fruit stand three years earlier, his father's plan in Grand Prairie comes into focus. Again: location, location, location.

Across the narrow two-lane asphalt of 10th Street, on the opposite corner was a grocery store. The only grocery store on the south side of Jefferson, Highway 80, serving the southeast quadrant of town that was convenient to the homes of the hundreds of families whose income came from the defense plant, the western access to which was four blocks east on Southeast 14th.

Also, 10th was the one street that accessed Jefferson from all the way to the south side of this fairly densely populated area. Neither 9th nor 11th Streets went from Jefferson all the way through the subdivision.

There wasn't a traffic light. But that was all that was missing from this location compared to the Oak Cliff location. There was a traffic light a few hundred feet to the west at 8th Street, and there were also vacant lots on each corner of 8th and Jefferson. But remember 8th Street was the first street west of 14th where the railroad could be crossed, and the traffic piled up when trains passed through town. It was a congested intersection that, rather than enhancing access, made it more problematic.

So a morning or two…no more…after finishing the interior dividing wall, his father left in the little Ford pickup, and returned a few hours later after a trip to the Farmer's Market in Dallas fifteen miles to the east. The pickup was loaded. Loaded with three hundred sixty-five dollar's-worth…at least that was what he paid for them… of over ripe, vine ripe tomatoes that would be beyond "over ripe" very soon.

His mother went ballistic, or what was more likely in her case, bonkers, since her usual state would have placed her already half way there. And being about eight months pregnant, without a bathroom or the usual contents there of, well..........

His father went about making some large signs on scrap pieces of sheetrock and plywood proclaiming in large red letters "VINE RIPE TOMATOES" and the price.

The next morning he opened the overhead doors to expose the stacks of crates of tomatoes with the top crates tilted forward to show the beautiful red tomatoes. The signs were leaning against the lower crates. Three days later he did not have a tomato. All he had to show for his three days and his investment was more than one thousand dollars.

⟞⟛⟝

Before September when Hank began the first grade at David Crockett Elementary School his father had made enough money in his new endeavor to permit them to move about a mile to the west and a block south of Highway 80 to a three room duplex on Austin Street that was only two blocks from the school.

The street between their duplex and the school was a narrow residential lane with little traffic and a sidewalk. So he could walk to school alone in less than five minutes without concern.

For the next three years life continued quietly with little change. He went to school and played like most during their sixth to ninth years without much knowledge or concern for anything going on outside their little worlds, including what their parents are doing in their workday when they are away from home.

Even summers and holidays were routine, except for the addition of his brother in June 1946, and the increase in the size of the Christmas tree and the number of gifts and toys under it.

Meanwhile his father was busy expanding the size and business scope of the little store as well as adding another store and some additional business interests while his mother was busy at home with his new baby brother.

There was little outward evidence of the increasing financial well-being of the family except the addition of a big grey classic Packard sedan in 1947, a new top of the line Schwinn bicycle, a nice scooter, and in late 1948 a new Ford pickup.

In fact the only experience of note for Hank was at school in the spring of 1947 when, still in the first grade, he got into some trouble of note for a seven year old.

There was a female classmate he considered his first girlfriend, ironically named Linda, who it would seem also held him in the same regard. There was also a stairwell on the west side of the south class-room wing of the school building behind the auditorium that was not directly visible from the playground outside the south entrance to that wing of the building.

One day during recess, he doesn't remember exactly how it came about, the two of them decided to go to the bottom of the stairwell and find out what it would be like to kiss.

Unfortunately some of the other snotty nosed, jealous little creatures saw them and ran immediately to the teacher to squeal on him and Linda who then ended up in the classroom standing in front of their classmates being made examples of as bad little boy and girl who were doing a terrible thing none of the others should ever do.

But that was it because it was 1947 in a locally controlled school in which the teachers were real teachers who were from the middle class and were themselves products of a rational and stable society, and were concerned with actually teaching children to prepare them for their places in a sane country and society, rather than indoctrinating them to accept government mandated norms of conduct and imbu-ing them with Marxist ideology.

Had it been 2013, it would have different. He would have probably been treated even worse than the little seven year old boy in Denver who was accused of sexual molestation and suspended from school for kissing his little girlfriend on the back of her hand in class by a school administration of those who had their education paid for with money from the government and who were themselves indoctrinated to perpetuate what their minds were filled with since they were Hank's age that kissing experiment day.

There is also much irony in the fact the stairwell was, and possibly still exists, less than one hundred yards from the spot in Crockett Park where one night only twelve years later he would engage in conduct with another girlfriend, not named Linda, for which the penalty was much more severe than the little Denver boy received.

That one changed his career plans and his life.

⊷⊶

1949. Three years after their arrival in Grand Prairie, the little store had been expanded to the front, west side and rear. There was an area at the front with two shuffle boards to the left of the entrance and iced coke boxes to the right. On the east wall was a large walk-in cooler and glass fronted doors for cold beverages, filled with milk, juice, soda and a whole lot of beer.

There was a butcher shop in the right rear with a door to a barbeque pit area. In the middle were nice shelves and glass fronted refrigerated cases with appetizingly displayed fruits and vegetables. Out the west side door, on the north side were fruits and vegetables, and on the south side was a large store room for cases of empty bottles, mostly beer bottles.

Strategically situated between the front and side doors and the butcher area was the busy check-out counter where Hank spent some time in the afternoons and on weekends standing on a box, manning the big, old National cash register.

To the west on Jefferson, on the east side of the old Interurban building at the intersection of Jefferson and Center Street was another little store. This one was like later day 7 Eleven stores before theft and crime became such problems they had to enclose the fronts, limiting access to one three foot wide door.

The entire front was open via overhead doors and it had a merchandise mix not unlike a 7 Eleven. There were the usual drinks, snacks and small grocery items. Iced coke boxes were rolled out on the concrete walkway that spanned the front of the store. The checkout counter was to the left, east end. Behind that was a huge walk in refrigeration unit with glass doors opening only behind the checkout. It was full of beer.

In the back wall near the refrigeration case and the checkout was a door. It was open to the covered beer "garden" with benches and a restroom. The "garden" was usually occupied by several people between the hours of late morning and closing time at night… an average of twelve hours a day six days a week.

A few blocks to the southeast of the corner of 10th and Jefferson, on a big, pie slice shaped lot was a newly painted and carpeted little house with a new, white, custom made, floral design, wrought iron porch railing.

The house was bought with Veterans Administration loan certificate number 41,018 and a loan of $3,425 from Murray Investment Company October 4, 1949. It was full of new furniture and appliances, including a big red circular sectional sofa to seat six.

In the driveway, under a new car port, was his mother's big, special order, battleship gray, 1949 Lincoln sedan. Parked at the curb in front of the house was his father's new black 1949 Ford pickup.

The little blue pickup that brought them to Grand Prairie and hauled that first load of tomatoes was relegated to a spot behind the store next to the Interurban building where it would play a large role in Hank's development the following year.

The two stores were the number one and number two largest volume beer retailers in the city of almost thirty thousand that was listed as the "Fastest growing city in the U.S.," thanks to the perceived need by the U.S. Government to build up for another war... in Korea.

⟨⟩

How does someone with a limited small country town high school education and sixth grade education wife do this in three years with only three hundred and sixty-five dollars?

The answer lies some distance farther east... and other places like it... where the thirty-six acres of strawberry growing, red sand where Hank's father lived from his birth to the age of fourteen, he also bought in 1949 because it was his "roots," is located.

> *"Perhaps in America, where nature has planted herbs that can heal the physical maladies of our continent, she may have also placed remedies of our hearts and minds. Perhaps in this new world there are men altogether differently made from ourselves, men who are not slaves to self-interest, men worthy to carry the noble flame of friendship."*
>
> *-Voltaire, Candide, 1759*

Shirley, Texas doesn't even qualify for the derogatory term "hole in the road." It's not on the road. And the road is not much of a road. It is FM 19, farm to market 19, one of those two lane blacktop ribbons running north and south in East Texas from Paris in the North to somewhere close to Huntsville, about two hundred miles to the south.

It is one of those arteries connecting what was farmland to the main highways that were the precursors of the Interstate highway system that fed into the cities of Dallas and Houston, smaller cities like Greenville and Longview, and the even smaller county seats like nearby Sulphur Springs, seven miles to the north.

It "was farmland" because, since the landowners have been paid by the government, for years, not to farm it, it is not now, nor has it been for decades, "farmland."

Sulphur Springs, the closest market town to Shirley, was where farmers from the surrounding area took the products they raised to sell to the people who came on Saturday mornings to shop and socialize in the center of town, which like so many in "Middle America" was built around the Nineteenth Century courthouse square.

This "market" really was more a social event than an economic endeavor. The bulk of what the farms produced was taken to the big farmer's market in Dallas about ninety miles to the Southwest via Highway 80 to which FM 19 connects twenty miles to the south.

Today, since there aren't many functioning farms, there aren't any farm products or farm families. There aren't any Saturday morning gatherings, and towns like Sulphur Springs have "dried up."

Thanks to federal government subsidies, the people with working families have sold out and left. Most have moved to the cities, and most of the land is owned by these city folks who just collect their small government checks for letting the land lie fallow, occasionally visit it on the weekends, or just rent it out as a place for some, usually receiving some kind of welfare, to park their mobile homes.

A way of life, an entire part of American culture, the people who contributed so much to the values that were an important part of the foundation of America has disappeared.

This began mid twentieth century. It has accelerated since the initiation of Lyndon Johnson's Great Society in 1965. This is how deeply the federal government and its American culture destroying policies have reached into American life.

At the appropriate spot on FM 19, about seven miles south of Sulphur Springs, if careful enough not to miss it, there is a small crossroad. There, if one turns to the west, winds back to the north about a quarter mile until the "hot top" plays out, then follows the red sandy remains of the road somewhat less than another quarter mile to the west, he or she, as is required speech today to avoid offending female gender self-esteem by using proper English, will find himself or herself, as the case may be, in front of a late nineteenth century white clapboard church that is, or was, the heart of Shirley, Texas, a community of two or three dozen farm families who lived and worked within less than a mile of it.

A few yards to the east of the church is the graveyard where on the cold wet January 1st of 1999 Hank and a few friends and family buried the remains of his father, P.W. at the age of eighty years, plus three and one half months; the last of his generation in his family and only one of the millions of his generation whose passing represents the end of a culture and the last defenders of its true history and character.

Hank, his brother and his son dug a small hole about three feet deep with the shovel he brought in the back of his Suburban along with the small bronze box containing his father's cremated remains.

Then, attended by his wife, two cousins and a few friends, he unceremoniously placed his father to rest among the graves of his mother and father, siblings, his mother's parents and more than a dozen other relatives. A few months later, his brother placed the headstone just like the ones the government has provided for millions of World War II military veterans.

In addition to this memory of this place, he remembers attending the funerals of his father's sister, his grandfather and of a couple of graveyard cleaning days that were once an annual, vernal picnic gathering for the families who resided in the area during the first half of the twentieth century.

For the last four decades, because of the lack of family of those interned there residing in the area, the place seems pretty much forgotten, but maintained by people who now live in the area.

About two hundred yards to the north of the Shirley church and graveyard, up the continuation of the sandy road is the rectangular, thirty-six acre, hard scrabble tract of red sandy soil that looks like the kind of place most contemporary Americans would think only good enough to park a "doublewide," leave it open around the bottom to avoid the expense and labor of building a doghouse, and make the trip into Sulphur Springs once a month to pick up their welfare checks and food stamps.

But these are not the people who settled this land in the early part of the twentieth century and before, managed to scratch a living out of the red earth, raise families without government assistance, edify them, and even have enough left over to build a relatively fine little church.

Hank's grandfather, Ira Thomas, who came to Texas from Tennessee at the age of fifteen in 1900 with his siblings, father and stepmother, managed to raise a family of five sons and two daughters on those thirty-six acres. He and his family accomplished this by growing vegetables and hogs for their sustenance, and strawberries to take to market.

His father's mother, Bertha Bell Jonas, passed away in 1931 when his father was thirteen. Being minus the contribution of wife and mother common among farm families of the time, his grandfather moved about forty miles west to Greenville with his father and some of his siblings where he began a truck driving job that took him out of town for days at a time, leaving Hank's father to fend for himself from the age of fourteen.

Still, even though he had to get up at 4:00 AM to work at the Coca Cola bottling plant during high school, he managed to letter in basketball and football, and graduate, as did his siblings and most others during the hard times in the middle of the Great Depression.

About ten miles north of Greenville is another small community called Celeste. It was there in 1912 Hank's mother, the last of eleven children, was born. It is the same place her father was born fifty-four years earlier in 1858, and wed Hank's grandmother in 1884 when she was only fifteen and he was twenty-six years old.

They managed to farm, bear a child every two or three years and successfully raise eleven of them for almost thirty years without assistance. Five of Hank's mother's brothers and sisters were old enough to be her parents. The oldest brother was twenty-seven years her senior. The oldest sister was twenty-two years older than she.

Owing to the age differential, the children were not particularly close. In fact, they had their own, mini Diaspora, spreading to California, Chicago, Houston, West Texas and other places. One Hank never met and two he remembers seeing only once or twice.

This family, like his father's, started with nothing, and without assistance from anyone, managed, through hard work, to make a living, educate their children, some with two years of college or business college, to become reasonably successful, and enjoy the benefits of upward mobility available in America to those who worked hard and persevered.

These two families are typical of millions that were the backbone of American prosperity. They produced the soldiers, teachers, postal employees, preachers, store managers, truck drivers, missionaries, corporate executives, entrepreneurs and others who contributed much to America.

Through hard work and provision of guidance to generations they provided the foundation for the America that was... before it began to disintegrate via the planned value desecration of Lyndon Johnson's Great Society.

These are the people who never owned a slave, did not own much of anything until the middle of the twentieth century after they were able to purchase it through hard work. Yet, it is their heirs many in urban Black America believe owe them reparation money.

These are the people the Rockefellers, Bushes, and others who consider themselves the East Coast "elite," believe have experienced an *"excess of democracy."*

Well, if they had a representative who truly represented and would speak for them, the millions of Hank's generation who have similar humble backgrounds, he would say to those among the generations of Black America and others who believe the country owes them something for nothing, and continue to slop at the trough of free food, housing, healthcare, cell phones, education and more at the expense of those who work and contribute while they do nothing except continue increasing their numbers and their burden on those who do work and contribute:

"Get a job. Go to work, and you might also experience the bounty of the country and the system that might continue to offer more opportunity, more of every-thing than anywhere if every able bodied, capable person would begin once again to pull his own weight and remove his burdensome weight off the weak-ening shoulders of the productive members of society, for the fact is your country is broke... bankrupt... and can no longer afford citizens who do not pull their own weight, but parasite off the working productive members of society who are not a non-contributory dead expense to the entire country.

"Parasite? Yes! By definition, that is what not working and receiving ev-erything you use, eat or spend from someone else is.

"It is not the government that is supporting you. It is other Americans who are working and productive. Those in government who pander to you, or Jesse Jackson, Al Sharpton and others who do so are merely the conduit of the largesse to you or are using you as a conduit of money to themselves... at your expense.

"Mark these words and remember them; your free ride is coming to an end due to lack of funds to support you... one way or the other. Either you take the action to remove yourself as a burden on others or there will come a day when it will happen without your consent, and your cooperation will be a non-elective. And that day is not far off.

"The people and the country are tired and weakened because even the productive are incapable of continuing to support you. It is best to act on your own behalf today before you do not have the free will or the ability to do so. You are warned. The Socialism and Marxism, no matter what they call it in American schools today, that you are benefiting from is historically proven to not be infinitely possible."

And *"pull his own weight"* is what Hank's father did, from the age of fourteen.

When they moved to Grand Prairie in 1946 he was not yet twenty-seven years old, but he had been working, supporting himself thirteen years, during which time he also supported Hank's mother ten years and him six. In 1949, after only three years out of the army, he had two places of business, new expensive Lincoln, new pickup, farm, new home and other business interests. He was thirty-one.

Those three years were good for him, as well as to him. They were also very good for Hank. But there were some not so good times.

His brother was born in 1946. Before he was a year old, he had to have a mastoid operation that required bone removal behind his right ear. After that, his mother devoted herself to, as she called him consistently, ad nauseam, *"my little ray of sunshine,"* in Hank's opinion, to his long term detriment. Unfortunately, the next sixty, plus years of his life have proven him correct in that assessment.

She was married and divorced before she met his father. During that marriage she had a daughter that died at the age of three, which reportedly was the reason for the divorce. That entire experience caused her to over react to his brother's illness and surgery for the fear of losing him and the consequences of that.

As a result, by 1949 she began to effectively ignore, actually seemed to resent, Hank. Her relationship with his father became stormy. It was disruptive of normal family life. From then on, it was never what could be called normal.

She also had to have serious surgery to remove a growth from her throat that required an incision at the base of her neck. The scar was very noticeable in the front from one side of her neck to the other, which did not make her happy. This was when his brother was less than two years old. She lived with that visible scar the rest of her life. The other three members of the family have had to live with the "scars" she created.

She was one whose life could be described as a life of asking *"Is That Really All There Is?"* daily, and complaining about her current situation, regardless of what it was.

Being the baby of ten siblings she was doted over. One of her older sisters told Hank when he was in his forties she was the prettiest girl she had ever seen.

She was spoiled. She was allowed to quit school in the sixth grade because she did not desire to go any more. She preferred art, playing the piano, the guitar and the mandolin, and singing, which she must have been pretty good at because in her twenties she had a radio program in Greenville in which she played the piano and sang.

When Gene Autry was in town, she dated him. Told Hank he was the biggest *"sissy"* she ever knew. She also dated one of the big band singers. Ditto: son of the local General Motors dealer.

Hers probably was, like so many others; a life that did not reach its full potential. But how many of us believe we have lived up to our full potential? Not many? Probably not.

We are all the product of nurturing we receive early on more than anything else. She spent most of her first twenty-eight years living with her mother whose *"baby"* she was.

But while on the subject of surgery, Hank also had a tonsillectomy in 1949.

All three of those surgeries were with no insurance; paid for without assistance from anyone during that three year period.

Today, we would be looking at a couple of hundred thousand dollars that would bankrupt most middle class Americans if the insurance costing thousands per year did not do it first.

CHAPTER 11

EARLY DEVELOPMENT

Partially because of his mother, Hank's father took a big interest in him, taking him "under his wing" most of the time he was not in school. Thus, he began spending a lot of time with him at work after school and on the weekends.

Early on, he would occasionally be awakened by his father miles from home at five thirty in the morning at the farmers' produce market in Dallas. By six A.M. he would have consumed a short stack of pancakes with sausage in the restaurant amid all the farmers and truckers who brought their products there his father went there to purchase. Afterward, he took him out to the sheds with him while he dealt with them to purchase their products.

Then, after his business was completed, they would visit either his grandfather, Ira, at his tomato packing plant, or his uncle Carney, his father's oldest brother, at his.

Both had what they called "plants" that were just buildings with large doors and loading docks at each end with a long conveyer belt in the middle.

What they both did was buy bulk truckloads of tomatoes... not the kind his father bought in 1946... then sort them into different grades of quality, size and ripeness, and box them in these categories for resale that same day, hopefully, making a profit on the spread between what they paid for the truck loads in bulk and what they could sell them for in smaller quantities to retailers after they boxed them according to these categories.

To accomplish this, both employed many men who stood on either side of the conveyer belt and hand-picked the tomatoes that fit the category assigned to each as they passed in front of them on the conveyer. They placed them into boxes with labels indicating the type, size and ripeness of the tomatoes. Other men would pick up the filled boxes, place another box to be filled and stack the filled boxes in their proper place.

All his grandfather and uncle did was the management tasks of buying and selling the tomatoes, and hiring and training the men who did the sorting and packing. Most were alcoholics and winos that would probably 'blow' their earnings before they were back the next morning. But these men were unlike many alcoholics and drug users today who do not work, are homeless and depend on the government to take care of them with money taken from those working. These were working and self-sufficient, because they had to be.

This was before Lyndon Johnson's "Great Society" implemented "welfare," food stamps, subsidized housing and other programs that eliminated a need to work. Thus, enabling those who are addicted, or just lazy, to avoid work, and spend their days just hanging out, drinking, taking and selling dope, breaking and entering, destroying their own neighborhoods, looting, rioting, stealing cars, or whatever they find more to their liking than working, while also producing more of their same demographic to continue their legacy... further burdening productive society with their "*weight.*".

Although it was intended, at least ostensibly, to reduce poverty and enhance the lives of those on the lower rungs of society, it has actually adversely affected the circumstances of them by greatly contributing to an increase in the prison population, the number of dependent, unwed mothers, poverty and crime.

Anyway, sometimes Hank would get to work a few minutes on the sorting line and talk with the men. Later his father would explain to him about them, which it should be noted, most were dependable employees who worked for his grandfather and uncle for years.

It was pre-pubescent experiences like this, having his own fireworks stand twice a year, New Year's and Forth-of-July, his own Christmas tree lot, operating a cash register at one of his father's two stores after school and on weekends before he was tall enough to reach the register without aid of a box to stand on, winning shuffleboard tournaments on Friday nights, operating a drive-in grocery, including ordering, stocking and doing the banking in the summer... being immersed in public life, rather than normal experiences of home and school of most children, that constituted what were different, broader, more diverse experiences.

His father, in addition to managing his stores, began buying a rail car load of Christmas trees and renting a prominent corner lot at 8th and Main streets.

At the age of eight, and later, after school and on weekends, he worked there selling trees in what his father referred to as *"Hank's lot."* There were always a couple of adults around, but he sold trees, collected and banked all the money.

His father also had a cabin built on the back of the little blue Ford pickup that brought them to Grand Prairie and hauled that first load of tomatoes.

A large sign proclaiming "FIREWORKS" was placed on either side. He can remember, not too pleasantly, many cold December and January afternoons sitting at the counter in the back of it selling fireworks.

To generate more business, sell more beer and generate more profits in the store at Jefferson and 10th there were shuffleboard tournaments on Friday and Saturday nights. There were cash rewards for the winners, so the turnout was good... lots of beer was sold.

Some days after school, he would stop by the store to practice. His father would play with and coach him. He got pretty good.

He could set up three pucks, upside down, put coke bottles upside down on each, and from the far end of the table, with one shot, take out all three pucks and leave the coke bottles standing upside down on the table.

On occasion, his father would bet with other players he could do it. They were usually grumbling as they handed their money to him. Hank also won a couple of tournaments.

⚊⚊

1950. Beginning at the age of ten, he spent summers opening and managing the store by the old Interurban building. He ordered merchandise, paid vendors and stocked. An adult manned the register because he could not sell alcoholic beverages. But it was he who was in charge, handled the money and did the banking at the bank that was only two blocks away at the corner of Center and Main Street. He can remember going to the bank and making deposits with wads of cash, and the tellers being somewhat amused about it.

At the same time his father paid one of the regular customers to take him and the little blue Ford pickup that brought him Grand Prairie to the alley behind the store in the afternoons and teach him to drive.

They would start at one end of the block long alley with Hank driving to the other end, learning how to go through the gears. Then his instructor would turn the pickup around and they would repeat the process over and over again until he was ready to take to the streets in the area. That is how he learned to drive at a much younger age than anyone else he knew... and with a four speed floor shift.

⚊⚊

The economy of Grand Prairie was continuing to boom in its upward trend and his father's two stores continued to do very well, even better.

The reason was the "defense" plant business that employed a large percentage of the town's population was booming because it produced the Vought Corsair carrier based low altitude ground attack fighter armed with four fifty caliber machine guns and napalm anti-personnel bombs, invented and tested just nine years before at Harvard University, that was one of the most terrible anti-personnel weapons ever invented because its purpose is to burn people alive.

This plane was the most successful piston-engine fighter plane ever produced in the U.S. in terms of numbers produced... 12,571 between 1940 and 1953. This success was a result of multiple modifications over the years to satisfy differing mission needs, including recent modifications to satisfy the then current need for it.

Hank remembers extensive local radio coverage in the summer of 1950 about the Korean Conflict that began June 25th as a result of alleged North Korean incursion into South Korea. The coverage began with reports of the Communist "*invasion*" of South Korea and quickly morphed into coverage of the new war the U.S. was involved in.

Never mind this was a civil war between Communist North and Right Wing anti-Communist U.S. puppet dictator Syngman Rhee who was put in control of South Korea after being flown into the country on General MacArthur's private plane when the country was artificially divided at the 38th Parallel by the U.S. at the end of WWII, five years before, or neither of the two had "free" elections the year before, and Rhee was kept in office over protests of a large segment of the country's population, or Rhee instituted laws designating his political opposition "Communists," and was engaged in a brutal campaign to eliminate "leftists," i.e., Communists, executing one hundred thousand, including entire families that summer.

As stated before; the concept of Communism was now the defined U.S. enemy and thus a ready-made target for the U.S. military/industrial complex whenever it needed more business and/or Communism might be advancing anywhere. So the U.S. got the U.N. to pass a resolution authorizing military intervention. Then immediately commenced bombing the country and put three hundred and twenty-six thousand U.S. military personnel on the ground there, joined by a relatively token British contingent, so quickly to cause one to wonder if they weren't ready to do this in advance of the alleged small Communist incursion, given its history with the country.

Considering the facts of Rhee's half century association with the U.S. Government at that time, including his purportedly being descended from royalty... as was Chiang Kai-Shek in China... being taken under the wing of U.S. "missionaries" at an early age, meeting with President Teddy Roosevelt at the age of twenty-nine in 1904, and having degrees (not necessarily education, but degrees) from prestigious U.S. universities... B.A. from George Washington, M.A. from Harvard and PhD from Princeton... even though he failed to pass Korean civil service exams multiple times, there is no question of his U.S. "puppet" status.

It should also be noted he was so corrupt and brutally authoritarian many citizens were fleeing from the South to the Communist North, which the U.S. could not tolerate. Therefore, since it is obvious the U.S. did not want to lose control of South Korea, the only question is; was there really a Communist incursion or was it another U.S contrived False Flag event excuse to start another war to endeavor to maintain control of its only foothold on mainland Asia.

However, wiping this aside, the magnitude of it given the size of North Korea and the potential long term cost to the U.S. economically and in human lives, or the continuing geopolitical consequences of this initial U.S. conduct that was to be ramped up again a little over a decade later, Grand Prairie shared in the short term economic benefits, as it would also that next time, as did Hank through his father's selection of Grand Prairie as a place to live and make money because of the "defense" plant.

Even though war is a terrible thing and Hank, as are most people, is opposed to it, he is grateful to his father for his astute decision to begin his post war business endeavors in a place that ensured him a very good lifestyle by benefiting via the continuing mainstay of the U.S. economy since Pearl Harbor... war and the growth of the U.S. weapons industry.

It was a business is business decision that could only be rationalized as *"When in Rome, do as the Romans,"* because, even then, the U.S. was beginning to look and act like the new Rome.

Not just for this, Hank has always been grateful to his father who was like a kid with a new toy in wanting his son to explore, experience, have knowledge and succeed.

In addition to general business experience, he is solely responsible for his pre-pubescent experiences of having his own gun, a 22 caliber target rifle, being taken for a ride in an airplane, taken to the ocean to wade in the surf, to the Barnum and Bailey Circus, visiting the mountains, attending Saturday, small town square gatherings, visiting old Western ghost towns, driving a car alone at a very early age, two of his own businesses, banking, having a variety of different animals to take care of, dealing with the public, and being able to operate a cash register and make change properly before he began school.

For years, after dinner it was routine for him to bring out one of the question and answer games about history and other subjects he bought for this purpose.

He would function as the "dealer." Hank and his little brother who usually was bored and left the table were asked to answer questions as long as they were willing.

During these sessions, he also taught math, but not the traditional type being taught in school where children were instructed to obtain the answer to 5 x 17 by multiplying 5 x 7, carry the 3, multiply 5 x 1 and add 3 to it.

His was the short cut method. Instead of multiplying 5 x 17 as being taught in school, he had Hank do (5 x 10) + (5 x 7) = 85, which is much quicker and can be done in the head, without the crutch of pencil and paper, especially as the numbers get larger.

All of this conveyance of knowledge by his father took place while he was running two businesses open 8:00 AM to 10:00 PM, he got up at 4:00 AM to go to the market in Dallas, and never got more than six hours of sleep, but was always home for dinner at the dining table, unlike contemporary Americans who usually work only eight hours but are so busy they don't have time for anything, including "*to eat properly*" as stated in television commercials.

What happened in the years since to Americans who don't even have time to know what their children are doing, or be close enough to them to recognize when they are affected by drugs or alcohol, being guided in the wrong direction by school curriculums, media propaganda, or associations with others whose influence may adversely affect their lives? Are they also the results of the same influences as their children, too self-centered, involved elsewhere, insensate, insensible, insouciant, or... you pick the appropriate "in" that describes "what happened" that is rapidly leading us on the road to cultural and national destruction.

⇒╬⇐

Hank is thankful parenting was different before those leading us to this destruction gained sufficient influence to accomplish their goals. Even his grandfather seemed to also like to get in on his nurturing.

He would occasionally take him home with him for the weekend to his big two-story house at 5300 Tremont in what was then a nice section of Dallas with large homes on tree lined streets. There, he and his wife, Hank's step grandmother, would spend time with him, take him out to dinner and the ice cream shop in the neighborhood convenience center where there was a laundry, small store and other amenities to which people could safely walk from their homes.

They also showed him old, sepia colored, tin-type photos of relatives his grandfather left in Cumberland Gap, Tennessee who looked like something out of an old movie. Log cabins on blocks. Pants cut off at the upper shin, suspenders, stove pipe hats, bare feet.

They were very unattractive. Also, they had first and middle names like, Andrew Jackson, born 1836, whose father, simply John Fletcher was born in 1796, Marvin Rufus, 1872, Eliza Harriett, Bertha Bell, Hank's deceased grandmother, Martin Luther, 1868, Delona, 1866, Annie Maletha, 1858, Andrew Gabriel, 1862, and others that seemed as strange over sixty years ago as they do today.

From what his grandfather showed to him of his long ago past in Tennessee, he had changed a lot. Surely, a lot more than the change Hank experienced in California that was just a geographical and slight cultural change.

His appeared to be a move from one century to another, which it literally was, from the nineteenth to the twentieth, from horse and buggy to automobiles, from barefoot and stovepipe hats to suits, white shirts and ties, and grey Stetson Hank never saw him without when outside.

He participated in his nurturing to a limited extent, but he tried and was contributory to Hank's understanding of much he would not have otherwise been exposed to.

Even later, when Hank was twenty-two and he was in the hospital near death, he asked him to come see him. Then he wanted him to comb his hair so he would look good. That was the last Hank can remember of him while he was alive.

At his funeral in the little white church he looked pretty good in his casket. His hair was combed nicely. The casket was closed and he was buried in the little church graveyard near his wife and mother of his eight children, Bertha Bell, his son J.B. who died in 1914 at the age of three, and other family members.

This was seventy-seven years after his birth in Tennessee, sixty-two after he settled in Shirley and a couple of years since he showed to Hank the hog wire protruding from the trunk of a large tree on the thirty-six acres a scant two hundred yards from his grave. This, he informed him, at the time, was a sapling that was a corner post of his hog pen forty-five years before.

⚊⚌ ⚌⚊

When he was a child Hank was, as are most children, like a sponge… absorbing everything heard, seen and experienced. But his childhood was different. He was not left to just absorb. His father immersed him. He put him into more and very different situations than most young children are exposed to.

It was thus, he was so immersed in life experiences that by puberty, figuratively speaking, his little sponge life was so full that had it been squeezed into a very large basin, that basin would have been brimming over.

He can remember going to school at David Crockett Elementary from first to fourth grades, then to the old four room school house across the street for fifth and sixth grades. But he does not remember ever studying.

First through third grades he lived in the Austin Street duplex only two blocks from the school where he played in the field next to the house and flew the kites he made from sticks and whatever paper and rags… for tails… he could find.

He planted a little garden on the east side of the house he remembers eating carrots from. But whatever he was doing while there, he remembers at five thirty PM his mother would call him in to listen to the "Lone Ranger," "The Creaking Door," "Captain Marvel" and other fifteen minute programs.

The family moved about the same time he began fourth grade. The store at 10th and Jefferson was only a block out of the way on his

153

walk home, so he frequently went there, rather than going straight home after school. But when he did go home, he worked in the shop behind the house, making things, or disassembling and assembling one of his two bikes.

After dinner there were the home schooling sessions with his father at the dinner table, which was the only place in the house suitable for studying. Then some TV and off to bed. He never had time to study. He was always too busy.

But there was some time for escape from the reality of his world at the Wings Theater on the south side of the first block of West Main Street on Saturday mornings.

Buck Rogers and his space ship that emitted from its rear what looked like the sparklers he sold out of the back of his pickup fireworks stand.

Lash Larue. Hop-Along Cassidy. Whip Wilson. Other, fifteen minute, concoctions of "Hollywood" that had to be seen every Saturday morning by the pre-pubescent crowd, so as not to miss an episode.

Of course, the purpose of these was to get kids to come to the theater every Saturday to see the feature movie of the week that was usually a western. Simplistic: good versus evil. Black and white... No gray. Not the color of the movies; white hat, good guys versus black hat, evil ones.

In addition to those mentioned above, added to the feature's list were Tom Mix and Johnny Mack Brown. All of these were always the good guys.

There was never a conceptually gray area, only good: white, and bad; black. But there was another color of bad: Although they were sort of in-between grey on the screen, the Redskins were also bad.

Hank wondered when he occasionally thought about this over the years; *"Was this 'entertainment' part of our conditioning? Were we being conditioned to accept a world that was either good or bad? No questioning. One where other, different people are always bad?"*

There were also the "Movie Tone" news reels. These were like propaganda. America was always good. Everyone else was bad.

The Germans were bad. The bad Chinese were helping the bad Koreans. The Japanese were bad. The Russians were bad.

He seriously thinks, today, after years of consideration, this indoctrination made it simple for most Americans to be easily led into unnecessary wars in the following years.

All in his generation grew up hearing about the Chinks, Gooks, Slopes, Japs, and Krauts.

Even after George Bush unnecessarily invaded Iraq in 2003, the words frequently used on TV "news" to distinguish Muslims from U.S. military personnel followed this theme: Muslims were the *"bad guys,"* ours the *"good guys."*

He even saw a U.S general on the "news" state about Muslims, *"Our god is better than their god,"* which he thought frightening. That a man of so little intelligence, so indoctrinated, could be commanding a large number of the U.S. military could not be in the best interest of Americans or their country.

Hank thought *"Isn't there supposed to be only one all powerful "God"?* That is what he was taught, and thought was what everyone was taught... until then.

He thought he even had one personal experience with the results of this indoctrination in the 1970s when he was going to East Asia frequently.

He took his boss on one trip. He was twenty years older than Hank. Top of his class at University of Texas. Rich. But obviously not open minded. He was carrying a lot of intellectual baggage imbued by something or someone.

They went to the Philippines and mainland China. This was the Philippines while U.S. puppet Marcos was still in charge. The U.S. had big naval and air bases there. He was a brutal dictator. Martial law, poverty, families scrounging garbage heaps for their livelihood, small children running around in ragged T-shirts and no bottom clothing.

Not being educated was normal. No future. Even slave labor on construction sites where workers were being overseen by military with loaded weapons. It was depressing.

Then they went to China. This was while Mao was alive, but things were already changing. There was much industry, construction, booming business. Everyone had decent clothing. Schools were everywhere with children in uniforms. English was being taught. It was easy to determine the Chinese were on the march to a better future. It was obvious. Or so he thought.

Upon their return, his boss decided to have a conference room showing of their trip to all office personnel. He had no idea. He thought his boss was pretty smart, until that day.

He was shocked he spent the better part of an hour telling everyone how great, good, it was in the Philippines and how terrible everything was in that bad country of China.

Hank was absolutely stunned. How could someone supposedly so smart be immune to the truth, even when seen through his own eyes? There was only one answer: indoctrination.

⊷ ⊶

During our lives, in our education we have always heard of the various art forms. Art in the form of paintings, photography, music, dance. "Hollywood" types always, especially at the Academy Award ceremony, refer to their movie making and acting as *"Art."*

"There is in fact no such thing as art for art's sake..." - Mao Tse-Tung

This is from the king of twentieth century population indoctrination on the topic of "education" who, based upon his times in China, Hank thought he knew of what he spoke. And obviously, so do others.

At the beginning of the 21st century, every day, there were advertisements broadcast on television by some organization named the *"Ad Council,"* promoting to parents how dull, doltish and unattractive their children will be if they don't get *"enough art"* in school. Just think, millions and millions being spent without selling a product, by whom?

Note. There weren't any commercials about how poor their child might be if he, or she, doesn't get a good education in something productive that will help them and the country be more productive and more prosperous.

No. There weren't any commercials about why children should study math, science, engineering, or other fields in which the country is falling behind the rest of the world. But there are other commercials, very expensively produced, attempting to get as many young people as possible to enter one field.

While those "bad" Chinese were graduating more engineers each year than the entire population of college graduates in the United States, the most prestigious engineering school in the world was in India, and the Chinese economy was forecast to surpass the U.S. to become the largest economy in the world in terms of Gross Domestic Product by the year 2016, what was the U.S. Government promoting?

Neither it, nor some obscure appendage of it was running commercials attempting to convince young people to study math and science. Instead, as has continued and expanded since, hundreds of millions were being spent by the U.S. Government every year encouraging young Americans NOT to go to college.

What is it spending all these hundreds of millions to endeavor to get young Americans to do? Join the military. Yes. Hundreds of millions of dollars spent not to cause our country and its people to become more productive and prosperous, but to encourage young Americans to spend four years learning how to kill people in a multiplicity of ways not for our defense, but in countries not a threat to us thereby exacerbating the potentiality of future threats.

When, even though it has a larger military than the next fourteen largest countries' militaries combined, and there is no credible threat to us, it is endeavoring to enlarge it and convince its youth who are our future that becoming mercenaries is the brightest future for them; when parents are being encouraged to ensure their children are being indoctrinated in the government's "education" centers that have been turned into holding pens and cultural battlegrounds, what has the U.S. become? Why this overt militarization of America?

Also, never mind the *"Ad Council"* has also been running commercials for years proclaiming that which has been empirically proven a blatant falsehood: *"Diversity is our strength."*

It has been proven over and over again, and again in contemporary times; diversity is not strength. Northern Ireland, Belgium, Spain, Yugoslavia, Czechoslovakia, the Middle East have all proven the divisiveness of culture, language and especially religion. *"Diversity"* is actually a weakness. It has a disruptive effect on the peace and harmony of any place in which there are large, culturally different segments of population.

Those who prefer young Americans join their military to help them in furtherance of their world hegemony via means of armed force have been at work endeavoring to ensure a strengthening of their position within this country. This *"Diversity is our strength"* program is a pivotal part of that endeavor.

They are fully aware of the old adage *"Divide and conquer,"* and have been assiduously pursuing the division of America for this purpose... to *"conquer"* in the literal sense of the word; to overcome, to defeat the people of America... for over forty years, as of 2014.

A divided America, one wherein there is cultural, racial, language and religious strife serves to strengthen the hand of the Federal Government. A government that is, clearly, no longer a *"government of the people, by the people, for the people."* It is a government of, by and for those in power and those whom those in power serve.

The cultural, racial, religious and language division of America for the purpose of strengthening the hand of the Federal Government over the people of America conceptualized by those behind the government was put into active operation under President Jimmy Carter who was either totally complicit or terribly out of touch with reality and naïve, which the jury, in Hank's opinion, thirty-six years later, was still out on.

It was during the Carter Administration that restrictions on receipt of welfare, food stamps and other benefits to illegal aliens were lifted resulting in the almost immediate, planned increase in the flow of illegal aliens from Mexico, people who are racially, culturally, religiously and linguistically different from the majority of the population of America; people who, if prevalent in large numbers, would *"Divide"* the country. This effort has proven successful in accomplishing this in subsequent years.

Carter also had an "open arms" policy toward Cuban immigrants who were immediately granted refugee status by his administration. But that was apparently insufficiently aggressive in the project to further expand a divisive population segment.

Therefore, between April and October of 1980 Carter cooperated with Cuban dictator Fidel Castro in shipping one hundred twenty-five thousand Cubans, many of questionable background, into the U.S. and granting them "refugee" resident status.

He employed the U.S. Coast Guard, Navy, Marines and Army in that five and one-half month effort to get all those Cubans into and settled in the U.S. Afterward, he awarded medals to many U.S. servicemen for their participation in this *"humanitarian"* effort.

To see one, "little" result of that effort, all one must do is go to the West Lake, Lafayette Park area of Los Angeles where Hank's office was on West 6th Street in 1962/63. Many of these "refugees" for *"humanitarian"* reasons were settled there.

This area of beautiful parks, once utilized by the people of Los Angeles, of upscale shopping and affluent residential areas has been turned into the most crime ridden, Rampart Division, area serviced by the Los Angeles Police Department. The parks have chain link fences around them. They are closed at night. The shopping is gone. The whole area is a crime infested, gang war ridden, combat zone.

In addition to efforts to divide and destabilize the population, it should be noted Carter was the president who created the Department of Education, paving the way for the Federal Government to take control of "education," ensuring the indoctrination of the people with what those in control want them to think and deprive them of everything they do not want them to know, including European and American history, which proves they are very much aware of the long ago stated fact: *"Lose your history, lose your culture."*

Since then schools have been provided curriculums for which money is the source of control. They must follow government curriculums and get students to perform accordingly to receive the funding they need to be able to continue their dirty indoctrination work.

Thus, President Jimmy Carter laid the foundation for strengthening the power of those in government over the people and formalized indoctrination of the people by the government. But why would a president supposedly elected by the people do this to them?

Laying aside for the moment the term "elected by the people" according to the English dictionary means "chosen by," which anyone caring enough about America and himself to Google Trilateral Commission will learn is a blatant falsehood the same dictionary defines simply as a "lie." Thus the answer is; this President was a member and whore of this organization formalized in 1973 to take control of the United States Government. And please note: this is not conspiracy theory. It is fact.

This organization, headquartered in New York City, was founded by David Rockefeller, head of Chase Manhattan Bank to whom the Americans have *"an excess of democracy"* quote is attributed, and Zbigniew Brzezinski whose name is not familiar, but should be given his role as the preeminent evil behind U.S. geopolitics, foreign policy and warmongering.

That Carter, the first puppet President from this organization owed allegiance to Rockefeller, not the American people, is substantiated in the afore-suggested reading and by his actions.

Less than nine months after assuming the Presidency in January 1977 he entered into an agreement to transfer to the country of Panama ownership of the Panama Canal built by Americans with American money and American lives almost seventy years before to facilitate ocean access between the Atlantic and Pacific and U.S. east and west coasts.

It is alleged Rockefeller's Chase Manhattan Bank that had a significant loan outstanding to Panama that was unable to meet its commitment to pay interest payments on benefited greatly from this agreement because Panama becoming the beneficial owner of the canal and its stream of revenue benefited the bank by collateralizing the loan, thus eliminating the probable write off that would have adversely affected the finances of the bank and Rockefeller.

Then two years later in February 1979 the Shah of Iran was deposed. This was partially due to his being perceived to be another puppet of the U.S., a perception enhanced by subsequent actions of the Carter Administration regarding the Shah, proving the validity of the perception. To wit: after the Shah was deposed, Carter illegally seized Iranian assets in the U.S. This seizure was also purportedly of benefit to Rockefeller's Chase Manhattan Bank.

Speculation aside, fact is none of Carter's actions benefited American people. In addition to his being a morally and ethically corrupt puppet for those who put him in office... his façade of Christianity aside... his administration laid the foundation for destruction of the "America" that was... the one we have witnessed the destruction of since his administration.

The seizure of Iranian assets occurred prior to the Iranian Hostage Crisis in November 1979. The tens of American citizens held hostage until January 1980 did not benefit from his actions, nor have the American or Iranian people, since.

Loss of control of the Panama Canal, the only connection between Atlantic and Pacific Oceans from the southern tip of South America to the north of Canada, has not been a benefit to Americans. Nor could it have ever been considered such... by anyone!

What are the additional plans for the future of America and its people by those in charge?

Unfortunately, we have been witness to their development since Carter, and what we have seen, and experienced over the decades has been an ominous foreboding. The answer is not favorable to working productive Americans, and it will continue to get worse.

⊫⊣⊢⊨

Hank happily spent his youth and formative years in simpler times when people running the country seemed not quite as evil as what we have had since, or at least were subdued in their actions because the people would not have tolerated what has been done to them since Carter, when simplistic plots of the movies were obvious, when the killing in them was not wholesale. When it was obvious it was not real, and frequently it was so obvious as to be almost funny, when they contained more character development, not millions of dollars of explosions and destruction to desensitize us to what the government has planned for us, when our schools were controlled at the local level, not by the propaganda mongers and indoctrinators in Washington, D.C. When there were also movies about beauty, music and culture, not predominately about police, murder, criminals and death. Movies that were romantic, that could leave us as romantics when we left the theater, and as we became older... not desensitized to real life bombing, killing and destruction our government has wreaked upon innocents in far off lands, and cooperated with, if not encouraged, "Hollywood" to present as appealing to the young.

Today beauty in all things is a precious commodity. It is no more revered, or despised, than in the human visage and form where it is desirable and admired at a distance, but undesirable when in proximity to those who do not possess it, or in contemporary television commercials.

The same is true of intelligence. Thus, we are exposed to less beauty, less intelligence, and more ugliness and senseless banality... to condition us for our planned future.

⟞⟨⟨ ⟩⟩⟝

But, in Hank's youth, life continued. Business was good. He continued to be tutored by his father. His brother continued to develop as his mother desired. She became a bigger *"pain-in-the-ass,"* more volatile, more belligerent. He more spoiled.

In addition to working on his bikes, drawing and watercolors, Hank built model airplanes. Not plastic ones. The ones that take a lot of time to construct with Balsa wood and tissue-like paper stretched over the wood frame, like the real planes in the early part of the century were built, using canvas over wood and metal frames. They were very light, very delicate. He hung them from his bedroom ceiling... at least a dozen of them that required hundreds of hours of work.

One day when he was ten and his brother four he came home from school to find his entire model airplane collection and hundreds of hours of his work destroyed.

There were broken pieces hanging from the ceiling, others on the floor. A small rubber ball his brother used to destroy the entire collection was also on the floor.

It would have taken a long time and been noisy to accomplish this destruction. The house was one of the small eight hundred square foot boxes. There was no way this could have been done without his mother knowing about it.

He immediately went to her. She said, *"He was just playing. They were only toys."*

This was a first in a long line of deliberate destruction of his possessions by both of them.

Over the next twelve years his brother would destroy much, deliberately, and she would make up excuses or lies to protect him until she began to engage in the destruction herself. She even did everything within her power to prevent him from having any friends.

His brother would lie about one of his friends saying something to him. She knew he was lying. But she would ban the friend from their premises on the basis of what he was supposed to have said.

She knew he was a born liar. He lied to her all the time. She knew it. Anyone could tell. She made a big deal of saying, in front of him, *"He wouldn't lie to his mother."* Then he would flash his slimy grin.

He could do whatever. She never laid a hand on, or disciplined him in any way Hank can remember. But he was not so lucky. His brother would lie that he hit him or did something to him, and she would come after Hank. No matter what he said in denial, she would not listen.

She tried to hit him in the head with a spike heel shoe. She would grab a belt and begin flailing away until he could get out the door and away from her.

One time she got him several times with a metal tipped western belt. In addition to the scar on his knee from the fall in Cheyenne, he still has the faint impression of that metal tip on his thigh.

It was as if she resented he was bigger, stronger and more capable than her *"Little ray of sunshine."* Or that he even existed.

She made his life at home a living Hell he was pretty sure his father was aware of, and the reason he took him to work and other places with him was to keep him away from her.

It was also the reason Hank went elsewhere...anywhere, other than home, after school until after he got a new friend the summer of 1951.

CHAPTER 12
WAR, FRIENDSHIP, RELIGION, HYPOCRISY, CARS AND ENVY

1951. But before we get to Hank's new friend.

As of the beginning of this year, the Korean Conflict was in its seventh month, and the U.S. was bombing North Korea with everything it had; enemy troops with Napalm from the low altitude Corsair fighter bombers and the rest of the country, including... it should be noted... its civilian populations with heavy bombs from high altitude bombers, all apparently with little effect on its adversary that did not possess an air force or Navy, and was comprised primarily of ground forces of manpower with only light and heavy ground weapons... not unlike U.S. preemptive conflict enemies since with the same results.

The U.S. dropped so many bombs on North Korea that before the short conflict of three years ended via armistice it dropped more tonnage of bombs on this small country than it dropped during the entire Pacific campaign of WWII.

The carnage was so great it was described by U.S. Major General William Dean as "*most cities and villages were either rubble or snow covered wastelands.*" Yet, all this death and destruction wreaked, seemingly in overkill response to what supposedly elicited it, yielded the U.S. little but causing China to provide large numbers of troop assistance to the North Koreans, resulting in the U.S. being driven south of the 38th parallel into a WWI-like ground troop stalemate by July of this year and for the duration.

Apparently U.S. frustration reached almost breaking point because it began threatening use of atomic weapons. This was conveyed to all U.S. allies. A nuke was even tested with some degree of public fanfare. Truman publicly stated this as a "consideration" and signed authorization for use although he never delivered it to the military.

The stalemate would continue two more years until July 27, 1953 when the U.S. had to accept the creation of the DMZ, a two and half mile wide demilitarized zone, along which it has kept thirty-five thousand troops the last sixty years at U.S. taxpayer expense.

The only big economic beneficiaries of the entire fiasco were those who provided all the material, equipage, weapons, aircraft, etc., i.e., U.S. military industrial complex companies, and the South Koreans who would be greatly rewarded along with these beneficiaries in the next unnecessary U.S. preemptive action.

Bottom line: this adversely affected most Americans except those like Hank and his father and others who derived economic benefit via the large primary beneficiary companies such as the Grand Prairie "defense" plant.

Given his age at the time, his awareness of this was limited to continuing radio reports, watching, frequently from his roof, the Corsairs... his second favorite fighter after the P51 Mustang... being test flown almost every day at the Naval Air Station two miles to the east of his home, and dinner table and in store conversations about how well business was going as a result.

Like most ten year olds, his concerns were mostly centered on those of immediate effect in his small world of day to day activities at home and his father's store... like this one.

⟜⟞ ⟝⟞

One day that summer while he was working in the store next to the old Interurban building a... don't laugh... plain looking ordinary white hen strolled into the front of the store that was only about forty feet from the busy Jefferson Boulevard, south section of Highway 80, and jumped up on one of the wire potato chip racks.

The store was in a highly trafficked commercial area. There weren't any farms for miles. But some of the turn of the century homes a few blocks south of the store inhabited by older people who had been there for a long time might have been inclined to keep a few chickens for eggs, or even to kill for food as his aunt Vida in east Texas did.

She would have had to come from one of those homes which means she crossed at least two or three streets and three blocks of residential neighborhoods, dogs and all, which, to say the least, would have been quite an adventure for a chicken.

This would have been an impossible feat for any of the chickens Hank had ever previously been close to, which were his Aunt Vida's that, although she kept them close to the house in the back yard, every time anyone went into that yard they quickly scattered, evidencing they were afraid of humans, unless whoever it was had a handful of corn or chicken feed and was slinging it to and fro. However, even then the chickens darted about warily picking up bits of feed while ensuring the person doing the feeding did not get too close to them. They were scared little animals, and for good reason.

He did not like going to Aunt Vida's, he did not like her or her son, and he didn't know where the hell that name came from.

She was married to one of his mother's brothers, and everyone in her family had fairly normal names like Alice, Bob, Sam, Helen, etc. So, he didn't know where his mother's brother found her, or why.

She was a huge, obese woman who quite obviously was partial to fried food, especially fried chicken. Thus, to satisfy her obviously ample desire for a particularly southern cuisine, she kept a flock of culinary chickens.

He did not care much for chicken as a food, primarily because the only way anything animal was... still is... prepared in the southern part of the country, including Texas, is to dip it in milk and flour and fry the hell out of it in either a skillet of melted lard or a vat of grease, which contrary to the facts; news alert to all those intellectually limited persons endeavoring to solve the obesity problem in America like the obviously "brilliant" Mayor Bloomberg of New York City by limiting the intake of sugary cola drinks:

Sugar burns off much faster than the high fat diets that are the primary food contribution to the obesity problem. Therefore, rather than endeavoring to limit the sale of Dr. Pepper and Coke, the mayor and all others demonstratively short of much knowledge about foods, or anything else, should smarten up and, if they must be the self-appointed food Gestapo, ban the sale of Crisco and bacon, order the closing of all Colonel Sanders and other fried chicken outlets, remove the candy and drink vending machines from schools and, rather than attacking soft drink sales ... as is said colloquially in the south; *"for god's sake,"* get all the little fat ass kids off their butts and start exercising them... because it has been proven obesity begins in childhood.

He did not like fried chicken before, but after his first visit to Aunt Vida's he was definitely off that particular food. He did not see how anyone could do what she did to those animals and then eat them... or do it in front of sensitive young children like him.

Although she resided... a term used here advisedly in place of lived because what she, Hank's uncle and undesirable cousin who almost killed him when he was five years old did would be unfair to the term "live" which means to have life... in, *"god help us,"* Daingerfield, deep in the piney woods of east Texas only thirty miles north of the metropolis of Longview.

However, that aside, where they resided was not sufficiently far enough from urbanization for her to have to brutally kill her only "pets" a few feet from the kitchen door in front of young children then plop them on the table in front of them as food within an hour of her brutal act. It was too much to bear, let alone eat.

When she had guests, and probably the rest of the time also, which Hank is sure had some bearing on the way his undesirable cousin turned out, she would get her coat hanger she had straightened into a long wire with a small hooked end, and proceed out the kitchen door to the backyard with a handful of chicken feed. Then rapidly, after tossing some of the feed to the chickens, she would hook one foot of one of the poor chickens with the wire hook held in her left hand then immediately grab the squealing and flopping chicken by the neck with her right hand and with a professionally practiced quality circular forearm and wrist action twirl the body of the poor chicken until it came off leaving the neck and head in her hand as the body fell to the ground where it would headlessly continue to run and flop about until it finally died on its feet.

She would repeat this act one or two more times, depending on the number of people to be fed, with the flopping and dying chickens bumping into their flock mates, creating pure bloody pandemonium among all the chickens lucky enough to be left alive until the head-less ones were dead still, picked up by Aunt Vida and taken into the kitchen to be plucked, cleaned, chopped up, dipped into milk then flour and tossed into hot grease.

Hank's position on this is; people can say what they want, like his offspring and others with the same belief... not thought... that *"God granted man dominion over all things on earth"* and man is the only sentient animal, but he is willing to guarantee anyone that Aunt

Vida's chickens were not scared little animals avoiding humans out of instinct.

They were sentient beings, as he says, *"scared to death"* of humans because they lived among the death and destruction they witnessed among their flock mates when his Aunt Vida committed her bloody ruthless deed among them.

This was proven in his mind when his little hen came into his store and jumped up on the potato chip rack proving she was not afraid of humans, just as she would later prove she had a brain adequate for analyzing and acting on the basis of what she observed, which had zip to do with instinct.

She was not afraid of him because she obviously was not treated badly or witness to conduct like that of his Aunt Vida, but was dependent for food upon some human who treated her well, probably because they wanted her for her eggs.

Thus, she was a sentient partner in a symbiotic relationship with a caring human upon whom she depended for food. None of Aunt Vida's chickens would have come into the store and jumped up on the potato chip rack in front of him, regardless of how hungry they might have been. They would have been too afraid.

He called her his little hen because she permitted him to pick her up and take her home where she became his first non-human "friend," which is the proper term for such a relationship.

It is infinitely preferable to the term "pet" because that connotes a one-sided relationship lacking a mutuality of care or affection.

"Pet" is improperly utilized because it supports the view of those who believe in their god given, stated right of dominion over, and lack of sentient ability on the part of all non-human species, which is empirically incorrect.

He put her in his chain link fenced back yard where he thought she was safe from harm. The fence was six feet tall. He put food and water bowls there for her so she did not have to wait for him to feed her and she could eat or drink whenever she desired. He treated her more like most would treat a dog they cared about. And, guess what. She acted as one would expect a dog to act under the same conditions.

When he came home from school and went into the back yard she would come running and rub up against his leg like a dog, and it was not because she was hungry for food. Her food was there all the time. She would also run and play and stay near him while he was in the yard, which was most afternoons after school, weather permitting.

There was a tool shed work room that was on blocks, so she had shelter under the shed where Hank spent most of his time after school at his little shop bench with tools organized in specific positions on the wall above.

He took his two bikes apart and interchanged the parts, as well as other really non-productive but much more entertaining and safe endeavors than being in the house with his mother and brother, which was not a pleasant environment for him.

One day he was on the ground in front of the shed with a board he was using to make something with that required him to drive a large nail into it.

After he began driving the large sixteen common nail into the board she came over and got in the way to the extent he almost hit her in the head with the hammer, and as he pushed her aside so he could continue pounding the nail into the board, she insistently came back and pecked the head of the nail, then looked at him. He hit it again and she again was insistent on pecking it.

She thought it was a game. Actually she created the game. He would hit the nail and she would peck it. She would not peck it again until after he hit it again with the hammer.

She would stand there, cock her head to one side and look at the nail with one eye until after it was hit. Then she would peck it again. He did this with her for many days.

This proved to him at a fairly early age animals, even chickens most humans don't give credit for being able to think, do, in fact, possess the ability to think, analyze and act as they do on the basis of experience.

Anyone who does not accept this is probably less capable of free thought than his chicken friend because they choose what they choose to believe. Rather than exploring, learning and accepting the world as it is, they try to impose their flawed concepts of the world, their place in it and what those they choose to believe tell them because of their unwillingness to accept their own position in the world as mortal creatures just like Hank's chicken friend was.

She was in the back yard for months during which he went to see her after school and spent a little time with her each day even if he was not doing something else there.

Unfortunately, early one morning he heard a terrible commotion in the back yard indicating she was in distress because she was making sounds like his Aunt Vida's chickens did when she was catching them. She had never done that before because she never had cause to be frightened.

He got up and out to the back yard too late. Just as he went out the door, he saw a neighborhood dog going under the fence where he dug a space to get in under it. He had her limp body in his mouth. It was a very sad day.

He didn't know where she lived before or why she left. But he thought he was providing a safe and good life for her. It really distressed him he was incorrect in that assumption and she died a terrible death, possibly even worse than Aunt Vida's chickens were subjected to.

She died fighting for her life with a damned dog after having braved what he thought would have been much more dangerous territory in getting to his store and back yard than he was sure that fenced back yard provided. She was totally dependent upon him and he failed to adequately protect her.

She was the first death of anyone or anything he had a close relationship with, and he thought it was his fault. So, that experience has weighed heavily on him since and affected him as Aunt Vida's actions on her chickens affected him as a child.

Just as they were afraid of her because they witnessed her killing their flock mates, he has since that time tended to be afraid of anything happening to… and overly protective of… anyone or anything in his charge. He has been mostly successful in that endeavor, but he has failed more than once and those times have also been disturbing to him.

Most would be denigrating in their thoughts and comments about him because of this, but anyone who would do that should be thought less of because it would be obvious they have given insufficient thought, if any, to others they consider to be something less than they perceive themselves to be, and also have never taken time to be as considerate or thoughtful toward other creatures as they should be. Thus they are likely something less than they perceive themselves.

He still does not eat chicken, but not for the same reason as before his little friend.

Before her he did not eat it because it was not on the menu at his house and he could not stomach it after witnessing his aunt's killing of her chickens. After her it would be no different than eating a dog, as most westerners would probably agree is repugnant

However over the years, since his little friend departed her mortality, many times when enjoying a great beef filet or tenderloin dinner he has thought how glad he is he did not have a calf as a childhood friend, and he has had experiences fifty years after her death that have caused him pause even when having one of those beef dinners.

On more than one occasion he has found himself in a cattle drive when the herds are being driven to lower pastures via the highway it is necessary for him to travel when he needs to leave the small town in which he has been living for several years.

Being stopped in the middle of a herd of two hundred or more Hereford cattle and have a large six or seven hundred pound heifer stop, turn sideways in front of his vehicle, let out a loud ineffable vocalization, hear an immediate little response from within the herd somewhere a good distance behind and look in the rear view mirror to see the little tyke running as fast as he can through the herd toward that sound causes him to have as much respect for his life as he did for that of his little chicken friend.

Only two factors permit him to continue consuming those beef dinners: one is his lack of a personal relationship experience with a bovine acquaintance to which his wife attests when she tells people it is a good thing he is not a cattle rancher because he would have the world's largest herd. The second is his ability to rationalize that unlike all the sickly looking vegetarians he has seen on the rare occasions his wife has been able to drag him into a health food store, if not for meat derived protein nourishment and its contribution to our brain development that sustained and contributed to the development of our non-farming ancestors for tens of thousands of years and ultimately to us, he could have the appearance and intellect of those health food store customers and self-proclaimed vegans.

⊷⊶

1952. In the 6th grade the girls got to vote for who they wanted as the leading man in the class play. Hank was home ill when the phone call came. It was the two prettiest girls in the class. He says he hoped he was picked for "beauty" or intelligence. Either one would do. But for whatever reason, it was flattering, even if deserved. However, it didn't enhance his relationships with the boys in the class.

This was the beginning of his not being so popular with the other boys which continued throughout school and beyond, except in the military.

He has always gotten along better with the opposite sex than with his own because there is something about most, but not all, fragile male egos that seem to never develop beyond their twelfth year.

This was the year his brother began school, and Hank could not imagine what his mother did without him there to dote over all day and continue to prep him on his course to success. Maybe that was the reason she got a new car; a 1952 Lincoln Cosmopolitan Sport Coupe. Expensive little thing; it cost almost twice the $3,000 annual income of the average American family at the time, but did not evoke any noticeable change in her attitude or conduct. His father got a new red Ford pickup.

His parents got new vehicles. He got a part in a play. His brother began to get some exposure to other children and the influence of other adults. But it was too late.

Also, probably because of the effect of the terrible death of his chicken friend, Hank got a new friend in early spring of the New Year.

Corky was a little brown and black bundle of joy, half Airedale, half Wirehaired Terrier. Occupying the same space in the back yard as his chicken friend, he became a constant for years.

After school he would greet Hank and play. He was the greatest jumper imaginable until a little female cat friend over forty years later.

He could jump straight up to shoulder height of a six foot adult time after time with non-tiring, seemingly boundless energy, which was a pretty good feat for a little pooch who never weighed more than twelve pounds. It was as though he had springs in his feet.

He was always there when Hank came home from school, and even years later, after he was away for months at a time when he was in California and in the military. Corky was always there in the back yard happy to see him no matter how long he was away.

Hank took his presence for granted and did not give much thought to his sentiency until many years later when he returned home and he was not there.

We have failed to mention Hank's mother was a "good Christian lady." But most could have figured that out from her adherence to the church's "Good Book" guidance: *"Spare the rod and spoil the child,"* which she employed selectively.

His father was intelligent in ways other than those previously mentioned. Probably as a result of exposure to the reality of the world after his mother died before he was out of puberty, he was not a believer. However, due to either a small flaw in his intellectual make up or, as is more likely, to endeavor to keep the peace at home, he put on a suit and tie Sunday mornings and went to church; a Southern Baptist Church.

Hank's mother found a new preacher who was in town from Florida for his health. He doesn't remember going to church before that time. He assumed she didn't have time for worship outside of home until his brother began school.

Then, the climate of the area, before construction of many reservoirs by the Corps of Engineers, was dry, much more arid than Florida. So, Brother Bill was there starting a church in some good believer's home where it was much easier for him to breathe. It did not take long for it to grow into a little church on 8th Street by 1952.

Hank thought Brother Bill was actually an O.K. guy... for a preacher. He came to town in a little, green 1939 Chevrolet coupe with everything he owned in the back, found some people willing to help him start a church and worked hard in getting it from meetings in a person's home to the building on 8th.

He worked hard and was successful, which Hank's father counseled should be admired regardless of whether you agree with what is being worked for.

This experience at the age of twelve with religion and church people was his first after his enrollment in the Cradle Roll Department of the First Baptist Church of Fort Collins, Colorado on April 17, 1940 which he doesn't remember, for obvious reasons. However, these two church associations at his mother's initiative do point to her proclivity to gravitate in that direction.

He quickly found the people in Brother Bill's new, little church to be as selective as his mother in applying the *"Spare the rod"* rule although it was a different rule they applied selectively. It was not a rule directly from God. It was the law, which it seemed was their opinion did not apply to them, probably because they were *"saved"* by accepting *"the Lord Jesus Christ as Lord and Savior,"* which he was later to learn; they thought absolved them from man's earthly laws.

In fact, he learned that directly from the mouth of one of *"God's servants"* when his mother and step grandmother took him to see a preacher they heard was one of those "must see" people.

He was in West Dallas, in a neighborhood where the people could have been excused for seeking a way... anyway... out.

This was not a preacher who could be considered in the same category as Brother Bill. This guy was a complete charlatan. He didn't believe in anything. He was there, where he was, simply to fleece people. He obviously selected a neighborhood where he thought the people would be as ignorant as he could find. Thus, he could tell them anything... no matter how ridiculous, and they would not question him because he was a man of God.

Hank heard this creep as he, slobbering, shouted and screamed, *"I can go out and kill a man Friday night and I will still see the pearly gates of heaven. Yes! I will still see God in heaven because I have accepted Jesus Christ as my Lord and Savior. All I have to do is to come into this building on Sunday morning and ask God for forgiveness. And that forgiveness will be granted..."* He kept on, but Hank, age twelve, tuned him out about there. He had already been going to church long enough to know where this character was headed.

He eventually got there. Promoting the tithe he told everyone they could also be exempt from man's laws if they came to that church on Sundays, accepted Jesus as he had, and gave ten percent of whatever their meager earnings were to him and his church.

During the services at Brother Bill's church there were deacons, as in every Baptist Church, who stood up front and prayed then went down the aisles passing plates into which everyone was supposed to place his tithe.

Hank thought these men were the biggest hypocrites he had ever seen, or naïvely, likely to ever see again because of their conduct immediately after Sunday church services.

It was against the law to sell alcoholic beverages in Grand Prairie on Sunday, a law in existence entirely as a result of people like the deacons and other people in churches all over town Sunday mornings.

He was raised to respect laws and thought they were also to be respected and obeyed by everyone else, including the people on whose wishes they were enacted, but based on his experience with the deacons at Brother Bill's church that was asking too much.

Apparently, since they were saved they thought they were exempt from man's laws like the slobbering creep in West Dallas told those in his church he was.

So he and his father did not go home with his mother and brother after church. Instead they went to one of his father's stores. There the deacons and other good church people met them to pick up their beer that was iced in coolers.

His father explained these hypocrites wanted their beer cold when they went to the lake after church, and most did not have large enough refrigerators at home to keep both their food and all the beer they planned to drink on their Sunday outings at the lake. Therefore, they arranged to meet him after church to illegally pick up their beer that would be ice cold because he had the facility to keep it that way.

Maybe they thought technically they were not breaking the law because they had already paid for the beer, and were there just to pick it up. It was doubtful law enforcement authorities would have seen it that way. It was obvious his father who was careful about doing this did not.

This first experience with Christian hypocrisy was not Hank's last. The next one would be much larger. It would also have a serious impact on his family's lives in 1953.

⊷⊶

By the beginning of seventh grade in 1952 he learned to drive so well he was permitted to drive by himself as long as he stayed on the south side of Jefferson Boulevard; did not cross the tracks to the north side of town.

Before the school year began, complements of his father, he had his own car; a 1941 Chevrolet coupe… two-tone paint; blue bottom, silver top. One of those metal visors over the windshield, snappy, top of the line for 1941, a nicer, newer one than Brother Bill's.

Shortly after it was given to him it was parked near the west end of the store near the Interurban building. It caught fire and was destroyed.

Supposedly a spark from trash burning in an oil drum used for that purpose not far away got inside it. But he wasn't sure of that.

Both his mother and his then six year old first grade brother who destroyed his model airplane collection two years earlier were present at the store that afternoon. As his brother would prove years later; this was something he was entirely capable of doing.

Also, his mother was not an early riser because her demons that likely played a part in destruction of his model airplanes kept her… and frequently the family… from getting a good night's sleep, and it was impossible to determine what she was capable or incapable of.

She did not have to get up. She had no place to go. She never worked. But the rest of the family had to either go to work, or school, regardless of how tired.

Occasionally, this worked to his benefit. His home and school were both in the same quadrant of town where he was allowed to drive. If he was going to be late, his father would tell him to take the

179

Lincoln. So, there he was, twelve years old, in the seventh grade, six thousand dollar Lincoln in the parking lot.

Beginning then and continuing today, compounded by cumulative experiences, something Hank swears he doesn't understand is women. This lack of understanding began this year with cars, which most females profess to care very little about, but if the cars are expensive or special in some way. That's different.

Seems there is always an exception to every rule.

With *"Bob's rule,"* it was a weight limit. With his mother, it was favoritism. With the Christians, it was their being closer to God. With most females and cars it seems to just be the money thing; cheap or inexpensive, no. Expensive, yes, please.

Whenever he drove the Lincoln he was extremely popular at 3:30 P.M. There would always be at least one leaning against the front fender. This was great, except for one thing.

His driving a car to school that cost more than twice their average annual family income compounded by the class play "election" the prior year did not endear him to some of the little male egos he had to go to school with, and since there was only one Junior High and one High School he went to school with the same kids, same boys, for six years.

The fact he never wore jeans and had really nice shirts did not endear him either.

But there were some nice guys he got along well with; the more confident ones whose families were financially secure, owned their homes and were in the majority, given the economic growth of the country at the time. But there were enough it was impossible to get along with to make life less enjoyable than it could have been.

There were two brothers who, after school one day, took one of his textbooks and decided to play with it like it was a ball. They lived in the first house behind the 10th Street store, had gone to school with him since the first grade, and were always a problem for him because his father owned the store and they demonstrated some envy about their perception of their financial differences.

He wasn't going to chase them back and forth to get his book back. So he went back into the school and informed the Assistant Principal what just happened.

He immediately went out front and brought them into the office. He asked them about what Hank told him. They denied it. Hank said they were lying. The Principal told him to shut up. He protested. The Principal jumped up, turning his chair over, and said he was suspended from school. Hank could guess which camp he was in.

He knew there were also teachers who resented his driving the Lincoln. One twenty something coach he heard make off color remarks to one girl who had ridden home with him made inappropriate snide remarks to him about it one day when he was getting out of his Ford.

Another twenty-something, homely female teacher made a snide remark, calling him *"gruesome"* as he was walking up the stairs between classes although he wasn't even in one of her classes.

It was amazing to him "adults" like this teacher would act this way, and obviously the Principal was also less than objective.

Today this causes Hank to think about his roommate who said, fifteen years later, *"When you are rich, smart, tall and good looking, don't' expect people to like you."*

He was talking about himself, and Hank has never said anything like that about himself, but it applies because it is what others think about you, not what you think about yourself that causes them to act as they do toward you.

It is not the absolutes of rich, good looking, or anything else that is important to them. How they perceive themselves relative to you monetarily, in class performance, the way you speak, if they are shorter, don't dress as well, if you have more or better looking girlfriends, or a more expensive car is what is important to them.

He stopped by the store on 10th that day as usual and told his father what happened.

He responded *"What?"* followed by *"They took your book, and he expelled you from school? Son, I assume you are telling me the truth, and as long as you do that I will support you one hundred percent. But if I ever catch you lying to me, I will beat the Hell out of you. So, here's what you do. Go back, confront that S.O.B., and tell him if he is going to stick with his decision to suspend you, he is going to have to deal with me. You are going to come back and tell me his decision. And if you are suspended, I am going to come back there and kick his sorry ass."*

Hank did that and was not suspended. But he was minus that textbook for the remaining months of the school year. Didn't matter much though, he didn't study anymore in Junior High than Elementary. But that was not the end of it.

CHAPTER 13

FIRST TOUGH TIMES

1953. The year Hank finished his first year of Junior High began less than auspiciously and ended under much worse circumstances.

After his father got two stores running successfully and the seasonal Christmas tree and fireworks businesses were a standard part of his businesses, he started another seasonal business.

For at least two years, maybe more, early in the spring planting season he had been running two small trucks... one north into Oklahoma and one to the south... selling wholesale onion and tomato plants.

He could never understand why anyone would want to buy onion and tomato plants at a grocery store then take them home and plant them. But apparently a lot of people did because the stores bought a lot of the plants.

His father had two men who drove these routes, but occasionally... probably to ensure the customers were being satisfied... he would drive one of the routes.

One morning, late February, he woke Hank up and asked if he wanted to go to Oklahoma with him. Must have been four A.M. and it was a school day, but why not?

They made it to Oklahoma. Just. Then they had a little problem.

Sometime before dawn they were crawling... not stepping, but literally crawling... out of the cab of the truck onto grass.

Something that would happen to him again, eight years later happened. The right rear axle broke. (Maybe the later change to Japanese steel was appropriate?)

They were going over fifty miles per hour. So, when it slipped out of the axle housing and dropped to the pavement it served as a pivot point. The truck swung around to the right, flipped over, all the way, and landed right side up, in a bar ditch, headed in the direction from which they were coming.

The truck was done for. What saved them was the bar ditch. When the truck made it half-way through its roll...when the cab was on bottom... it was in the bar ditch. The truck bed and the front supported the cab, keeping it from getting crushed and injuring them.

Onion plants were scattered over a hundred feet up and down the highway. Fortunately most were off the road on the shoulder and in the grass beyond because they did not come off the truck until it began its flip. Crates were everywhere. Some were destroyed, but the soft landing prevented most of the plants from being destroyed. They were still in their little tied together bunches. His father was fast on his feet. He immediately began kicking, tossing and scraping the plants that were on the highway off into the grass.

The highway patrol showed up. Gave them a ride into town where his father quickly went into action. Not to dwell on the details, but before noon, about six hours later, they were under way again, in a new, almost fully loaded truck.

Within that period of time, his father found a replacement truck, purchased new crates, hired four or five men to pick up and repack the good plants at the roadside, made arrangements for their truck to be moved into town, got all the undamaged plants reloaded, and they were off with ninety percent of the load they had prior to the accident.

Two mornings later, after they finished the planned route and returned home, he entered home room, gave his father's excuse note to Ms. Hulsey and took his seat.

She sarcastically said to the whole room, *"Can't your father take care of his business on his own, or does he need you to help?"* Hank responded, *"Sometimes"* not bothering to elaborate regarding which question. She didn't pursue it any further, as he expected.

Even at the ripe old age of barely thirteen, he was not too concerned about what teachers thought about him. He did his best within the bounds of his own rules, made decent enough grades, worked some, had a childhood none of the teachers and few others would understand, tried to stay out of trouble, have a broad based, entertaining life, and not take too much crap quietly. He is pretty much the same today.

"Not to worry," as an Australian friend used to say, followed by *"They don't have a clue."*

He was right. There is no point endeavoring to explain yourself to others or be much concerned with what they think. Just grin and bear it. Make the best of it. Live with it and enjoy the benefits you are able to derive from life, regardless how much those who are resentful try to cause you trouble over them.

He learned in the seventh grade having a nice car is one of those benefits. In addition to just liking cars… drawing, designing and having a nice one…one of the benefits of nice cars is due to the un-understandable attitude of younger females toward them. We just have to make the best of this, live with and enjoy the benefits. That's "all there is" to it.

There was one "benefit" he can remember in the seventh grade: lovely blonde with great blue eyes, golden tan skin and long blonde hair; the California girl of later years, in the wrong place, at the wrong time. But he was happy for her misplaced timing and location. She really was lovely and a real pleasure.

He can remember two things about her other than those already stated: Her father was in the Navy, stationed at the Naval Air Station for only two years. Then she was gone. Also she sat really close to him with her left hand on the inside of his right thigh… in the seventh grade.

Given his inability to disassociate memories of the Lincoln from her, it was probably for the best she was around for only two years. Otherwise he might not have just failed to finish college. He might not have finished high school, and that would have put a damper on the rest of the life he has enjoyed… although that is ignoring the possibility he might have enjoyed his life just fine without knowledge of what he would have been missing. Others have.

Then there was Paula. Although not exactly a benefit of the car he also can't forget her when thinking about the Lincoln, or maybe it is the other way around. Ditto the blonde.

Her father worked for his. Nice guy, educated, but alcoholic, worked only part time and spent a lot of time with him and Paula when they were sandbox age.

They had two sandboxes, one at her home and one at his. Her father built both of them, hauled the sand and everything. He was a mellow guy much like Robert that Hank would have experiences with fifteen to twenty years later. Alcohol had the same mellowing effect on both although it almost killed Paula's father over a decade later.

Her mother was different… a straight laced teacher, maybe a little up tight… a non-drinker. They were a strange couple.

As Hank and Paula got older they didn't spend much time together because of her mother.

Early one evening they had a date to go to the movies. This was shortly after his restriction to the south side of Jefferson was removed and he was permitted to drive to the Uptown Theater on Main Street.

He drove over to Paula's in the Lincoln, went inside and chatted with her mother. Then they departed…almost. Her mother went to the door with them, looked outside, asked where his father was, and went almost apoplectic when she saw her daughter and he were going off alone in the Lincoln at the age of thirteen.

No date that evening or ever again… a real shame, but not a stopper for him.

He and Paula could have had a future, having been together a lot from pre-school, and liking each other a lot. He remembers her writing in his senior year book about their having known one another longer than anyone else they went to school with.

But what are those French words that seem so appropriate for much of Hank's life? *C'est*.…

⚜

Rita was a tall brunette he met in the seventh grade about this time who, like the out of place at the wrong time California blonde, he also had a memorable Lincoln experience with, plus many experiences to follow over the next fifteen years… another of his unrequited love stories that could have also yielded a more than satisfactory life, if not for his Is That All There Is? craving from an early age.

Her mother and father were divorced. Her father moved to Grand Prairie. Her mother stayed in New Mexico. The plan was for her to divide her time between them with every other year in Grand Prairie.

She would be gone for a year after the seventh grade. Then she would be in Grand Prairie for the ninth and eleventh grades.

They met in art class. Hit it off immediately. He liked her. She seemed to have picked him out of all the boys to be the one. She called him *"Boy!"* And if he remembers correctly, she was his first real, official date that unlike the one with Paula was actually consummated even though there is a good chance it might have never happened if not for Paula's mother.

This was the first one he was able to pick up in the car and take to the movies at night. There was only one problem. His mother decided to strike again in her continuing effort to do whatever she could to screw up his life... to make it as miserable as possible.

When he was ready to leave on the date she informed him at the last minute he could not go in the car unless he took his miserable little six year old brother with him.

He explained who his date was and how important it was to him. How it was not right for her to do this. But it was all to no avail. She would not permit him to leave in the car unless he took with him his little six year old brother whose only ever obvious objective in life was to destroy as much of Hank's as he could.

An important fact about this is it was only a short while before this that his brother and he were at their father's store no more than five blocks from home. It was daylight, shortly after noon. The brother was bitching and complaining about something. Their father got tired of it, pitched the keys to his pickup to Hank and told him to take the little *"pain in the ass"* replication of his mother home.

As he drove up in front of the house their mother saw her *"Little ray of sunshine"* in the truck with him and became almost hysterical. Hank was going to kill him. What was he doing?

Then she jumped into her Lincoln and raced to the store where she confronted their father, hollering at him in his place of business, threatening who knows what, all because his *"little ray"* brother had ridden, during daylight, five blocks with him.

But when he was about to drive across town... at night... less than a month later, it was a different story: night time, no problem, across town, also no problemo.

The little destroyer had to go with him, or he wasn't going. Just a little inconsistent and obvious what her priorities were. She was even willing to sacrifice *"Little sunshine ray"* if it would hurt Hank. So he had to take the little S.O.B… literally, or not go. No choice.

Rita was somewhat surprised about their little chaperone. But she was nice about it; they ignored him, had a decent time and continued to get along well.

That summer, after she went back to New Mexico, they wrote letters frequently. Did that until graduation from High School for the three years she was in New Mexico. When she was in town the other years they spent a lot of time together, going out frequently. She was even protective of him, and was a great friend and companion.

Longest human "relationship" he ever had outside his current marriage. But she wasn't around his senior year or the summer after it. Had she been there then, his life, and hers, might have turned out a lot differently.

She got married a year after he did… in early 1960. Then she was back in town visiting her father one time while Hank was still in town… must have been late 1961 or before he went to California in early 1962. She called. They made a date for dinner. He was surprised when he picked her up. She was seven months pregnant.

Next time he saw her was 1965. She called shortly after he got out of the army. She was visiting her father again. Another of those one day deals. Then she was gone again, until a couple of years later when she called at the beginning of summer 1967.

He went to see her. Her husband was in the military, and was going to be in Alaska for a couple of years. So she decided to move back to Grand Prairie for those two years. Told him she told her husband about him, and she would need a companion some of the time he was away.

Although her father still lived in town, it sounded as though she moved back because of Hank, but she had two kids by that time.

He saw her for a few months, spent the night with her frequently. But it was not comfortable... two kids, husband.

They had been as close as few young people their ages ever were, even though physically apart most of the time, for almost fifteen years, from the ages of twelve to twenty-seven... long time, strong feelings on both sides. But he did not want to be involved in a potentially family disrupting situation, didn't want two kids, and was not interested in getting married again. No future, or not a good one, in his opinion, anyway.

So he went to Georgia for a while for business, moved from Oak Cliff to North Dallas, and did not go back or call her. Although he thought about her and planned frequently to call, he got involved in endeavoring to change his life, working on going back to school.

Then about four months after the last time he saw her he met someone else who caused him to put calling her on the back burner. Four months later he left Texas never to contact her again, and has been regretful about that ever since.

She was a great friend, companion, caring person, one of the nicest people he has ever known... and he still thinks and wonders about her occasionally all these years later.

He is sure, no matter what, they would have been best friends for life had he just gone back and explained everything to her. Not doing so was a big mistake on his part.

Although he has thought about it many times, he has never been able to determine why he did not just sit down and talk with her about his thoughts and feelings because he is sure she would have been alright with his decision, and they would have continued to see one another to this day. He is sure she would have even been a friend to his wife.

Probably the biggest personal relationship screw-up Hank ever made as a result of his "bad habit of not going back."

━╬ ╬━

At the end of the school year 1953, he was not given his report cards. He went to the office to see what the problem was, and he was directed to the same Assistant Principal.

It was the book. Hank reminded him he was informed when the textbook was taken, and, further, because of that, he was not going to pay for it.

The Principal insisted he was going to pay for it. He insisted he was not, pointed out to him he was not being fair, and he wondered why.

Principal got really upset and tried to make more of his comment about his not being fair than the simple statement of truth it was. They stalemated. He refused to give his report cards to him. Hank refused to pay.

All students always received report cards at the end of the school year, so his father asked about his grades. He told him he didn't know. His father wanted to know why. He told him. He then told Hank he did not want to go see the *"Son-of-a-bitch"* principal because if he did, he and Hank would both probably be in trouble. So he directed Hank to go back and tell the principal he had better give his *"Goddamned report cards"* to him, or his father who has to pay the bills would come to see him because he was tired of his *"crap."*

He got his report cards, and the *"Son-of-a-bitch"* assistant principal never bothered him again, even though he moved to the high school the same year he did, and he had to deal with him five more years after these two incidents, but never had another problem.

———

1953 was also the year Hank's knowledge of religion… maybe we should say predisposition toward it… was greatly expanded.

He was not big on it previously because of Brother Bill's deacons, but events in 1953 put him over the edge regarding religion.

What he encountered affected him personally and confirmed in his mind that without any doubt for one to be a confirmed Baptist, or maybe a devotee of any religious group… he didn't know about… *"He must be willing to reject the reality of the world, even the universe, become an unquestioning sheep,"* and maybe even like the Baptists of Grand Prairie or Judy's family he would later meet in Los Angeles…*"a bigot and a hypocrite."*

Today he says *"I have met a lot of nice people, and most of my friends over the years, who have been adherents of one religion or another. I don't really care. Unlike the Jews I encountered in Los Angeles who persecuted me because I did not share their religion, it doesn't make any difference to me what anyone believes… as long as he does not try to force his views on me, or affect my life in any way. I might add gratuitously that on that point the Jehovah's Witnesses come to mind. I don't like them intruding on my property and telling me what a bad person I am because I don't agree with them. That's personal."*

Let's deal with this, but let's take the *"bigot"* and *"unquestioning sheep"* parts first, for which he has to be thankful to Brother Bill for this knowledge when one night he was having dinner at Hank's home and they had an informative exchange.

He has always been one to ask questions about anything he doesn't understand or to find out something he desires to know. Even in his consulting and management experience, he always found the Socratic Method the quickest road to enlightenment.

Therefore, he asked Brother Bill, *"considering the unending and un-fathomable vastness of the universe,"* which he pointed out to Brother Bill; he frequently referred to, why would he always point up? Why did he and everyone refer to Heaven as *"up"*? Couldn't it be below, right or left, or all around us?

Brother Bill did not appear to be too enthralled with his inquisitive nature. But here is where Hank says he is obligated to him for showing him the way.

He reached out, tousled Hank's hair, and said, *"Son, we are not supposed to ask questions like that. We are just supposed to believe."*

There. In one short statement, he had the proof... directly from a man of God.

Everyone is supposed to be a member of the herd of *"unquestioning sheep,"* to be "blindly" and obstinately devoted to his religion; in other words, to become the human embodiment of Webster's definition of *"bigot."* That is: "a person who holds blindly and intolerantly to a particular creed, opinion, etc."

That, in the simple specificity of the English Language, confirms bigotry to be synonymous with being a devout adherent who "blindly" believes without questioning and is intolerant with those who may differ with him. Don't blame Hank. Blame Webster.

The *"hypocrite"* part is a little easier. We have already seen it proven by the deacons. They assumed a false appearance of virtue every time they stood before the church podium, prayed and passed the plates to collect money, which in doing they appeared virtuous. But as they went out to illegally purchase their beer an hour later, they confirmed their display of virtue to be false. Ergo, *"hypocrite,"* again according to Webster: "a person who pretends to be what he is not; one who pretends to be better than he really is, or to be pious, virtuous, etc., without really being so." Thus, it would seem, for anyone to be a devout religious person he must be either nonhuman or a hypocrite.

O. K. Hank could accept a small group of, possibly rogue, deacons being hypocrites, but the majority of an entire town, maybe the majority of the entire country of almost one hundred and fifty million "good" Americans at that time? That was difficult to believe. It was incomprehensible to Hank... until 1953.

Thirty years after it was thought the majority of Americans learned their lesson and repealed national prohibition, permitting the sale of alcoholic beverages again, the majority of the thirty thousand plus ignorant souls in the little city of Grand Prairie, Texas proved their hypocrisy and stupidity. They voted to make the sale of any alcoholic beverage, including beer, illegal within the town, and for what reason?

To answer that question, it would have been necessary to go into all the churches and ask the stupid beings there pointing, or looking up, declaring their unquestioning devotion to their god: *"What does beer have to do with your religion of worshiping a god whose son was sent to save you and who was believed to consume wine when he was here?"*

"Stupid" was added because after their vote it was necessary to drive five miles to cross the county line to buy beer in Arlington, or find a restaurant where it was possible to have a beer with a pizza or a Mexican dinner. And that's what people began to do. But more importantly, guess where the restaurants moved to, and all the new ones opened.

Further, guess where people, including Brother Bill's deacons, who wanted to go out to dinner, shopping, or to a ball game where they could buy a beer built their homes and began to live, which in turn, resulted in retailers opening new stores, a theme park and baseball stadium being built, and so much more.

Thus, the hypocrisy and stupidity of a few thousand Christian hypocrites in 1953 killed the city of Grand Prairie and enhanced the prosperity of the tens and tens of thousands of people who chose to make Arlington, Texas the place of their businesses and homes.

It also did what at the time, was very important to Hank's family and circumstances. It required the closing of the number one and two retail beer businesses in Grand Prairie, rendering the cash flow of his family kaput and their future dim.

But before we get to the specific consequences of this for him and his family; a further example of Grand Prairie Christians potentially destroying lives, income and the future of other people is warranted. This was another experience with hypocrisy in Brother Bill's little church.

A couple of years later Brother Bill was so successful he was able to have a much larger, red brick edifice with a good sized white steeple on it built on the church grounds. It was needed because the congregation outgrew the original little building that became the Sunday school classrooms after this new edifice was finished.

The expanded congregation included an attractive divorced young lady. She and Brother Bill "hit it off." Unfortunately they began dating. That was too much for all those "good Christians."

What, their preacher dating a divorced woman? That was just too much un-Christian-like behavior for them to tolerate in "their" church... never mind some of them were divorced and remarried.

So these "good Christian" people, including those Sunday beer buying and drinking deacons, began holding meetings planning to throw Brother Bill out of the church he built from scratch.

That was a bit too much for Hank's father and, to her credit, even his mother. Because of that they ceased going to church regularly.

Somehow Brother Bill survived the wrath of God delivered through all the "good," God fearing Christians in his congregation. Hank doesn't remember how, but he knows he did because his fourth encounter with Christian bad behavior would involve Brother Bill again, six years later, that possibly wouldn't have occurred had Christian Mingle been available to find *"God's match for"* him... assuming that for pay miracle service can actually prevent people from making the wrong choice for themselves.

But after the election brilliantly reinstating alcohol prohibition in the insignificant little dot on the planet called Grand Prairie, his father was busy closing his two stores, getting rid of equipment and trying to find something else to do to generate income. One endeavor was a fairly short stint as an appliance salesman in Dallas. That didn't work out.

For some reason... wonder what... his father just soured on the town. He also ceased the Christmas tree, fireworks and wholesale plant businesses.

That rendered Hank unemployed when he was not in school for the first time since he was ten years old. He had no place to work, but that turned out not to be a problem, as it seemed there was always something for him to do even if it was not something he wanted to do, or for which he was compensated.

That summer someone decided to paint the family's house. It wasn't Hank but guess who did most of the climbing up and down the ladder with a bucket of paint, garnering more experience that would surely be of some benefit later in life. Certainly not his seven year old brother, but that was not a problem for him, either.

Hank also had the duties of carrying out the trash the mornings the trash truck came, and mowing the yard... with a push mower, no less... that was great exercise in the hundred degree temperature Texas summer heat. No wonder he did not demonstrate a great deal of enthusiasm toward either of these endeavors. But he did not need to.

His mother made sure he did not fail at either of these duties, while also proving what a great trainer she was.

If she did not think he was getting the garbage out soon enough, or didn't get after the lawn mowing as quickly as she thought he should, she had a standard approach of prodding and shaming him, she thought, into moving more quickly. This also included some training, of sorts, for his brother.

She never simply suggested Hank needed to do something right away. No. She also had to belittle him while demonstrating what a great judge of character she was, and at the same time predict what benefit this "character" would be to her in the future.

Boy! Did she miss the mark on that one? She really was not a good thinker.

Her standard approach was to direct the ire she was feeling toward him, while expressing her admiration for the "character" of his brother... always in his presence.

It went like this: While talking at Hank, not to him, but motioning toward him, she would say, *"I don't know why I have to always go to so much trouble to get you to do anything. When your brother gets older, I won't even have to ask him. He will just do it for his mother."* (Note the third person reference to her, as if someone else was saying this.)

Maybe she used third person to save herself the embarrassment of that prediction because down deep inside she knew she was just talking trash.

When he got older she did not ask him to do anything. She knew he would not get up soon enough to carry out the trash, and he was too weak to push the mower. She didn't even bother to ask him. She just did both, herself.

⋙⋘

There was a ten day respite from all of this that was intended to be a good time. This was when Hank's father took him to Colorado to see where he was born and a few other things; Cripple Creek, the Royal Gorge Bridge. Pike's Peak. They were also going farther north, possibly to see Mount Rushmore. But they hit a little hitch in those plans and returned home well before the planned route was completed.

They went with Hank's uncle Carney, his wife and youngest daughter, them in his Cadillac, Hank and family in the Lincoln.

Somewhere near Cheyenne his mother got mad at his aunt Halley and insisted she, Hank, his father and his brother terminate the trip, which they did, of course, and hurried back to Grand Prairie and the joys she delivered at home.

Maybe because of his newly created position of not having any income and possibly his older brother Carney thinking it would be good for him to get away for a while he asked Hank's father to go on the trip. It was a spur of the moment thing that was decided and they were off, all within one day.

Possibly the fact a few thousand religious bigots to whom he had been catering for years *"moved one of the ends"* of what he spent the last seven years building made his father susceptible to wanting to get the hell out of Dodge… as far away as he could for a little respite from his closing down activities.

On the other hand, it could have been something else.

For the first time in their married lives of about fifteen years, his father was spending much of his time during the day at home with his mother. Possibly he was not aware of what days and days with her could be like, he developed some empathy with Hank and just needed to get away somewhere... anywhere.

For whatever reason, not long after their trip being terminated as a result of his mother's demons, his father decided they should take another trip; this time to the south to Houston where two of her sisters lived. Maybe he thought if she was with her family members rather than his she would be happier and he would get some relief.

If that was the case, Hank could not imagine what could have made him think that unless his desire to change the scenery and daily proximity to his mother in the confined space of home without other adult companionship overwhelmed his better judgment.

His mother and her sisters never got along. Their wiring was as faulty as his mother's. In fact, one of them was much, much worse, which she proved only two years later when she was fired from her many years long position as an executive secretary with Humble Oil Company in Houston for the same paranoia frequently exhibited by his mother, and then a year after that ended up in a sanitarium receiving shock therapy at his father's expense.

The other one was nicer, at least to Hank, but apparently not to everyone else.

Years before, she deserted her then three year old son and his father... from what Hank was told; with the little boy bawling his little eyes out... to run off with another man who was her then current husband and the father of her two daughters at the time of this trip.

Hank thought the guy she left was the lucky one because she drove the current husband to drink, turning him into an alcoholic.

He said this uncle was one of the nicest men ever knew. So he did not have it in him to reciprocate. But since he could not take her sober and he did not want to leave his daughters, alcohol was his refuge.

Fortunately Hank's father did not even drink beer. He said it was not possible to be a successful vendor of it and drink it also. So Hank never had to contemplate how much worse things could have been for him if his father was an alcoholic.

His mother and her sisters were all selfish, self-centered and crazy, which prevented them from getting along with one another even as well as they got along with everyone else. So he could not imagine what his father was thinking unless desperation might have altered his cognitive ability regarding this a little.

But whatever his reasoning, Hank was amazed he had a decent time on this trip.

For some reason unknown to him to this day, his father went off course two hundred miles on the way to Houston to the Dixie Dude Ranch in Bandera, Texas, northwest of San Antonio.

He could not imagine how his father even knew about it unless having bought a Quarter Horse from the King Ranch the year before resulted in meeting someone who told him about it.

Anyway, however it came about Hank got to go horseback riding for the first... and definitely last time.

It was a slow ride on horses trained to follow the tail of the horse in front of them.

Had he any prior knowledge of what this would be like, he would not have gone. But he did not, and his father was strongly promoting it as another experience he wanted him to have. Also it took him away from the family, away from harm for the entire day.

After over twenty miles the slow caravan to nowhere returned to the residential part of the ranch with him so sore in the crotch he could barely walk and was certain his ability to father children was eliminated, which based on subsequent events might have enhanced his life.

He doesn't know what his mother, father and *"sunshine"* did back at the ranch while he was off blazing new trails, but whatever it was, he doesn't remember any negative results.

They left the dude ranch, family still fairly intact, and continued on their journey to Houston.

Amazing! There weren't any problems in Houston between his mother and her sisters or between her and his father who must have been a genius to have pulled that one off.

A road trip of some duration, and his mother for more than a day with two of her siblings without any major problems or arguments was a rarity... no, a miracle only God could have pulled off because... after all... they were his creations, weren't they, Christian Mingle guys?

It probably seems strange to normal people for Hank to have been thinking about what bad things could happen, but viewed in context it is really not so strange.

When soldiers are in a combat zone they are always on guard for incoming rounds or invading enemy. Not to be doing so would leave them open to a surprise attack or caught out in the open when rounds hit.

Well, that was the way Hank learned to think about life with his mother. A stray blast or attack was just a minute away at all times. He literally grew up in a war zone in which there was rarely a cease fire.

The highlight of the trip for him was a day at the beach in Galveston. It was the first time he saw the ocean. But unlike Thomas Mann, he was not "unburdened with life's tribulations" nor did he envisage "an unobstructed future for himself."

He was only thirteen years old... six or seven years junior to Mann when he first viewed the ocean and wrote his story about it. Thus, he had not a clue about existentialism or anything else that intellectual.

All he had as a frame of reference was life with his mother, father and *"Sunshine."* As a result, his future concerns were about the next few hours. His youth was a plus. He was immune to disillusionment. His future had to be brighter than his present.

However, with this metaphorical reference to "soldiers in a combat zone," "incoming rounds," and "a cease fire" during this summer sojourn, we would be remiss not to address the reality of these being endured by young Americans, many no more than "six or seven years" older than he, in that far away little country of Korea.

Here his youth was also a plus. He did not have to endure that solely because he, luckily, was not born six years earlier. Also, if not for what happened regarding this that summer his future might not have been "brighter than his present."

⇌ ⇋

During the past short period of only three years his government chose to risk the lives of one million eight hundred thousand young Americans unnecessarily in that far off insignificant little country that was in no way a threat to America or its citizens. Even if its leaders had a desire to harm America they could not. They did not have the means.

Therefore, the "leaders" of America chose to risk the lives of almost two million young Americans who had the misfortune of being of age to be conscripted and used as cannon fodder for one or both of two reasons... or excuses. Also, let's not forget the probably hundreds of thousands of lives of Korean men, women and children that were obviously not thought of as human beings, but only as *"collateral damage"* by America's "leaders."

"Communism," whether a real imminent threat or not, was *"bad"* and had to be wiped out at any cost wherever it raised its ugly head... or the economy was perceived by them about to turn south, and a good sized shot in the arm of the military/industrial complex in the form of an unnecessary little war that would cost billions of dollars would eliminate the manifestation of that undesirable slowed economy virus that was almost as distasteful to them as Communism.

Whichever or both of these is fact, it is empirically proven what happened to those one million eight hundred thousand young Americans during the three years between the summers of 1950 and 1953 was caused by forces entirely beyond their control residing in

Washington D.C. thereby, again proving the assertion "the freedom of the individual to act, and be responsible for his actions, is the primary source of whatever events and results thereof encompass him in the course of his life" is manifestly untrue... hogwash, bullshit. Ask some of them! Hank has.

Fate of time, place, to whom born, resulting socioeconomic status and connections determined who was among those sent to Korea. It was also fate that most who survived and were still there July 27, 1953 when the armistice was signed got to come home.

And although unknown to him, this armistice also... at least temporarily... ensured Hank's near term future could "be brighter than his present." But also unknown to him was the fact he was not out of the woods where those who considered him no more than one of millions to be sacrificed in whatever quest they dreamed up next would continue to seek fodder for it.

It would be only six years later when the worst post war recession the country experienced would send these scavenger hyenas in search of another military solution to that which they caused. And this time their quest would be larger game, and preparations would require more time. Hank would not be so lucky then. He would be the right age.

However, for now, thankfully summer finally ended and he could be away from family and home five days a week... not just away from home with family.

But for now it was a good "thing" he did not have the pleasure of being home during previous summers. Had not his father been keeping him occupied away from home, he was certain he could have easily become a runaway.

He is also certain his mother's conduct toward him toughened him up, but more importantly, for better or worse for him...he still doesn't know which… it imbued him with an extremely low tolerance for taking crap from anyone.

Before he was old enough to leave home, he already had a lifetime of it. The last trip of the summer was a welcome respite from that, as would be getting back to school.

CHAPTER 14

LIFE BROADENS

1954. School was much more of the same Junior High routine… a continuation of the fall semester with one small change. In history class the teacher was somewhat more aggressive in his favorite new subject and the latest U.S. Government created scare and fear strategy to condition the people for the war plans it was already cooking up: Communism in Asia and the *"domino effect"* of Asian countries potentially "falling" into its sphere being a threat to America..

This was obviously a result of the Korean Conflict, its status as stalemate and the resulting armistice 38th parallel concession of the U.S. he viewed as a victory for Communism, which Hank agreed it sort of was, since the under armed, and "under" almost everything relative to the U.S. forces could not be defeated by its overwhelming bombing and fire power, which should have been a warning for the future about endeavoring to defeat, or dislodge an indigenous population that is politically, religiously or in whatever way strongly nationalistic and homogenous. (Subsequent events indicate it wasn't.)

The teacher seemed to be, as kids expressed then *"eaten up"* with this. He continued to point out on the world maps in the class the potential for Communism to continue to move to take over Southeast Asia. He seemed to always focus on Indochina, the area where Vietnam is located. It was more like a geopolitical class than history.

When thinking about this Hank, suspiciously, relates it to his thoughts about the Saturday morning movie serials and movies of the years prior; was this government indoctrination for what was to come, or was it just one teacher's obsession?

Probably the latter, but the action toward Vietnam ten years later, after... we now know... the U.S. military being in Vietnam years before the Gulf of Tonkin raises concern.

However, this class is actually more memorable to him for another reason, which is likely the reason he can recall so much of the foregoing... memory by association.

One day just after the bell rang, as he was getting up from his seat, two of the girls in the class quickly approached him. One of them was one of the two who phoned him about the leading man role almost three years before.

One on either side of him, they immediately began fingering and turning down the sleeves on his short sleeved shirt he had folded up two turns while asking him why he did this. Then one of them asked him another question: *"Do you know why bees buzz?"*

Before he could answer, the other one did as she faced across in front of him to the other girl laughing, *"You would too if you had your honey between your legs."*

Then they both scurried off laughing as though they were embarrassed and wanted to get away as quickly as possible before he could respond.

Maybe they were harassing him because he was somewhat shy or maybe, given one of them demonstrated what she thought about him in the sixth grade in her phone call to him, they had another idea, which he considered probable given what Paula said to him also in the form of a joke about *"balls"* when they were alone in her bedroom one afternoon a few months earlier.

It is a fact girls mature earlier than boys. At fourteen all three of them had reached womanhood.

Certainly that physical change elicited some thoughts and curiosity. Maybe they were expecting him to follow up. But he was too shy for that, and probably fortunately because, as he previously stated about the out of place blonde before; he would have likely had to drop out of school before graduation, as did at least two of his male friends who also were married and working to support three by their seventeenth year.

One thing was certain though. All three of these girls were liberated before "the Pill." One of them demonstrated that by getting pregnant and having to drop out of high school at the beginning of her junior year and marrying one of the afore mentioned friends.

Hank probably missed something on all three counts, but that was O.K. He at least got his high school diploma and was able to progress beyond that. Also these three were just three of many he would miss out on for various reasons in subsequent years.

But since he did not get enticed off course these early years he also honed his contrarian attitude about most things a little more finely. He did not go with the herd. Not much studying. Spent most of his time drawing and painting in watercolors. Did a lot of designing cars and drawing what he thought future airplanes would look like. He did a good job of this, also.

As proof, when he heard Ford was going to be producing the top of the line Lincoln Continental again, after over a half decade hiatus, he set about designing what he thought it should look like, and nailed it. When it came out, his design was better than ninety percent correct. He still has the drawing.

Although he was having a pretty good time in 1954 his dear old Dad was not. A year after closing his stores he still had not found anything to get some income rolling in.

At the age of thirty-six, after being in business successfully and profitably for seven of the last eight years, he was about to run out of money, and rather than let that happen, he took a big step down and took a job as a labor foreman with a company doing contract construction work in the "defense" plant less than a half mile walk from his home.

He really was an amazing survivor. Shortly after he got the foreman job he convinced the superintendent he could save money for them by replacing some of the hand labor with equipment. They agreed.

He did that by buying a small Ford tractor with a hydraulic bucket on the front and what is called a "box blade" on the rear, trading one of the pieces of refrigeration equipment from one of the stores for an old dump truck and renting both to the company by the week. That quickly more than doubled his income, and he was off and running in a new direction.

The previous summer of Hank's painting also paid off for him.

Just after school was out for summer after the 8th grade, Mr. Smith who owned the Jones Blair Paint Store on Main Street, where they bought the paint for the house the prior year, called and offered him a job, which he thought was great because he was not going to have to be stuck at home with you know who for the summer.

Mr. Smith, his real name, was at least sixty-five years old, or close to the age of Hank's grand-father, so he had a good rapport with him.

He had the largest wholesale paint business in town supplying most of the painters. The Main Street location of his store was great... between Center Street and the Wings Theater. So he also had a great retail business, including picture framing, blinds and shades... overall, a good profitable business... not nearly as good as beer, but good, and given the variety of the business, Hank got a lot of training in new endeavors to add to the experience he got working in his father's stores. Additionally he received "training" in another new endeavor. He began paying income tax and Social Security.

As his father and grandfather were doing for years, Mr. Smith taught him a lot of new "stuff" like how to use a mitre box to cut picture frames, to mix paint and install blinds. He also opened cases, stocked shelves, and made deliveries some of which were not what he expected.

Mr. Smith's wife was ill, could not drive and had to go to the doctor in the Oak Lawn area of Dallas that was over fifteen miles away, north of downtown, through a good part of Dallas city streets with a lot of traffic.

One day Mr. Smith asked him if he knew where Oak Lawn was... not had he driven there, just where it was. Of course he said, *"Yes"* because he had been there and he did know where it was. He had never driven there, though. But before he could add that important bit of information Mr. Smith tossed the keys to his almost new 1954 Chevrolet pickup to him and told him to go pick his wife up at home and take her to the doctor.

Another time he showed a big stack of Venetian blind boxes to him took one out and asked if he thought he could install it.

He told him he didn't think that would be a problem, he had them at home, knew how they worked, and used tools working on his bikes and other things, as well as a lot of work was done on his house over the last few years, and he'd helped a little on that.

Mr. Smith then told him to load the blinds into the pickup and gave him the name and address of the man he should see in Arlington.

There were half a dozen houses in which Mr. Smith contracted to install blinds that Hank spent the next three days installing, which required him to drive to and from Arlington, about a fifteen mile round trip. Not a long trip, but the first time he could recall driving alone with sufficient time to think... which could have gotten him into trouble.

At the age of fourteen, he didn't have much to think about except things or experiences in his little life to that time, and pleasant thoughts prevailed over the unpleasant. Also at that age the most pleasant thoughts, driven by the post pubescent surge of his hormones, were of girls.

Those thoughts have a physical effect... a creative one. They elicit an immediate physical response that reminds little boys they really are favored over females. They are born with their own special "toy," which when stimulated only by certain pleasant thoughts becomes one that demands attention. Sometimes it is very demanding.

This time his was thinking about the out of place little blonde blue eyed California girl in the Lincoln with her hand on the inside of his right thigh and what might have been had he followed up on the two young ladies earlier that year in History class when he suddenly had a problem literally on his hands and elsewhere.

Thankfully, there was a box of Kleenex in the glove compartment, but that still required some quick action resulting in erratic movement of the pickup's steering wheel that resulted in movement of the vehicle that could have gotten him into trouble had one of the local constabulary seen him since he was too young to have a driver's license. It would also have been an insufferably embarrassing experience.

He took Mr. Smith's wife to the doctor another time, and did quite a few deliveries. Then one day Mr. Smith raised the subject of his age for some unknown reason... maybe his wife said something, given women tend to be more sensitive to age.

When he replied, Mr. Smith said *"You are only fourteen? I thought you were sixteen. Do you have a driver's license?* Hank said, *"No."* At which time Mr. Smith looked at him, sorta smiled and said, *"What the Hell? It's too late to worry about that now."*

He continued to drive his pickup, make deliveries and do everything else for the rest of the summer, just as he was doing before their age conversation.

It was a good job, kept him out of trouble at home. He made a little money and gained more experience, including learning to control his thoughts, or at least not to deal with them inappropriately while driving, and he did have another good time summer of 1954, including this.

A classmate friend introduced him to either a friend or relative who was visiting for a while, a very, very pretty young lady his age with whom he got on well, immediately.

After their meeting she decided they should have a picnic. The next day they had a nice picnic at a lovely shaded spot in the edge of the woods in the city park.

He says he doesn't remember anything else, just that really nice day in the park. But he does admit recalling this experience gets him to do more of that thinking; this young lady, the out of place California girl of the two previous years, Rita, even Heidi.

It seems as though the ones he always liked most were the ones who were different, from elsewhere, short times with them. They were exotic. Even one tall *"brown haired girl"* in Greenville his aunt May introduced to him when he was visiting her.

Different, exotic was more appealing. Grass is greener? He says he doesn't know, except they were certainly confirmation there really was more out there. That what he had been experiencing definitely was "not all there is."

Even though he was certain there was much more out there… somewhere, he knew it was a long way off, in time. He still had almost half a decade before he would be leaving, getting out.

He had just barely departed puberty in 1954. Still had another year of Junior High and three years of High School. At that age, four years was like an eternity. Almost one third of the lifetime he experienced to that date.

But before we get too far beyond puberty, there are other experiences of his short life before and around this time that are important.

Although we have addressed the contributions of his parents and other life experiences and observations that provided the foundation upon which his adult life was built, other small parts of his life prior to departure from puberty did contribute, somewhat.

As we have addressed, his mother quit school in the sixth grade then spent most of her time learning to play the piano, guitar and mandolin, and singing.

When they moved into the little duplex on Austin Street she was thirty-four years old and had not had a piano handy for a decade. Thus, one of the first discretionary purchases his parents made was a piano.

Then it seems they decided; "*since we have a piano*" we should see if another family member might have any talent in that direction. Thus, he began piano lessons at the ripe old age of seven.

It should have been readily apparent had Beethoven, who was composing at the age of three in 1773, been Hank he would have still been playing "From a Wigwam" those one hundred and seventy-four years later.

Apparently it wasn't. He continued to take piano lessons for about two years until, he moved.

He rode his bike to these lessons at the teacher's home in Indian Hills that was in the southwest quadrant of town, about one and one-half miles one way, up and down a couple of small topographical rises... ergo the "hills" part of the name. These trips were after school. Thus, his lesson days were full from school in the morning, until about dinner time. No play time. But he did get to participate in one recital in which he played "From a Wigwam."

During this same period, it was decided he should also have some exposure to dance. Thus, off to Mrs. Breitcamp's dance studio for tap and ballet, which was located about as far to the southeast from home as piano lessons were to the southwest. But he didn't bike to these lessons. His mother took him. He didn't know why. This trip was flat land all the way. Possibly, it was because she perceived an hour of dancing and three miles of bike riding in the afternoon after school would be too much for his little legs. But that is giving her the benefit of the doubt in his mind about this.

Dance lessons did not last as long as piano lessons. The classes were all girls, but for one other boy... and thus uncomfortable!

Imagine; a young boy trying to do ballet among those girls then having to see... or be seen...by them in school the next day... or their telling the other boys.

Also, he did not possess the proclivities assumed to be innate in most male ballet dancers, However, had he known at that age what mature female ballet dancers have as legs, bodies, muscle tone and stamina, he might have thought more about pursuing this course. One thing is certain. He would have had little competition for their affections.

What he took away from his short piano and dance careers were the following: stronger legs from all the bike riding, a lesson from his piano teacher that his shoes should always be shined. A basic knowledge of tap, that he had rhythm and a decent ability in this endeavor, a lifelong dislike of "the ballet." And he learned to read music.

Any influence of these endeavors in later life was probably minimal.

The shoe shinning bit may have been of some assistance in the military where it seems it must be impossible to kill the enemy without one's shoes glistening, mirror finish black.

In the Army more time was spent shining shoes and combat boots than practicing on the rifle range or in hand-to-hand combat, which seems inconsistent, given the concern about the enemy being able to know where one is if he has anything reflective on him.

But that must be offset by the possibility of being able to disarm him visually if he gets close enough for hand-to-hand combat. He could be disarmed, so to speak, by the reflection of the sun in his eyes from shiny boots.

Also, he can ride a bike, do a little shuffle step and a mean soft shoe. Then there is the ability to recognize EGBDF, center C and the rest that did contribute to his Junior High experience that included another musical adventure.

Although he doesn't remember whose idea it was, he signed up for band in the seventh grade. He thinks it probably his father's idea because he bought a really nice, professional grade coronet with real silver trim and pearl keys for him. Then he encouraged him to learn to play "Melody of Love," which he never did master.

In fact, he didn't master much. He played for the first two years of Junior High. Played second chair to a guy named Gary who was determined to become a professional trumpeter. Was probably second chair because, as with everything else, he didn't study much. But second wasn't bad. It wasn't third or fourth. Those were filled by guys who possibly practiced more than he did.

But he had an excuse for not practicing the coronet. We have referred to the houses in his neighborhood as "little box houses."

That is literally true. They had wood exteriors and drywall on the interior with no insulation in between. No central heat or air conditioning where it was so very hot at least six months of the year the windows had to be open...day and night, and it was embarrassing to have everyone within two blocks hear the blasting sounds of the coronet, which is a slightly more mellow version of the trumpet or bugle, during his feeble attempts to become proficient playing it.

But there was a real reason for not practicing the coronet more frequently he could not disclose. He was afraid his top lip could begin to resemble that of Louis Armstrong. Now, that would have had an impact on his later life experiences, especially with the fairer sex. That was more important than blowing a horn... in his opinion, anyway.

Besides, he thought what is wrong with second? Gary worked his butt off trying to become a professional trumpet player, continuing through High School and probably college.

Hopefully he made it. But he has not heard any recordings, nor his name mentioned among famous musicians, and that's the problem.

Hank was also, according to his art teacher, number two in art class. There was a kid who was much better than he who was number one. But he, like Gary to his trumpet, was totally devoted to his art...

to the exclusion of everything else, and Hank also has not seen any mention of him among the great artists of the twentieth century.

When he began the study of architecture in college he was also number two in his class. The number one guy was just out of four years in the military where he was stationed in Europe among all that great architecture. He was consumed. He had hundreds of slides of European edifices to prove it. But neither has his name appeared among famous twentieth century architects. Ditto the military. Years later, when Hank was in Officer Candidate School, he was called in and told he was number two in the class.

His nick name should have been *"Deuce."* His opinion is too many people are unwilling to recognize their limitations. They refuse to accept the reality of what they are... what their true capabilities are. They choose to operate on hope. Reality is too real for them to accept.

That doesn't make much sense to him, but it seems few can accept reality. They choose to believe and hope their nick name is going to be *"Ace,"* and conduct themselves on the basis of the way they believe things ought to be rather than the way they are

He would be the last person in the world to tell anyone not to try to reach as high as they truly think they can reach. But that must include acceptance of reality. Hope doesn't enter into it.

As his father told him, *"Son, hope in one hand and [choose your material means of filling] the other. See which one fills up first."* That was good, realistic advice.

People should be able to recognize whether they have talent of the kind required to make it to the top. The work and talent of those who are, shall we say world class, is all about us. All anyone has to do is look at it and objectively compare his talent. There are books, art museums, architecture, recordings available to everyone.

In the case of Gary, when he and Hank were in the eighth grade he could have paid fifty cents to go to their gym one day to see the North Texas State Lab Band with Pat Boone. There... if he could be objective, which most cannot... he could have determined how his talent would stand up against those musicians.

Hank did, and he could tell: no way. For him to devote himself to becoming first chair in his little junior high band would have meant excluding almost everything else and having very little, if anything, to show for it later.

Disappointment? That is the ultimate feeling of most who devote themselves to just one thing, whatever that may be, unless they have obvious, superior talent. If someone has the talent to be the best, it is comparably obvious fairly early in life. They may not be willing to admit it, but to devote themselves to becoming the best at something and not achieving it must be disappointing.

Second best at many things AND well-rounded is better. It affords more opportunity. If someone really enjoys art or music he should pursue it, but not to the exclusion of broadening his abilities and options.

Not to have more than one option in life is just not smart. Think of devoting yourself to playing the piano for years and years, hoping for the big break, finding yourself at forty playing in a dinner play-house in Kansa City or some similar venue because that is the best gig you can get, and you can't do anything else because you did not devote a little of your time to studying English, History or something that would provide a fallback position. That would have to be disappointment, as all the tears on the T.V. show "America's Got talent" from those who have *"worked my whole life for this"* while working as a waitress sadly prove over and over.

To each his own, but for Hank second place and the versatility to do other things was a better choice than the possibility of "disappointment and disillusionment." He would have been happy to be referred to as *"Deuce."*

His view is; art and music are best enjoyed, not practiced, by ninety-nine point nine percent of the population. We can enjoy those arts by looking, listening and, in some cases, joining in if it gives us and others pleasure.

Being able to sing, to play the piano, to paint, to dance well enough to please ourselves and others is one of the pleasures of life. Singing in a church choir, playing to entertain friends at a party, helping your children or their school with an art project, being a good dancer... those are worthwhile endeavors. One of them is even expected, normal social behavior. Or so his father thought.

When he was twelve, before seventh grade, his father began dance instructions. He added a large one room addition to the house in 1950 or 51. Then he bought a nice piece of furniture that contained a radio, a record player with a multiple record changer and a recorder that permitted him to make records.

Over the next two years he added a large Wurlitzer Juke Box... one of those with the bubbling lights in multiple colors, a pin ball machine and some other entertainment. But the most important part of the room was the large space for dancing. He liked to dance.

He had Paula's father and mother bring her over, and he taught Paula and Hank to ballroom dance. Waltz. Fast. Plain slow dancing. He spent a lot of time on this until they were proficient.

Then he wanted to make sure Hank was properly attired, so he taught him how to tie a tie... both four-in-hand and Windsor knots. He even instructed him on how to ask a young lady to dance and Paula how to respond yes and no. Speak of all around guys.

This was beneficial because the major social event of Junior High School was the Sock Hop. The dance was frequently held in the school gym. Boys who could not dance were not in great demand. He was grateful to his father, again.

This is another example of where being raised under his father's tutelage provided a foundation of knowledge, self-sufficiency and self-confidence that would prove to be the foundation upon which his future would be built. His time in L.A. proved the value of it. In the future it would bear even more fruit.

His growth was not the only place his father was effecting growth outside his business endeavors. His home grew along with Hank. As he grew, it got larger.

In addition to the room addressed above a new master bedroom and bath, a bedroom and bath over the garage were added and the size of the kitchen was doubled. The house grew to three times its original size.

No wonder after his business success of seven of the prior eight years, he was running out of money in 1954. For him, money was for spending, and he did a good job of that too.

From three hundred sixty-five dollars only eight years before, a new house, filled with new furniture and appliances, additions costing a multiple of the original cost of the house. all for cash... no credit cards back them... a lot of large landscaping and fencing, two new Lincolns, ditto new Ford Pickups, couple of trucks, equipment for the stores... too much equipment, which would prove to continue to be a problem for him even a decade later in his new business, nice platinum diamond and ruby ring and platinum watch for Hank's mother, Christmas expenditures equal to about twenty percent of the average annual family income at the time, including electric trains, bicycles, expensive perfume, Neiman Marcus dresses, silk underwear in every color the store had, the farm, bad investments in a couple of oil wells, etc. etc. He knew how to spend it. And he enjoyed it.

Wonder how much money just "went"? Consider the two cars and pickups equaled four years income for the average family of the time. House additions another four. Christmases and travel another two. Then there was clothing, food and miscellaneous.

Hank is certain he spent at least thirty years-worth, probably more, of the average family income of the time in seven years.

If he only had any idea about investing in 1949 through 1953 he could have socked away enough to let it grow for decades, died pretty well off, and he would not have been so pressured about income in

1954. But that was a result of his background and maturing during the great depression.

Surely many of his generation were affected in the same way, so Hank could not take him to task over this. Buying too much equipment, yes, but on this subject Hank would be on pretty thin ice because his conduct has not been much better.

He began investing as soon as he had sufficient income to live well and have quite a bit left over. Most years he never spent more than fifty percent of his net income, and invested the rest. But his problem was taking profits short term, which he attributes to the nature of his nurturing and the financial ups and downs of his youth.

Over the last four decades he left more than his current worth on the table just in real estate he sold that he didn't have to because he did not like tenants, and was not sufficiently prescient to even come close to predicting the amount of real inflation we have experienced during this time.

CHAPTER 15

LIFE GETS BETTER

The last year of Junior High that began in 1954 was uneventful – more of the same except Rita was back and he continued to use the car for dates, minus the little chaperone. His mother was relatively quiet.

He spent most Friday and Saturday nights going to movies at the Uptown Theater and having burgers and malts at the Griddle System hamburger joint where he also frequently had lunch, including great Boston cream pie, and if he didn't have a date, to the Dairy Queen and cruising. More Sock Hops where his friend Bill who was a fabulous dancer frequently put on a one man show doing the Bop. It was a pretty good year.

⟨⟩

1955. Business continued to grow for his father. He quit the foreman job. Went on his own, bought more equipment and trucks, and began doing work for other contractors.

He was outgoing, gregarious, very likeable. Hank remembers one of the regular customers in the store at 10th Street telling him, *"You could put a store behind a rock somewhere, and people would still find it because of you."*

In his new construction business that would also prove true. Some of the people he began doing business with in the first year were still customers fifteen years, or more, later.

He really was sort of a "man's man." Strong. Five ten. Forty-six inch chest, great, strong legs, about two hundred twenty pounds. Smart. Tough. Not bad looking, tremendous amount of common sense, great dancer, gambler and fabulous shot.

He would bet a hundred dollars a shot…a week and a half wages for the average person at the time… he could hit a small French's Mustard jar thrown as far and as high into the air in front of him as the person foolish enough to take the bet could throw it. And he would shoot it with his forty year old, single shot twenty-two caliber rifle that looked like it was just retrieved from a junk pile. Hank says he doesn't think he ever missed.

What the unsuspecting bettor was unaware of was he and that rifle were inseparable for a quarter of a century since his father gave it to him for his twelfth birthday when they were living on the farm at Shirley. He began shooting with it then and he continued doing so.

He kept it in his pickup, at the ready. He would go out south of town and practice at least once every week.

He had been having Hank throw the bottles for him since he was able to throw them far enough. But he could throw them himself, shoulder the rifle and pick them out of the air.

He had that gun for sixty-eight years. It was his prized possession and he gave it to Hank shortly before he died. He still has it leaning against his desk only a few feet away.

He doesn't know what he will do with it before he dies. He doesn't have anyone to leave it to.

Beginning of summer 1955, end of Junior High, for the second time in Junior High Hank could not get his report cards at the end of the year. But this time, for a good reason.

After ninth grade, at the age of fifteen, he began a business at O.L. Nelms Farmers' Market out on Highway 80, half way between Grand Prairie and Oak Cliff where he employed the lesson learned from his father nine years earlier in 1946.

He rented a stall at the Market then went to the Farmer's Market in Dallas on Friday, bought produce that was close to going bad and, using his father's 52 Ford pickup on which he helped him install a flat bed, brought it back to the market, repackaged it in smaller retail sized packages and sold it on the weekend... at one hell of a profit... to families who came to the Market to buy fresh produce.

This was a win-win for the farmers in Dallas, for him and for his customers who paid a fraction of what they would have paid at the grocery store,

He made great profits, the farmers did not have to throw away products foregoing potential revenue, and with the products he did not sell on the weekend, he drove to the various restaurants in Grand Prairie on Monday and gave them a deal on produce that had to be used ASAP.

The two Mexican restaurants were big customers for the left over lettuce and tomatoes.

That summer he made five hundred dollars a week. That was a lot of money for anyone then, especially a fifteen year old and a pickup truck. He wished he could have done it all year, but it was strictly a seasonal... summer only business.

His mother was unusually kind enough to pick up his report cards.

The highlight of the summer, other than the money he made, was O.L. Nelms was frequently at the market, and he got to know him.

He thought Nelms admired a fifteen year old doing what he was doing. Maybe he thought he had the potential to replicate what he accomplished.

In the interest of maximizing the profit from his investment, Nelms built a bar at the east end of the covered boardwalk that was the "market" where Hank and the other vendors backed their trucks up to the boardwalk, off loaded their products and placed them on tables in the smaller, retail sized packages.

It was good merchandising all around. The customers could see Hank and the others had a lot of merchandise on their trucks. That provided more credibility. Some thought all those selling the produce were farmers, which some really were.

At the east end of the boardwalk, maybe a hundred feet across the parking lot, perpendicular to the boardwalk, Nelms also built a large two hundred foot long metal building that housed a flea market where vendors rented spaces much like on the boardwalk in which to market their antiques, junk and all sorts of stuff on which people like to see if they can find a deal. It was like a huge garage sale.

People wanting to go between the flea market and the produce market had the choice of the easy way between the two by going through the air conditioned bar or having to make the deliberately difficult step up to, or down from, the boardwalk.

Nelms sold a lot of Pabst Blue Ribbon on those hot, Texas summer days… probably to Baptists from Grand Prairie. He also spent more time at the place than he might otherwise if not for his bar manager.

He was in his mid-fifties, at least. His bar manager was an attractive thirty-five year old… max… female with whom he apparently had a "thing" going.

She always wore those shorts with the little tied bows on the outside of either leg that enticed you to want to untie them.

Hank heard halfway through the summer, she was living with him in his penthouse apartment atop the five story building he owned on Gaston Avenue, a very good part of Dallas at the time.

When he came to the market he drove a nifty little black Allard sports car. It was the one that had a grill like an Indy racer and motorcycle fenders, a two-seater.

He took Hank for a drive one day with his bar manager in her little shorts between himself and Hank. It was a tight fit he found enjoyable even though she did not put her hand on his thigh. He also enjoyed the ride.

Toward the end of summer he purchased his second car, a black 1946 Plymouth four door sedan with a huge interior, especially in the back seat, he bought with some of the money he earned that summer.

His father's new business, begun the previous year, continued to grow. He was doing a lot of contracting at the "defense" plant as a result of the business it was getting due to the post war rebuilding and rearming of Europe and the ratcheting up of the Cold War that officially began coincident with the end World War II.

It was a good summer. He made a lot of money, had a good time and bought a "new" car. But autumn did not begin so well.

He always had bad colds that eventually worked their way into his chest twice a year. At the beginning of autumn and spring he would usually miss several days of school each time. This was the problem in the sixth grade when the girls phoned him to relay the news about his part in the class play.

The beginning of High School was not any different. He had an attack shortly after school began. But this time it was different. The girls didn't call, but the doctor was called.

The doctor his mother liked diagnosed him, incompetently, with asthma. Probably a quack... his mother really liked him.

She operated on the basis of whether she liked someone, rather than competence. Her opinion of the person was more important than competence. But it really didn't matter. She probably could not have recognized competence, anyway.

Hank remembers, many years later, in 1976 when Jimmy Carter was elected and his mother just had to phone his office to let him know how happy she was about Carter being elected because she knew he thought Carter was a jerk who was promoted specifically to appeal to the viscera, rather than the intellect, by constantly showing him on TV with a Bible held prominently in front of him.

This was usually outside his Georgia, small town church, as he was departing the Sunday school class he supposedly taught.

Those behind getting their first official puppet into office... primarily Zibigniew Brzezinski who has boasted he picked Jimmy to be President... knew most of the American electorate were a bunch of non-thinking Christians who believed, not thought, anyone who was a Christian was their guy. Ditto twenty-four years later when in the Presidential debates another of their jerk puppets was set up to answer a question to ensure his election.

Hank knew as soon as he heard the question then the answer; Bush II was a winner in the eyes of the huge non-thinking, Christian voting-block. You know. Those who vote on the basis of what they believe, not what they think because that would require... well...thinking.

The moderator asked Bush Junior... as if he ever thought of this, or anything else... *"Who is your favorite philosopher?"*

The little Shrub... actually weed... answered, *"Jesus Christ!"*

That answer pretty accurately summed up Hank's thoughts on what he just witnessed.

Ladies and gentlemen, we have a winner!

Who in the hell could vote against that? Well, apparently a lot of people. He still would not have become President if not for certain members of the Supreme Court placed there by his father. But this is getting way ahead. So let's get back to Carter, Hank's mother, his ailment, and doctors.

His mother was also one of those who believed, rather than thought.

When she phoned him with her good news he asked her a few questions, going through several of Carter's expressed positions, asking her whether she agreed with each.

She answered in the negative to every one of them. So he asked her how she could be happy a guy she disagreed with on everything was going to be President.

She responded, as one might expect from a member of the non-thinking, *"Because he is a good Christian man."*

At this point Hank rested his case... possibly forever.

❦

The results of the misdiagnosis of his affliction as asthma by his mother's doctor, unlike the results the American people received as a result of their misdiagnosis of what they might be afflicted with by the two presidents, was actually good for him.

In addition to his misdiagnosis the doctor provided a prescription-like piece of paper for him to take to school informing the staff he was not to participate in strenuous physical exercise of the type required in Physical Education classes.

Thus, only a few days into his first year of high school he was excused from Phys Ed class for the rest of his high school days over the next three years.

This was good because it opened up a slot for him to take another solid subject enabling him to graduate with more credits than the number required. This was almost the equivalent of another year of solid subjects.

Thus, the misdiagnosis enabled him to receive a significantly broader high school education than he would have otherwise received, which was of great benefit to him later, in business, the military and in providing a broader base of knowledge for his further academic endeavors.

How does he know the doctor misdiagnosed him?

As soon as he departed the confines of Grand Prairie, he ceased having the spring and fall afflictions. For years, in California, the military and elsewhere, he engaged in strenuous physical activities, including running, without the problem that did not recur except when he returned to the Dallas/Fort Worth area.

Then, because of its recurring and he suddenly had serious headaches like he never experienced before he went to a doctor who diagnosed him with serious allergy problems.

This was confirmed, years later, when he was once again back in the area and having the same problem.

He went to an allergist whose tests determined he was allergic to three plants prevalent in that part of Texas. Further, he stated because of the severity of his allergic reaction to these plants, *"If I were you, and did not have to be here, in this part of the country, I would get out."*

Think about that. Two decades later. Just over twenty years after he reached his definitive decision to *"Get out,"* a doctor gave the same advice to him.

What difference could it have made in his life had that doctor been his doctor when he received the asthma misdiagnosis?

Maybe he would have provided a prescription that required him to leave home… and go somewhere else that would maybe have given him a better "leg up" on life?

Obviously neither he nor we know, but it is interesting to contemplate the universe of possibilities had Hank spent more of his formative years with someone less ignorant and more interested in helping him get ahead, rather than resenting him because of *"Sunshine."*

But speaking of his mother and considering her conduct, maybe he was a little too hard on the "quack" doctor she liked. After all he had been around awhile and was called whenever one of the family members was thought in need of his services. That provided him some fairly intimate knowledge of Hank's family.

He remembers at the time asthma was thought to be the result of psychological problems manifest in the nervous system as asthmatic symptoms. Thus stress was considered a "trigger" for asthma attacks, and *"God knows"* there was plenty of stress that maybe the doc took into account, resulting in his misdiagnosis.

Knowing Hank's mother, he may have concluded she was part of the problem.

It's possible. Some really good doctors include the psyche of their patients in their diagnosis. Maybe his doctor did this.

He did not know. But he did know one doctor who, under stress from his mother reached a decision that amounted to a prescription for himself, which he related... more like, announced... to Hank in a hallway of Methodist Hospital in Oak Cliff.

He was a doctor married to a high school classmate of Hank's, and he was his mother's doctor when Hank was in his early forties and his mother about seventy years old.

She had back problems diagnosed as requiring surgery. This doctor did the surgery, and a day later Hank encountered him in the hallway as he was leaving her hospital room.

He knew Hank, so he stopped and announced to him as he motioned toward her room, *"I never want to see that woman, again!"* He never did.

Hank and his wife were in town because his father was having triple bypass heart surgery. It was just happenstance his father and mother were in the same Methodist Hospital in Oak Cliff at the same time.

She was getting out the next day. He was still in fairly serious condition and not going to be released for several days.

His mother was living on the farm at Shirley at the time, and she did not have anyone there to take care of her so he and his wife decided it would be better for her if she stayed in their condo in Fort Worth that even though they had been living in Los Angeles for several years they kept because they were occasionally there on business.

It was a nice two bedroom two bath, condo in the best part of town with a pleasant courtyard and view, in a nice quiet neighborhood, and they stocked it with some of her favorite foods.

After her first night there he and his wife had to leave for a while the following day.

They told her they would be gone for the afternoon, but would be back before dark… within three or four hours. Should not have been a problem. It was a much, much better place than she was accustomed to, and had everything she could possibly need.

But he and his wife were stunned when they returned later in the afternoon… at least an hour before they told her they would. In the living room was his father.

Hank immediately asked him what he was doing out of the hospital two or three days before he was to be released after heart surgery. He did not get a chance to answer.

His mother started in on him about how she called his father to come get her because he and his wife were mistreating her, leaving her alone, etc., etc.

When he attempted to address the fact his father was seriously ill and should not be out of the hospital, ignoring that; she demanded he take her home, right then, driving over one hundred miles one way while seriously ill… just because she wanted to go home.

He learned later; she called his father immediately after they left. Told him they were mistreating her. She had to leave, did not have anyone else. He had to come get her. Never mind his condition.

He knew she was lying. They had been divorced for at least ten years. She took his farm through lies about him in their divorce. He decided to just walk away, rather than continue to deal with her. But she, for obvious reasons, really did not have anyone else who would put up with her. So whenever she called he was there.

She really did not… how can this be said tactfully?… give a damn about anyone except herself and "you know who," but she did not call him because she knew he would not come. So his father was the one in the so called "barrel" that day and many others until he died almost a decade and a half later.

That day he drove her to Shirley. A few days later he was back in the same hospital with pneumonia for a longer stay than after the heart surgery. During that time he almost died, but Hank's mother never came to visit.

—⊱⊰—

Back to the autumn of Hank's first year of high school.

When he began tenth grade, he was driving his recently purchased "new" Plymouth when only shortly after football season began he got into a bit of trouble with it.

Since it was 1955, he was only fifteen and the legal driving age with a learner's permit was sixteen. He had been driving almost five years, illegally, but was never stopped by the police.

After a football game one Friday night, he was driving south on Stadium Drive, away from the stadium. Just as he stopped at the stop sign at Stadium and Hill Street his friend Bill who was in a car that came around the corner from Hill Street and headed back down Stadium blew a bugle out the window of the car.

The next sound and feeling he remembers is a thud and the feeling of the impact.

Someone rammed into the back of his "new" Plymouth. Then suddenly there were flashing red and blue lights behind him. When he got out of the car he could tell what hit him in the rear was a police car. The cop turned on his lights after he hit him.

He asked for Hank's driver's license. It went downhill from there. He was pretty nasty about the whole thing, blamed it on Hank, and wasn't happy when he pointed out he was the one who hit him. He wrote tickets to Hank for driving without a license and negligent collision.

Then he became even more upset when Hank complained about the negligent collision ticket because it was impossible. He was sitting still when the police car hit him. How could he have collided with anything? The cop said he would see him in court. Hank said *"Absolutely!"* and away everyone went.

⊫⊰⊱⊨

The courtroom was a riot.

When his case was called the officer and he walked up in front of the judge sitting up on his "bench" behind a podium-like thing above Hank's head.

The officer was a lot taller, but he still had to look up at the judge. So, there they were… the three of them in front of a court room with a lot of people in it, some of whom were fellow classmates who came to see what might happen to Hank.

Of course the officer got to speak first. He blamed Hank for everything, said he caused the wreck by being there, should not have been driving, etc. Then the judge asked Hank his side.

He said, *"Well, I was stopped at the stop sign, like I was supposed to, sitting still, and this officer ran into the back of my car with his police car."*

It was possible to hear the beginning of chuckling in the room.

Then he said, *"After he hit me, he turned on his flashing lights."*

There were some low boos and hissing. The judge called for quiet, and Hank said, *"Then he got out of his car, blamed me for the accident and gave me two tickets; one for driving without a license and one for negligent collision."*

More, louder, booing and hissing.

The judge asked if that was all, and Hank responded, *"No, sir. The back of my car, I bought with money I made working last summer, is caved in."*

More, booing and hissing.

The judge then turned to the officer, found him guilty of negligent collision and fined him for that… louder cheering and applause. Then he also told him he was responsible for paying for having Hank's car repaired.

More, cheering and applause.

Next, it was Hank's turn again. The judge turned to him and, Hank swears, it was like he wanted to get in on the action.

He dismissed the negligent collision charges against Hank to the sound of a lot of cheering and applause. Then he said, *"But, Hank, I must find you guilty of driving without a driver's license because if you had not been sitting there at the stop sign, this officer could not have run into you. Now you go over to the courthouse and tell them to arrange the repair of your car to be paid for."*

The cheering, whistling and applause got louder. They were dismissed. Hank walked down the center aisle to the back of the court room rather jauntily while being applauded.

Meanwhile, the officer... he says, *"If he was just mad at the scene of the accident, the best way to describe his attitude after this is; he was really pissed off."*

While on the winning side Hank's attitude was *"Look at me. I met the law and I won."* It would be the same next time... years later. But he would be a little more subdued.

That aside, while we are, sort of, on the subject of cars, Hank's parents got another new one in 1955 for no apparent reason other than his father's new business was doing well, he had more income than he needed, and "investing" was never a consideration... unless it was in something that required maintenance, rusted, broke down, depreciated, burned fuel or consumed food, needed taking care of or died without ever contributing to income.

It was only three years since the purchase of the '52 Lincoln that was still perfectly good, so one could expect his father and mother... given its color she definitely had a hand in this one... would have experience purchasing expensive automobiles. But this purchase did not go so well.

They bought another Lincoln Cosmopolitan Sport Coupe. This one was a fleshy pinkish with a cream top. Not a lot of difference between it and the "52. It was just three years newer, a different color, and "new," or so they thought.

He had to give it a thorough check out, considering he was also going to be driving it even though it was a pink that would not have been his choice.

While he was giving it a detailed inspection, he noticed something peculiar: the little half-inch wide piece of vertical metal molding at the front of the right door opening was a different shade of pink than the other, similar molding pieces in the car.

He went inside and told his parents about it. But before anything else could be said about it, his mother took the lead, telling him he didn't know what he was talking about. It was a new car.

At that point, less than happy with the usual *"You don't know what you're talking about. You're just a kid!"* crap from his mother, he went back outside where he began to really check out the "new car."

Behind the spare tire, he found a set of architectural drawings for a house. They had the architect's name, address and phone number on them.

He took them into the house and gave them to his father before his mother could intervene again. He also said he thought the car was not new. It had probably been wrecked because the car company would not put a mismatched piece of molding on a new Lincoln that cost that much.

This time his father went outside with him to check out what he was attempting to convey to them. After looking at it with him, his father went back into the house and told his mother, *"Honey, I think Hank's right."*

After that there was a discussion about what to do, during which Hank chimed in with something about a lawyer and a free new car at which point his mother told him to be quiet and... you guessed it... *"You are just a kid."* Then something else about how little he could know about anything to which he responded, *"Call the guy."*

He doesn't remember which of them… but he can guess… listened to him. Anyway, one of them did and they decided to phone the architect whose name was on the plans.

His mother, of course, was the one who called the guy and told him what they decided. That was; they were looking at buying the Lincoln and the guys at City Lincoln Mercury said they should call him because he could tell them about the car.

He did. He said he owned the car a short time because he had an accident, it had to be repaired, and he did not have time to wait, so he got another one. After thanking the previous owner of their "new" Lincoln his mother went ballistic, saying she was going to call City Lincoln Mercury and give them a piece of her mind.

He counseled against that, mentioned the lawyer, again, as well as a free, new car. She shut him down again with more of the *"kid"* crap, and called them, anyway.

After she told them what bad guys they were, and agreed she and his father would go to Dallas to meet with them to determine what could be done, she hung up; very proud of herself for giving to them, regretfully, a piece of something she really did not have a sufficient amount of to be giving any of it away.

They went to City Lincoln Mercury met the crooks and, ignoring the counsel of the *'kid"* again, came back with a downgrade; a new Mercury.

Later, Hank asked his father what happened. He explained how she really had left some of what she should not have there, and how he ended up paying hundreds more than he should have for the Mercury because it was not possible to deal with his mother who was stupidly happy for days about how she really *"Let them have it."*

"Jesus!" he thought. At fifteen, he had more experience in business and dealing with the public than she had at forty-two, not to mention a fully functioning mind and common sense.

He is certain, to this day; if it was left to him to deal with, his family would have gotten a new Lincoln, and his father would still have had his money in his pocket, minus a few hundred for the attorney. Logic and common sense argue in favor of his opinion.

Something he learned years later was at work in this little horror play. That is people only know what they know, and the less they know, the less likely they are to listen to anyone who knows more than they do because their limited base of knowledge prohibits them from recognizing this fact.

Thus, they go through life leaving little acts of stupidity and a trail of little disasters, if not big ones, behind them... happy in their ignorance.

What most of us do is learn from experience. Build on our knowledge. Know more next time. Avoid making the same mistakes again. But those in possession of little knowledge, combined with a lack of common sense and a big, falsely inflated sense of self-worth usually have some sort of mental, computer-like pop up blocker that keeps anything from getting through to them.

Their mind is made up. They are too damned smart to learn anything. They already know all they need to know. But it seems like the "Spam" doesn't have a problem getting to their already "Spammed-up" minds. Maybe that is why they don't mind giving a piece of it away every time they have a chance.

Hank's mother continued giving pieces of hers away for far too long.

For most of us life is but a series of events. Thus, the sum total of life is an accumulation of all its events and the results of how the individual dealt with them.

That sounds simple enough. But it overlooks something very important about life and its events that are also contradictory to Mann's theory "The freedom of the individual to act, and to be responsible for his actions, is the primary source of whatever events and results thereof encompass him in the course of his life."

For several years, the formative years, we encounter events over which we individuals have little, if any control or ability to act on our own. Our parents or someone else has control over many of our actions until we reach an age of accountability...whatever that is, since there are confusing points of view and many opinions about it.

There are academics, "doctors," specialists, psychotherapists, child psychologists... a whole stream of these quacks... who have appeared on the scene in recent years to answer all the imponderable questions parents, teachers, nor anyone else had until these charlatans filled their perceived void in the marketplace for their unneeded services, including approval of drugging American school children into submission with controlled substances like Ritalin.

They throw about opinions about children like the mind is not fully developed until twenty-two years of age and twelve year olds cannot be held responsible for their actions without considering differences in individuals; frequently tossing this bullshit out to the vast TV audience that is "dumbed down" to accept anything presented by an authority figure, as they have been indoctrinated, and either parents believe this crap or they are unwilling to accept responsibility for anything, including their own children.

As a result of this, children, normal children who are more active than the rest of the herd, and would have been considered normal before these "experts" were brought into their lives are being drugged in public schools for any perceived notion of these charlatans.

Because of this, it is becoming impossible to determine what a normal child is, or what his age of accountability is. It is like a science fiction film in which all children must be the same little sheep, or be drugged into submission to the all-powerful state. That's probably the reality.

They are never accountable. Everything we see today indicates very few are willing to accept responsibility... accountability... for their actions, and no one is willing to assign responsibility for anything. Therefore, we have reached the age of no age of accountability.

But before these whores to the state of submissiveness appeared on the scene, children were children. They were under the control of parents and other family members, and, to some extent, teachers who were closer to families of their students than to the government, as they are today.

The adults who grew out of the children who were the products of their immediate families and the culture in which they were immersed really were the unfettered products of their environment... for better or worse.

Hank's Mother was definitely the product of her environment. She was out of school by the age of twelve, probably rarely attended prior to that. Thus, the environment she was a product of was primarily her family, and being the baby of eleven children, she was most definitely spoiled. Her siblings confirmed that in comments more than once in front of Hank while he was growing up.

There are many spoiled children. But one difference between most of them and his mother is they probably interface with many people outside their immediate family during their formative years. Thus, there is a compensating factor for whatever kind of attention and reinforcement they receive from family members.

Their world of experience is broader, probably exponentially, considering the number of students and teachers they would normally come into contact with over the course of a half dozen years.

His mother, on the other hand, living on a farm during her formative years and not attending school, had an experientially deprived youth wherein she rarely interfaced with anyone outside a doting family constantly complimenting her on her beauty and talent.

She was not exposed to objective commentary from outside the family. Thus, most likely, in addition to compliments from family members about her beauty and talent, she received reinforcement of her negative characteristics, or her negative characteristics were a result of a continuous stream of complimentary commentary.

Either way, she was experientially deprived when it was not healthy for her psyche. As a result, she never felt... dislike that term, "felt"... a need for, nor was she challenged in any way that would have resulted in the introspective reaction of most when confronted about what they have, or have not, done or said: Why did I do, or say that?

Also, being deprived of formal education... whether self-induced or not is irrelevant... she was knowledge deprived, i.e., ignorant about so many things. Thus, we have a product... a human being... whose best attributes of beauty and talent were reinforced and whose worst characteristics of ignorance and lack of exposure were also reinforced by silence about them.

So why would she listen to a fifteen year old... or anyone else? She was convinced she was too damned smart to learn anything from anyone.

She also demonstrated a little mean streak that, from what Hank heard from family members, could have been inherited from her father. But whatever its source, combined with other unfavorable characteristics that manifest themselves in conduct dysfunctional to familial harmony, it did not create the perfect home environment for his youth.

His mother's dysfunctional personality and conduct affected more than the home environment. As evidenced by his brother, it had tremendous impact on her offspring, Hank included because he was under her control and influence during his formative years.

The cause of his and his brother being as they are and acting the way they do is, to a great extent, a result of the way she treated each of them, as well as their individual inborn traits, which influenced the different ways she treated each of them.

She recognized his brother inherited more traits from her, and Hank more from his father. Thus, given her disdain for demonstrably strong personality members of the opposite sex, which was imbued in her by her mother, she bestowed her favors on his brother while demonstrating in every way possible her dislike of his inherent traits.

Since his brother was more like she, he liked being spoiled and spent most his formative years catering... actually "sucking up"... to her, and encouraging her to create him in her own image, although, obviously, he could not have foreseen the negative and dysfunctional impact this would have on him and his life.

Fortunately for Hank, in most ways, her less than loving motherly treatment of him after the age of six was, in his opinion, positive for him because it caused him to be stronger, more self-sufficient, more resilient and thus more capable of dealing with the world and others in it. But there were, even early in his life, some negative impacts on him that affected how he views the world and others, and thus the way he conducts himself that negatively impact his life, as they have that of his brother.

Unlike his brother, because of his treatment by her, she elicited negative responses from him. She caused him to view her, as she demonstrated she viewed him; with disdain... even subconsciously, her physicality.

Of course, like his brother, Hank was unable to discern this at the time, but even during his early years this was evident. The image of her as she was mistreating and even on occasion abusing him was indelibly imprinted in his subconscious.

She had a thirty-six triple D bust line and much less… to the average normal male… attractive derriere and legs. The extent to which he is cognizant of her physical appearance, coupled with his feelings toward her due to her treatment of him, he thinks, affected his likes and dislikes in the female form.

Although he is more concerned with the person than the form, he is much less impressed with large breasts than the average male. To put it bluntly, as it is normally stated; he is a *"legs and ass"* man, more appreciative of a female form that demonstrates something about the person.

Any female can have large breasts… whether God-given or by surgeon. Ditto, to some extent, the derriere, but the combination of it and legs in well-defined condition requires some amount of effort by their possessor. Anyway, whatever its source, this orientation on his part would result in a very negative impact on Hank's life not too many years distant.

⊷⊹⊶

1956. In addition to the traffic "accident" and court room drama, Hank did have one other somewhat exceptional, little related experience his sophomore year.

In January 1956 after he turned sixteen he did what most other sixteen year olds did.

When it was announced Driver's Ed classes would be available on a certain date, he decided to go because that was the traditional way to get a learner's driving permit. However, that did not work out as well as his courtroom appearance.

When he walked into the class, the coach who was the designated "teacher" for the course said, *"What are you doing here?"* When he replied *"I am here to take the Driver's Ed class"* the coach responded, *"Get out of here! You've been driving for years."*

There was some laughter from others there to take the course. But his protest was for naught. The coach said he was not going to waste any time on him. So, he left. Went to his Plymouth in the school parking lot, and drove away. Later, his father took him to get his learner's permit. He has been driving legally ever since.

The balance of his sophomore year was, as he recalls, relatively uneventful.

School continued normally. He still didn't study much, continued to draw cars and airplanes during class. The "defense" plant continued to flourish, resulting in his father's business continuing to grow. In fact, the second half of the school year, early spring, he took a fairly large leap forward in his business.

He made a sizeable investment, relative to available funds and income, in a new piece of equipment. He bought a tractor with a new to the industry piece of equipment attached to it that would soon revolutionize the small excavation business. He was sure he could make a lot of money with a hydraulic backhoe.

As usual, he was correct. The "defense" plant kept expanding, adding new production to supply the growing weapons industry of the U.S. in which it became the world's largest supplier of weapons to every dictator on the planet, if it had not already achieved that enviable position by that time, which was probably the case.

In fact Hank recently heard... almost sixty years later... seventy-five percent of all arms sales worldwide are by the United States. How's that for a war based economy?

Anyway, what was not necessarily good for the rest of the world was good for Grand Prairie and all the rest of the towns and cities reliant to any extend upon the success of the industry and to those directly benefiting from the "business" that generated.

Hank's family was not an exception. The backhoe and most of the other equipment and trucks his father bought were busy every day of every week, almost from the first day, for years to come. The backhoe even generated additional business for a truck or two. Thus its purchase was a very good call.

CHAPTER 16

CHARACTER BUILDING

After the tenth grade, Hank benefited directly from the business at the "defense" plant when the first Monday after school was out he was awakened at 7:00 AM by a tugging on his right foot.

It was his father standing at the foot of the bed with his hand around his ankle saying, *"C'mon. Get up. Put on your work clothes."* He questioned, *"Why? I don't have a job."* To which his father responded, *"You do now. C'mon."*

He got up. Dressed and tagged along as his father took him to the "defense" plant, which was then Ling TEMCO Vought, or as it was called; *"LTV."*

Since the late forties, the old North American Aviation was taken over, renamed, combined and expanded. But it was still in the expanding business of building airplanes for the military.

Hank questioned why he couldn't do what he did the previous summer, making a lot of money and having a good time. His father, having a good construction business going and some contacts in the business decided he should get his feet wet in the new family business, as he had when in the retail business.

Since he was living in his father's house, he made the rules. So, there he was about to get some more experience.

After they cleared security his father took him to a construction site where people were engaged in building something. There, he introduced him to the foreman and left.

Fortunately, he provided some necessary information to Hank before they got there. He told him he lied about his age to get the job for him. It was necessary to be eighteen to work inside the plant and belong to the laborer's union.

The foreman took a few minutes with him to fill out the necessary forms to put him on the payroll and the union rolls. He had already been told Hank was eighteen. Thus, technically, he did not lie. His father did. All he did was answer the foreman's questions, he filled out the forms, then took Hank to another place in the plant, got out of the pickup, handed a shovel and a sledge hammer to him, drew a square of about three feet on the concrete with a blue marker, told him to break the concrete out of that square and left.

It was eight inch thick, steel reinforced concrete. So when he came back two hours later Hank had broken some of the surface off, but not much. He told him to keep at it and left again.

A little later he came back. This time he had a black guy in the truck, a jackhammer in the back, and he was towing an air compressor.

Hank was "set up." It was obvious. The foreman and his father conspired to have a little fun at his expense. But he passed the test of whether he would work his butt off at manual labor, for the first time in his life, to accomplish nothing just because he was told to do so, which he didn't know at the time, but it was great training for something similar he would encounter a few years later that was also not at his initiative: the Army.

They got back into the pickup. The foreman drove to the south side of the plant to an area that was not developed but some concrete walls had been poured that would eventually become some kind of buildings. Also there were about a dozen black men digging with picks and shovels.

They were all ages… from about twenty to over sixty.

The foreman introduced him around then left him to begin digging with the rest of the men. He spent the rest of the summer with a shovel digging ditches with those guys.

It was a unique experience, not unlike we have seen in movies. They actually sang to keep a rhythm going, and to pass the time. They worked and sang, and talked.

One of the youngest asked Hank one day what he was doing out there digging with them. Hank asked him what he meant. He said something about he didn't understand why he was there when he could be in an office with all the other white people.

Hank told him most of his classmates were working downtown in shoe stores and other places in air conditioned comfort making ninety cents an hour. Then asked him what they were making.

The questioner began to smile as he told Hank what he already knew. So Hank asked him which he would rather do, make less because it was easier, or have more money to spend.

Laughing, he replied with something like, *"Yeah, man. I understand. I agree wit you."*

He spent the rest of his summer of 1956 working with a bunch of black guys, digging, talking and eating lunch out of a paper bag while sitting on the side of a ditch in the one hundred degree, plus, Texas heat and hot sun, earning $1.62 and ½ cents per hour.

By the end of the summer he was in such great shape a couple of classmates commented on his arms and asked how he got them so built up over the summer. Then they acted like they didn't believe him when he told them.

It was a good summer financially, physically and experientially. His wallet was fuller. His body was also… in the right way, if only for a short time, and the experience was one he will never forget. It was humbling.

He also had another first experience that summer he has not forgotten that was partially a result of his developing physique.

━┽┼┾━

He only worked the usual five days a week, having most weekends off for himself to do whatever he wanted... no yard mowing or other chores, and also, since he was being such a good boy doing all that hard manual labor during the week, he occasionally got to drive around in the not so old, spiffy Mercury.

One weekend afternoon, as he was driving by the home of a young lady schoolmate who lived in the same quadrant of town as he and who was also fairly spiffy herself... actually a hot little Italian heritage looking young lady a year younger than Hank... she and her boyfriend, a classmate of his, were on her front porch, she wearing short shorts with the same little tie bows on the sides of the legs as Nelms' girlfriend wore the previous summer. So he stopped for a little friendly visit.

The lawnmower was in the front yard. After a couple of greeting-like comments she informed him she was trying to get her boyfriend to mow the yard for her, but he was not being cooperative, so she suggested Hank might want to do her the favor.

He responded with something like *"Possibly. It depends on what is in it for me"* leaving that open for her response.

At that, probably for fear Hank might actually be so stupid as to volunteer to mow the yard to get in her good graces or receive some sort of reward, her boyfriend reluctantly said *"O.K.,"* went to the mower and began mowing.

Then she said since he was mowing there was *"no point in us sitting here watching,"* and asked Hank to take her for a ride in his spiffy car; another time a nice car paid off.

Of course he obliged her. They got off the porch and headed for the Mercury. As they walked past her not so bright boyfriend, she told him she would *"be back in a few minutes,"* got into the car with Hank and rode away, leaving him mowing with a push mower in the hot summer sun.

It did not take long to determine a ride was not all she was interested in when she suggested they go park in a nice cool place under a big shade tree Hank was familiar with because it was a place south of the junior high where his art teacher used to take his class out for nature sketching.

He was unaware he was about to have another nature experience, a new one in the cool shade of the tree, until they started doing a little of what came naturally. She took it to the next level when she untied the little bow on the left leg of her shorts, took his left hand and pulled it into the now loose leg and over her leg to you know where.

Although it was another new experience for him, he was not at a loss as to what to do. He further obliged her, thinking that with the satisfaction she was demonstrably getting from her part of the experience, he was surely about to reach an even higher level of new experiences until when he made that suggestion she suddenly changed her mood, removed his hand and said, *"We better get back."*

He reluctantly obeyed and drove back to her then finished mowing and visibly upset boyfriend because it had been a tad longer than *"a few minutes"* since they left.

He did not get out of the car. He just let her out, waved good bye to the boyfriend and drove away... not upset.

The boyfriend never spoke to him again. Even when they were at their thirtieth high school reunion over thirty-two years later, the only exchange between them was the dirty, unfriendly look he gave Hank who thought he should have told him not to blame him, *"It was the car."* But he thought it best not to do or say anything that could spoil that pleasant memory for him.

The last work week of the summer when Hank left to go back to school he felt bad because he knew the men he worked with all summer would continue to be out there in the heat, or cold, digging, lifting and laboring away... most for the rest of their lives, which for some of them would not be that long. Yet, he knew he would not face a similar future.

The scene really was one of "despair and disillusionment" with lives lacking "fulfillment and meaning." It was a depressing realization he will never forget.

It bothered him that two of the men were at least sixty years old and had never done anything to earn a living except physical labor, and that was all the younger ones had to look forward to.

Obvious to him from working with them all summer was the fact their futures were not so much a matter of intelligence or personality, since most of them seemed reasonably intelligent and were nice and companionable. It was simply a matter of circumstance.

They did not choose by whom, when and where they were brought into this world, so to Hank it was another vivid example that "the freedom of the individual to act, and to be responsible for his actions, is the primary source of whatever events and results thereof encompass him in the course of his life" is manifestly untrue... nay hogwash!

He got along with them well because, thanks to his father, unlike most of the kids he knew, he had been working in public, meeting and talking with all kinds of people since he was six. But he had several classmates he knew would not have succeeded... if that is the correct word... at what he did, that summer.

That they would not was not because of who they were, but because of who they thought they were, and he couldn't stand the arrogant bastards himself. So he could imagine how it would have worked out had they been in his place for the summer: It would not have been for the summer. Probably one day, if that long.

He, unlike they, was somewhat prepared for his unplanned interface that summer because in the summers of 1950 to 1952, when he was managing the store next to the old Interurban building he spent some time with an old black man. Also, later, in '54 he had the opportunity to talk with a black female, who was about his age, several times.

⸺⋅⊹⋅⸺

"Blossom" was over sixty, either the son or grandson of ex slaves. Every day, weather permitting, he walked over two miles, one way, from where he lived in the black community west of the disused WWII Air National Guard base on the west side of town to the store where he bought a quart of beer, took it outside to the west side of the building and sat there... taking his time... drinking his quart of beer.

He did this because he was not allowed in the beer "garden" at the rear of the store, and he came to Hank's store for his beer because he had credit there.

His father set up credit accounts for many customers, "Blossom" and others.

There was also "Sarge," a WWII Vet with some psychological problems who, like "Blossom," wore an olive drab Army jacket with NCO stripes on the sleeves and came almost every day to drink beer.

There was an insurance agent who was a future mayor of Grand Prairie. There were many who were good, honest people in need of a little interim help, and who paid their bills religiously... if that is an appropriate comparison.

When "Blossom" came, Hank occasionally went outside and talked with him for a while. He doesn't remember anything they talked about. Just remembers talking with him, and he was different. That gave Hank some ability and basis to converse with his summer workmates.

The girl who worked for his mother sometimes on Saturdays helping clean house lived where "Blossom" did, between three and four miles from his home. So, she had to be picked up and returned home.

He was the one who did that, and alone in the car with her for as much as a half hour on those days, they talked. Nice girl; just shared the same misfortune of whom, when and where, as his summer workmates.

He actually wished some of his classmates had similar bad luck... especially the ones who saw him with the black teenage girl in the car and made wisecracks about his new *"girlfriend"* and some really unnecessary remarks he can honestly say caused him to think he would have preferred spending time with his summer workmates and his new *"girlfriend"* than these worthless, arrogant ones.

CHAPTER 17

BROADENED EDUCATION

Shortly after school began junior year, Hank's Plymouth quit. He guessed last year was too hard on it. Whatever... he was without transportation. That left him dependent on his mother to take him across town to school, or frequently permit him to drive the Mercury because her demons still were keeping her awake too late for her to be able to get up early enough.

It was just fine with him when that was the case. As previously stated; the Mercury was pretty spiffy, as his little Italian friend proved that summer. It was a black Montclair... the model with the sleek, low roof line. It had a yellow strip under the windows, a matching yellow and black interior, a Continental spare tire kit and dual exhausts. It was actually better looking than the Lincoln... it was sporty.

Also, some days he got to ride to school with Pat, a smart, popular, senior girl who lived a block behind his house.

One morning, as he was going to get into the car with her, his mother came out of the house to caution him about something. As she frequently did, she spoke at him, not to him, in her acerbic tone with her *"Hank Henry!"*

Pat, immediately upon hearing this, said *"Hank Henry"* in a very sweet sounding little modulation, *"I like that."* So did he.

For the rest of the school year, every time attractive, sweet Pat saw him in school hallways, she would greet him with that sweet, melodic *"Hello, Hank Henry."* It was a pleasant experience he could look forward to. He really grew to like the new "handle."

Also, Rita was back for the eleventh grade. So he had one good-looking young lady calling him *"Boy!"* and another calling him *"Hank Henry."* Either one was O.K. with him.

He was like the old TV comedian of the time who said *"Youse can call me Jackson. Youse can call me* [some non-memorable other names], *I don't care what youse calls me, as long as youse calls me."* That conveys his attitude about it, but he really did like *"Hank Henry."*

But other than the exceptional attention of the two ladies, eleventh grade was much like the previous year. He still didn't study much, continued drawing in class. Added some reading not on the curriculum he managed to read in some classes, and added some more breadth to his studies… some of it practical.

He began taking mechanical drawing and architectural drafting in which he designed a house and produced a complete set of architectural drawings.

Toward the end of the class, the teacher in this course, Mr. Lowery, suggested he should continue studying architecture and plan a career in that because he seemed to have a talent for it.

He agreed. He still liked art, but design of buildings was more interesting than what he was exposed to in Art Class.

He also took typing. Seemed like something that could be useful. He did not plan on being a secretary, but thought being able to type his own correspondence might come in handy.

Apparently he was one of few boys who thought that way. It was populated almost like his ballet classes years before. There weren't many boys in the class. The classes were larger, but the boy, girl ratio was about the same as those dance classes.

He guessed most of his male classmates thought they would have secretaries. But he also thought that *"Not likely"*… unless the trucks he could envisage them driving had desks.

He decided to take Latin over Spanish. He couldn't see any need to know Spanish. But Latin, being the foundation of our language, seemed to him something that could yield dividends later.

He had a little problem in Latin, though. Maybe two problems; he should have studied more, and he could not get along with the teacher, which was one time he was in the majority.

Any poll done at the time would have yielded the same results as the unofficial poll; she was the most disliked teacher in the school.

⟞⟝

1957. That aside, she refused to even give a grade to him until he translated Caesar's Gallic Wars. Therefore, during the last two weeks of school he was busy "studying," writing this translation requested by her, but he did not finish until a couple of weeks into summer, which during he thought he should have spent more time in class paying attention, rather than practicing his drawing by creating on paper in pencil the many slow and painful ways his mind could conjure her meeting her demise.

He faired only somewhat better in math. In Junior High, there was mandatory Algebra I. In the tenth grade he added Algebra II and after that Plane Geometry, Solid Geometry and Trigonometry.

Although he knew, given his study habits, he would probably only squeak by, he thought these would be useful in architecture and engineering.

That was accidentally prescient… if that is possible… because that year, his father began bidding some jobs on a "Turn Key" basis… meaning the amounts of earth needed to be cut out and removed, or cut from one place and moved to another, the amount to be trucked in, the amount of gravel, road base and other materials needed had to be calculated and some quantities expanded based upon the required compaction factor. Then all the prices based upon the determined measurements and unit prices for each had to be extended to determine how much to bid on the job to make a profit, all of which his father did not like doing.

Thus the added math was handy when his father asked him to begin doing this "take-off" work on the plans he was given to determine all these quantities. And, it was critical he do a good job because if the bid was wrong, his father... and the family... would have to "eat" the resulting loss, which was not appealing to him because he had already gone through that mini depression-like period of tough times in 1953 after the Christians took away his family's income. For that short time he learned what eating less was like, and he did not like it.

Also he was really happy to do this because he preferred the real world over games and academics. Thus this was more enjoyable and rewarding than studying. It was like he... at seventeen, in the eleventh grade... had already graduated to the level he heard addressed in the terms *"Those who can do and those who can't teach."*

Even before that time he had already decided he was a doer... not an academic.

So in many cases the *"Kid"* who according to one parent was not worth listening to about simple matters was being depended upon to determine whether the family would make money or lose on some fairly significant amounts at risk.

He derived a little sadistic pleasure thinking how much that must "frost" his mother, especially since she knew it was something *"Sunshine"* would most likely never be able to do.

This difference in the attitude of one parent versus the other toward him, his intellect and the trust placed in it was a vast, conceptual abyss. One example of which was a job in town where some doctors he knew wanted to fill-in a large gully to increase the size of their parking lot to accommodate the expansion of their practice and their building.

He did the take-off from the plans for all the quantities. His father provided the unit prices, and he then calculated the bid to be presented.

Saturday morning they went to the doctors' office. His father went into the office to present the bid. After a while, he came back out, walked up to the pickup and said, *"Son, are you absolutely certain about the bid?"*

He asked him why he asked that. His father told him the doctors had three bids and his seemed too low compared to the other two. So the doctors, being honest guys, said they didn't want to give the job to him, and have him be unable to finish it because he was losing money. Nor did they want to have the trouble of finding someone else to finish the work, which was really their concern.

He assured him he was sure the bid was correct. His father said, *"O.K.,"* went back inside, got the job and made good money on it. He trusted him, whereas his mother would have hired a professional, something, or maybe two, rather than trust him.

He continued to do this work for his father and expand his ability in this area that would pay off later in California, in the military, and in business after the military.

The combination of academic training and real world experience at the same time at that age was invaluable. It provided a breadth of knowledge and experience, and appreciation for the combination most never gain. He would have this reinforced by others later.

He proved the combination of his father's math lessons, the math he studied in school and architectural training was a better foundation for much of this work than what engineering students were being taught in college. Also, it put money in his pocket when general contractors gave jobs to him because he could do this.

They said they had to do it for other earth moving contractors they dealt with… who he thought were probably like the other two who bid on the doctor's parking lot… and they preferred not to do that.

He did have another memorably bad experience with his mother in the eleventh grade that was partially his fault because by that time and age, he frequently just reached the point where he could not sit quietly and take all her demeaning crap.

One morning when he was unlucky enough to have her drive him to school, she had been on his case all morning about something. She would not shut up. He had enough. He quietly and calmly said, *"You know that old song; 'I Want a Girl Just Like the Girl That Married Dear Old Dad'? Well, I don't."*

Good thing he saw it coming. If not, she could have broken his nose, or, at the least split his lip. She took her right hand off the steering wheel and with one swinging motion, as hard as she could, backhanded him across his face with her knuckles.

That was the last time he remembers taking any abuse from her. There were a few times after that, before he left home, when she tried to hit him. But those times he just grabbed her wrists, as he learned from seeing his father protect himself from her unexpected, out of nowhere attacks.

Then, of course, she would tell his father how he bruised her wrists. Fortunately, he understood and empathized with Hank because he knew they both had to do the same to protect themselves when she physically attacked them.

She got worse as she aged. There was no helping her.

Hank managed to get her to a psychiatrist twice in later years, and even in front of a judge to try to help her when some of her neighbors complained and threatened to try to have her committed, but it was to no avail.

Somehow, he has never understood, unless all these people are the quacks he always thought them to be, their conclusions were there was nothing wrong with her.

Either she was truly brilliant enough to fool them, or their licenses should have been taken from them. Hank's opinion is it was the latter.

⊶ ⊷

He and Rita continued to date, went to the Uptown, the scene of their first chaperoned date four years before.

She, for some reason was protective. He doesn't know why, but he remembers one time when he had words with one of his male classmates, which was not an uncommon occurrence. She did not like it, really got on the guy's case, called him a jerk and something worse.

He had been having problems with some of his male classmates since he began driving the Mercury to school early in the school year shortly after his Plymouth quit. In fact, it was not long after he just spent the summer digging ditches for three months that it was a few words and more with a couple of his classmates one afternoon at another classmate's house when, as he was about to leave, the two ex-friend classmates also came outside and started hassling him.

It was apparently a manifestation of envy about the Mercury because that's how they started it.

One of the classmates who lived around the corner from him and was he thought, a "friend" since they were in the fourth grade, until another occurrence with him at the beginning of sophomore year about twelve months before, waited until Hank got in and started the Mercury. Then he calmly walked to the front of the car and popped the hood.

Hank got out of the car, went to the front, closed the hood, and quietly asked him to please not do it again, explaining he had to leave. Then he got back into the car just in time to see, in the rear view mirror, the other classmate, the football coach's son, pull the handle that loosened the continental kit where the tire could be removed when needed.

It was not possible to drive the car with the continental kit tire unsecured, so he went to the rear of the car pushed the covered tire back into the locked position so he could depart and also quietly asked the coach's son to please not do that again. Then again he got into the car to leave.

At that time the ex-friend who was previously a friend since pre puberty unlatched the hood again, and again Hank went to the front of the car, closed the hood and told him in pretty firm and not so quiet terms he *"better not do that again!"* Then he again got back into the car preparing to leave when, as he looked in the rearview mirror, he saw the coach's son do the same as before to the continental kit.

At this point Hank, shaking from madness… a state he can remember being in no more than three times in his life… turned off the car's ignition, got out, gently closed the door, and began walking to the rear of the car.

As he rounded the rear of the car, coach's son, standing on the opposite side, smugly said, as he motioned downward toward the continental kit, *"There! What're you gonna do about it!"*

During this Hank covered the distance of the two steps between them and let the coach's privileged prick son have an answer to his question.

After the word *"it!"* seemingly without a pause between the words, *"You broke my nose!"* spewed forth from the same pie hole as his other words concurrently with the blood gushing forth from his other, referenced orifice.

Hank who had not done so before terminating the conversation reached down, secured the continental kit and quietly got back into the car to depart the scene, which he did without any further meddling with the hood of the car by his oldest ex-friend.

As he was driving home, recalling what the same two did the year before at the beginning of sophomore year that put them into the ex-friend category was something that required conniving between the two of them and one male senior class member that no one could do to a friend, he wondered *"What the hell is wrong with these guys? What have I ever done to them?"*

Apparently for years, some of the redneck seniors... mostly the ones Hank could envisage driving trucks after graduation... thought it their right to catch incoming sophomore boys, especially the ones with more hair on their heads, away from school property and "initiate" them by physically holding them while using scissors to chop off as much of their hair as possible, leaving hair butchered and gapped and occasionally some blood on the scalp.

He had not been caught and still had his nice full head of hair because he avoided going out anyway except in his own car so he could get away if the initiators tried to initiate him. But unknown to him these two had already suffered the shearing when they phoned him at the beginning of their sophomore year and asked if he would like to go to the Dairy Queen, which was a normal occurrence.

As soon as he got into the back seat of coach son's old Kaiser that night he knew, but they were moving and he could not get out.

When they drove into the Dairy Queen's gravel parking lot, three seniors headed directly toward the car, scissors in hand.

He immediately got out and headed for the car lot that separated the Dairy Queen from the A&W Root Beer competition, ran across the hoods of the front row of used cars in the lot and, still running, jumped off at the other side onto the also gravel A&W parking lot just as the three seniors who were running in front of the cars along with him caught up with him.

Unable to stop short on the gravel the three seniors plowed into him literally pinning him sideways… as he tried to turn to avoid it… against the left front fender just above the wheel well of the new car of an A&W customer who was sitting quietly enjoying root beer floats with his family in their new car.

The side of Hank's hip seriously caved in the thin metal of the fender above the tire, the car owner got out, looked at the damage and lit into the three he could tell were responsible for the damage because one of them was still prominently holding the scissors. Meanwhile Hank went into the A&W and watched the commotion through the window.

The police were called. The parents of the seniors responsible for this "negligent collision" had to pay for the damage to the customer's car. He was never initiated. His two classmates were immediately relegated to "ex-friend" status and he did not have any further dealings with them until they decided to play with his Mercury that afternoon. Also, he does not recall hearing about any further initiations after that night.

⟞⟝

He got up at 5:00 A.M. Easter Sunday 1957 to take Rita on his first Easter date, dressed in suit and tie… she in dressy dress, hat, gloves, the works, as was the custom then even though it was a sunrise service Rita saw advertised in the local paper. But unlike his later important Easter date in 1963, they never got there. They could not find it. So rather than going back home they just enjoyed some time together since she would be leaving again in less than two months.

He doesn't remember exactly when he first thought of departing Grand Prairie, but he is certain by this time in the eleventh grade that idea was firmly implanted in his mind because he remembers sitting and talking with Rita about it then, and also his friend Neil when they were discussing what they were going to do when they graduated from high school.

Having already developed his interest in architecture, he began seriously looking at books and magazines, and determined Brazil was worlds ahead of the U.S. in the field. So he was considering the possibility of going there to study and practice.

The remaining couple of months of school were uneventful after that morning. Then the summer of '57 was a replay of the previous summer in which his father ensured he had a job the Monday after school was out, though this time he didn't do much digging.

He was a plumber's helper, melting lead and carrying it to the plumbers who were making the connections between the pieces of pipe by pouring the melted lead into the bell end of one pipe to secure it to the next piece in the line. It was still hot, physical work.

Again, he made some money and gained more experience that provided knowledge about jobs he did not desire. But he enjoyed having the additional knowledge about the workings of things... unseen things... that are a part of our everyday lives.

⤙⟊ ⟊⤚

Twelfth grade was a continuation of the previous two years. Not much different. Not much studying. He continued drawing and reading books that were not part of the curriculum during classes. One he read... started and finished it in English class... was "Peyton Place," a good, controversial piece about people and life.

Good thing he occasionally made A's in English. Ms. Hulsey, the one who questioned him in the seventh grade about involvement in his father's business, was his twelfth grade English teacher, and she liked to stroll around the classroom.

He sat in the back of the class, his favorite place. One day she caught him reading Peyton Place, reached down turned to the front of the book where she could see what it was, didn't say anything, and continued on her way toward the front of the class.

He is certain he received a very good education in the Grand Prairie Public School System, for which he has always been very grateful to the teachers and those behind it.

Between those people and his father, he was provided a much better foundation for life than most have been provided, certainly much better than American students have received since the institution of the Federal Government Department of Education by President Carter.

⟞⊹ ⊹⟝

1958. Beyond academic education, Hank learned some important facts about life during his last school days. One lesson was how important politics are... everywhere... that politics, not reality, even determine who is the most beautiful or most handsome.

Judy was the most beautiful girl in school since the first time he saw her when she was twelve. He is sure she was the most beautiful from day one, and she is still one of the most beautiful women he has seen to this date. But she was not the choice for the title of "Most Beautiful" in senior year. Another young lady who was reasonably attractive, but not beautiful was honored with the title.

Ditto for "Most Handsome." The one upon whom this distinction was bestowed was far from handsome... by any measure. There were many upon whom this title could have been bestowed without any obvious bias being on display.

It was politics, pure and simple, nothing else, in both cases.

The girl inappropriately named "Most Beautiful" was the daughter of a previous mayor of the town who was dating the son of another previous mayor of the town, and would, not too long after graduation, become her husband.

The "Most Handsome" was a star football player who was on the All-America high school team for two years. But there was another who was also on that team for two years who was definitely much more handsome.

The "Most handsome" was bestowed for reasons in addition to football.

Hank didn't begrudge the "Most Handsome" for his title. He did not choose to be "Most Handsome." And he contributed much to the school. Doubtful the other All American Team member would have achieved that distinction without him. Also, since it was probably the first time ninety-nine percent of America ever heard of Grand Prairie they should have made him Honorary Mayor of the city, but "Most Handsome"? No.

The title even received some chuckles, which Hank didn't think was good, especially for the "Most Handsome" one. He was really a nice guy. Continued to be that way the few times Hank has seen him since they graduated.

It is his opinion he was given the title because he was not from a family of means and the deciders wanted to do something for him. Hank did not think they did.

He did not contribute anything to the school. He just went to school to get an education. He was not there to be the most popular or class president, or for recognition.

He never thought about it. He had other things to do, was happy being involved in his father's businesses and getting absorbed in drawing and other means of self-satisfaction. He did not have a need to be admired or recognized for anything.

He also did not try to "fit in." He was just who he was, never a joiner, nor tried to be accepted as a member of anything. He did not buy into any party or group… and still doesn't… being willing to separate the good from the bad without having to consider who they are, what they are, or what group or party they belong to.

Just like today, when he is unwilling to abide by, or support any party line because that is what is expected of a member; when in school, he had friends among the popular group and friends of the "greaser" variety members of the popular group would not even recognize existed.

It was obvious many were not there just to get the best education. They traded off some education for fame and admiration. Possibly more importantly: many parents pushed their children to be recognized so they could participate vicariously in their recognition.

The fact they should have been encouraging them to obtain more education than recognition is evident in their lives after school.

It is a shame. So many people peak at their High School graduation.

When Hank looks back through his high school Year Books, maybe twenty percent of the stars have carried their high school glory beyond their eighteenth birthday.

Few who were in different clubs, played football, baseball, basketball and were on the track and field team did anything of significance after they graduated, including excel financially.

Seems to him that, rather than competing in every sport possible, belonging to every club and running for every office... all of which are very time consuming... an old rule would have resulted in a better future for them: *"Moderation in all things."*

But Grand Prairie and Hank's school experiences there were probably just a microcosm of what the U.S. is like... probably always has been. Politics rule in most aspects of life.

⇥⇤

He did not peak at his graduation. But he almost did.

Too bad Rita was not there to look after him. Had she been, his life might have been very different. He might have followed his plan to be an architect. He showed promise. His grades reflected that, as did his work.

He even began the study of architecture at Arlington State College that was one of only two schools in the state that offered it.

It was only fifteen minutes away and his father gave one of his old vehicles… a rusted 1951 Ford pickup with a broken right front spring that made it list in that direction… to him to drive to school. He also had the bedroom over the garage to himself, away from the rest of the house, where he could get more sleep and study relatively undisturbed.

The other place offering architecture was the University of Texas in Austin that would have been more expensive and unnecessary, since he had zero interest in the reasons others chose to go there.

He was only interested in learning, and carried a heavy academic load that would have either precluded his participation in the other activities, or reduced the learning experience due to less academic concentration.

At the time he was unaware of other distractions in Grand Prairie that would accomplish that undesirable result and permanently derail his architecture career plans. So by being thrifty and more focused, rather than the typical college student, he destroyed his planned road to success in which he was showing significant promise.

To satisfy a course requirement to design a commercial building that would be a unique or innovative design, yet also satisfy its commercial requirements he conceived a new business, a combination bakery/pastry and coffee shop with a new feature for 1958 that would not become common until at least twenty years later.

He included a drive-up window that was more advanced than the ones installed since at McDonalds and other fast food purveyors. It had a porte-co-chére over the window that was incorporated in the overall contemporary and innovative design of the building with the structural steel frame on the outside and above the roof of the building. It was not just tagged on as an afterthought like the ones we see today.

He still has the large two panel color presentation with a view from an angle above to display the structure's unique design features.

However, based upon later dissatisfaction with experiences in his architectural endeavors, maybe he would not have followed that career choice, anyway, even if he had the choice. But he doesn't know about that except to say he is certain he would have gotten his degree and missed out on some very unpleasant experiences no one needs, and are definitely not contributory to a better life.

Between puberty and his eighteenth year, in addition to normal school and teenage life, and extracurricular activities, his cup of life was heaped toward fullness with experiences – both good and bad. But it was nothing compared to what was yet to come.

CHAPTER 18

A GRADUATION PRESENT?

In addition to what Hank learned about politics in 1958 he learned another important fact of life: It is not the heart that distance causes to *"grow fonder."*

She was what John Updike referred to in his novel *"Run Rabbit Run"* as one of those *"proud ass"* women, or girls, he described as having an attitude and self-confidence one can see when they are walking down the street that is rooted entirely in their knowledge of the shape and appeal of their derrière. It is the female version of self-confidence attributed to men who are described as *"swinging some pipe."*

She frequently wore dresses of the time that were about calf length and had a little bow, not unlike the ones on the legs of the two young ladies' shorts previously discussed, at the small of the back, the purpose of which was to gather the fabric so it would flow appropriately over the hips disclosing their rearward protruding roundness.

He should have been more wary. She was definitely after him. It was flattering. She was good looking, in demand, and apparently had a plan: Hank.

She began to want him to feel her wetness frequently at the end of the evening as they were kissing good night, but there was no sex until a week after his graduation.

That first week after school his father again ensured he would not be without employment. He was at the construction job his father was just starting at East State Teacher's College in Commerce, Texas not far from Sulpher Springs where he was going to be during week days for the duration of the summer, returning to Grand Prairie only for the weekend late Fridays, as he did this first week he was away.

The first time was her idea, his first, but not last time to be seduced by an attractive female. But it was the one with the worst consequences.

They were at a popular late night teen parking spot northwest of town they called "*Twilight Lake,*" after the popular song of the time "*Twilight Time,*" engaged in the usual passionate but controlled "necking" of the time when, while she was telling Hank how much she missed him during the week, she surprisingly said "*I want you to fuck me,*" and began pulling up her skirt, removing her panties and lying back in the front seat of the Mercury.

Then during the act she chanted "*fuck me, fuck me, fuck me*" in a low passionately pained high pitched whisper... something she would continue in the future.

The second time was the next night at her best friend's house... actually outside.

They were in the house when she asked him to "*Come outside with me*" where they ended up by the side of the house on the thick, soft St. Augustine grass.

He remembers both times and others well... how could he forget them?

She pursued it, sometimes in very inappropriate places; like in the den of her house while her father was napping in the next room.

It was almost like she wanted to be caught.

In retrospect, he thinks she did because she was afraid he was going to leave, leaving her behind, and she did not want that.

Therefore, she was endeavoring to secure her long term relation-ship with him the best and only way she knew, or could, by demon-strating how physically fond of him she was with action to back up her words.

He should have caught on. But he was young and unwary, and she did a hell of a job of proving she was physically fond of him whether he believed her words or not.

━◁ ▷━

1959. They were issued a Marriage License two weeks, to the day, after Hank's nineteenth birthday. It was then he encountered his fourth episode of Christian bigotry.

He decided if he was going to be married in a church, as she and her family demanded, he might as well have Brother Bill he had known since he was twelve years old do the deed even though she wanted the pastor of the church she and her family were members of to do it. They compromised, his pastor, her church. But, oh no!

Turned out not all Baptists were created the same. There are even different versions of what Jesus may have been... according to the literature one branch distributed at the time.

Even though the Baptist part of the Christian milieu did not ap-pear on the scene until sixteen hundred years after his purported death, they issued these little tracts asking, *"Was Jesus a Baptist?"*

Hell, no! He died sixteen hundred years before you were invented and the King James text written. But most were not smart enough to understand.

Never mind that reality. The important reality was; they were mar-ried two days later, on January twenty-ninth 1959, just past midway of Hank's first year of architecture study, in her church, by Brother Bill after something Hank doesn't remember was negotiated.

So he quit college after his first year, got a job as a laborer, worked his butt off, eventually got a promotion and began making good money, bought a nice car, the little house, and with the company car, left her with a metallic burgundy Super 88 Oldsmobile convertible to drive while he was working. Made more money than both her parents, got into the role of working father with a decent job, a pretty wife, a young son.

⚜

1960. He recalls a Saturday when he, his wife and young son were driving to visit his wife's father's parents who were nice people he liked, but lived on a farm in north Texas where they lived most of their lives without indoor plumbing... nice Victorian house but they were in their sixties and having lived all their lives without it, never thought about having it installed.

Although, he was not looking forward to two days without plumbing, he remembers looking at his pretty wife and his son while driving along in his nice Oldsmobile convertible on a bright fall day thinking how happy he was with his life

He was satisfied with his unplanned life to the extent he would have never thought about changing the course he was on at the time. But he didn't have to.

In November, one year and ten months after they were married and two years after the Thanksgiving weekend night in Crockett Park that was the genesis of his marriage and the death of his architecture career plans, he came home to find she and his son were gone. There was a B.S. letter, as she later proved. *"Will always love you, but..."*

As before they were married, Hank says he should have seen it coming.

Her mother was a real bitch, fat, mean and nasty.

One night when they were having dinner at her parents, they were talking about work... theirs and his. The only one at the table who did not have to work was his wife. So they were aware that at twenty years old, he was making more than the two of them.

He didn't mention it, but was sure she told them, and, besides; since she did not have to work, had a home and a nicer car, he knew they knew, which it was obvious her mother did not like.

She was one of those people who cared more about her position than her daughter's life, and for her over twenty years younger daughter to be doing better than she was without having to work, as she did, was probably intolerable to her.

She was a hair dresser. Her husband was a guard at the "defense" plant. The future was mentioned, as in what they might be doing in the future.

In response without really thinking about it, Hank said he hoped to be making twenty-five thousand a year by the time he was thirty, a decade thence.

Apparently that was just too much for her. She quickly threw her head back laughing and responded with *"Who do you think you are?"* in a nasty snarly way.

He never expected that. He assumed she would be happy her daughter was doing well and could possibly do *"more better,"* as the son-in-law of his west Texas travel mate Robert of the red eyes was fond of saying. But this was another of many learning experiences for him.

He was amazed how self-centered so many are... even parents to the exclusion of their children. But there was another indication of what he had gotten into by permitting himself to be led astray by that which grew fonder while he was away.

Her father was a member of the Masons, the secret society of misfits rumored to be heirs of the Knights Templar who are strongly anti-Catholic. He... a real intellectual heavy weight... mentioned several times how bad the Catholics and the Kennedys were. Said if Kennedy was elected the Catholic Church would rule the country.

Hank, like his father, was a good little husband, going to church every Sunday, to her church, of course. But as the 1960 election was drawing near, he was growing tired of the anti-Catholic rhetoric he was being subjected to every Sunday by room temperature I.Q. preachers... hers and others brought in from other Churches to "preach" the same Masonic, anti-Catholic, Knights Templar holdover nonsense from a millennium before.

He thought he had to listen to this crap from her father for familial peace, but to have that similar I.Q. in law's views spewed forth from the church pulpit was intolerable.

He was not a fan of either the Kennedy family or their playboy son, but he decided enough was enough. He was tired listening to this. So one Sunday while getting dressed for church he said, *"O.K., I'll go to church today, but if they start the anti-Kennedy, anti-Catholic, intellectually insulting, nonsense again, I am going to leave... right then."*

Sure enough, they did the singing, passing of the tithe collection plates. Another visiting preacher was introduced. Then he began the anti-Kennedy, anti-Catholic rhetoric.

Hank and his wife were sitting in the middle of the church, half way up the center aisle between the pulpit and the main doors, in the center of one of those long pews. But, true to his word, as is his custom; as soon as this started, he said, *"Let's go,"* got up, *"excuse me, excuse me,"* his way to the center aisle, out the front door, and has never been back.

Thus this whole marital experience, in addition to life changing, was a real eye opener for him wherein he learned; being good, honest, dependable and hard-working, does not guarantee respect or any advantages in life.

He demonstrated all those characteristics he was engendered with, and thought were attributes and proper conduct even though he was in an education and life plan busting unplanned marriage. He even designed a small contemporary home he planned to build for them when finances permitted. He was definitely in for the long haul.

It would have taken more than he can imagine even today to have caused him to leave his son and shirk his responsibilities. But then he never had a need or chance to consider doing what would have been unthinkable for someone of his character. The decision was made for him... by someone of obviously less character.

He doesn't think that decision was good for but one of the three lives affected by it, especially not, as he would learn many years later, his son's, given the way he was raised and the improperly skewed, limited perspective of life resulting therefrom. But in retrospect it was a decision that was good for Hank.

Being freed from the bonds of one who proved she was so limited, dishonest and constrained by the inertia of small town Texas culture and values... exactly what he was so desirous of getting far away from... probably saved his sanity by enabling him to *"get out"* and participate in the world he knew was outside of that where he would have otherwise spent the rest of his life asking *"Is this all there is?"*

CHAPTER 19

CULTURE AND NURTURING

Even in a seemingly fairly homogenous small city with only one high school, the degree of intellectual and socioeconomic diversity is amazing... if one has sufficient exposure to cause thought about it.

It really is a small or micro version of the macroeconomic "melting pot" we have always heard so much about, and therein lies a cautionary tale for the unwary young.

With that in mind, based upon Hank's experience and other similar horror stories; should a young man encounter a young lady and find she is wearing cotton underwear when his family is accustomed to silk, he should move on, which he should also do if he is the young lady's first. For the cat is not the only fatality of curiosity.

If a young lady is in a relationship with a young man who is providing better for her than her father is for her mother, and her mother begins talking negatively about him, she should decide whether she prefers to continue to live better than her parents, or would prefer spending the rest of her life working, as her mother has.

If the decision is she prefers the former, she should either kiss her mother goodbye or cause her to cease interfering in her life.

If her decision is the latter, she should leave and get a job. But before she can make that decision, she should also decide which is more important to her, religion or world realities.

If the wrong decision is made, she may be walking away from a good "thing," someone who is more intelligent than what she grew up with, and who she can depend upon to take care of and cherish her and her child for the rest of their lives, as opposed to spending it with someone who has never run his hand over the silk of a young lady's underwear.

⊷⊹⊶

1961. By the seventh day of February, approximately two years and eight months after his graduation from high school Hank had completed a rigorous year of college, been married, a father, a union member... not by choice, met with some success in business, bought a home, separated and experienced divorce court wherein one of his *"ends"* was definitively moved... for good.

During his time with him, his father was responsible for his working and learning about business, knowing much about construction and retail, knowing how to build a house, to bid construction jobs, and to run a business on his own.

That and the after dinner games and question sessions about geography, history and math that were his contribution toward his education... probably the most important part of it... had already paid dividends during the time he was married, supporting himself and two others. But he failed to educate Hank about what just happened to him because he had no experience or knowledge of it, yet.

However, when he was having a tough time after his divorce, his father assured him, *"Son, you can do whatever you think you can."*

This and his advice to *"forget about hoping"* were, as intended, helpful for direction in life.

The encouragement and advice were especially helpful during this year when he lost all hope about everything, primarily because of the way he was treated after the divorce, as he continued living in his house, working and trying to spend time with his son on Wednesdays for dinner, and Saturday and Sunday every other weekend.

Those were his visitation days. But he was put through sheer Hell all the time by his ex-wife, and her lovely mother and father who did everything possible to prevent his exercising his visitation rights. He was even locked up one Wednesday afternoon.

The police came. Hand cuffed him, threw him into the rear of a police car. Took him to the Police Station and locked him up, ignoring he was within his court ordered rights.

He was constantly harassed and his rights abused. But what was worse, they were willing to mistreat a two year old baby just to try to get back at him for something he knows not what to this day, over fifty years later.

It was very trying every time he returned his son to his ex-wife. He would cry and cling to him until they physically pulled him away causing Hank to wonder what they could have been doing, or not doing, to cause him to not want to be with his mother and grandparents he was living with almost ninety percent of the time.

It was difficult to deal with and not be able to do anything about it thanks to the warped view of the courts that always took the position children should be in the custody of the mother regardless how bad or non-caring she was.

This went on for the better part of the year until his ex-wife and her family decided to move away from Grand Prairie to a town north of Dallas, a good sixty miles away.

That put an end to the Wednesday visitations, as he was sure was intended because the move was far enough away that he would have difficulty exercising his weekend visitation rights, but it was rumored there was also another reason for their move.

He endeavored to continue his visitations, but it became impossible. Another incident one Sunday afternoon when he was returning his son to his ex was the end of his exercise of his legally conferred visitations.

After he handed his son off, as he was going back to his car at the curb three men came from around the sides of the house. One went to his car and restrained his then sixteen year old brother who was with him for witness purposes while one attacked Hank and the other stood guard close by while his ex, standing on the porch between her mother and father who were at that moment obviously complicit in arranging his being attacked on their property, which, had he pursued it, was felony assault, holding their two and one-half year old son yelling *"Kill him, Kill him, Kill him"* in succession more times and with more passion than her customary *"Fuck me."*

Fortunately a neighbor across the street was aware of Hank's schedule and seeing what was planned prior to his arrival, phoned the police who arrived shortly after the attack began.

They took all involved to the local police station where the sheriff privately told Hank he wanted him to cease coming to his town because his ex was involved with these people who were *"known"* to him and other local law enforcement, and his continuing visitations were not going to work out well for anyone because it was his opinion that with these people *"someone would get killed"* if he continued to come.

So, with this stern warning from the Sheriff, Hank ceased exercising his rights. Thus their goal of depriving him of his rights he thought was one of the reasons his ex, her mother and father quit their jobs, took her little sister out of school and moved sixty miles away from their home and that of many of their relatives for many years was accomplished.

But he later learned there was possibly another reason, if rumors were true, that could have been an even greater incentive for them to move: his ex was rumored to be pregnant again.

He can't confirm the truth of this, but he thought she did appear to have gained weight and refrained from holding their son. He was also aware she was having an affair with the owner of the beauty salon where she worked after spending her child support money to go to beauty school while every time he picked up his son for visitations he was handed to him with nothing but the T-shirt and diaper he was wearing, no extra clothes, diapers or anything.

Although he cannot confirm why they left town, he did have first-hand knowledge of the affair because the salon owner's wife called and invited him to her house to talk about this he did not think was any concern of his until the salon owner's wife insisted it might have some bearing on his son's well-being.

She said the reason she informed him was she caught his ex engaged in sex with her husband one evening in their salon on his office desk, and she planned to seek a divorce, the proceedings of which were going to include suing her for alienation of affection and whatever else she could get her attorney to pursue, which she thought, plus the loss of her job, could adversely affect his son's well-being.

In addition to this fact, there were also rumors his ex was seen wearing maternity clothes after he ceased exercising his rights, and the reason for the family's sudden departure was a get out of town or be sued financial settlement, which is plausible because the salon was the most successful in a town of forty thousand.

That and the home where the wife was living when Hank met with her indicated there could have been a significant amount of money involved, and she conveyed to him how determined she was for revenge in the form of financial compensation.

She intended to get everything she could. That would have likely destroyed the guy's business and affected his livelihood to an extent that would have been intolerable. Thus, it is plausible a sufficient amount of money to cause the move could have changed hands.

Hank doesn't know what happened, but he does know the salon was still in business and doing well over three years later when he returned from the military because he used to have breakfast with the owner and two friends.

Neither he nor the owner ever mentioned this, but both knew of the other's tangential relationship to him. Small town! Small world!

However, to this day, Hank has no idea what generated such hatred toward him. Why they, the entire family did what they did. He was never mean to either of them in any way; did not mistreat his ex, their son or her parents. Nothing! No real reason ever cited.

He was nothing but a good husband and father, gave up his education and career plans, worked hard as a laborer to overcome financial adversity and provide the best lifestyle he could.

Why he and his son were treated as they were and deprived of a relationship is another of those unanswered questions Hank says he will die with.

But this episode of his life does confirm his belief people are like water. Both seek their own level. He is happy she found hers and what she received as a result. However, he is not happy she took his son downstream with her.

———

At the time of these occurrences the wife of his ex-wife's uncle who owned the shop where her mother worked expressed to Hank what she thought about him versus her sister-in-law and niece, and what they did to him when she advised *"Don't spend a lot of time worrying about this. When your son is old enough and finds out what happened about this, he will seek you out."*

However, it was too late to be of benefit to either when that happened because he was lied to about his name and his father, and was even enrolled in school for years under a false name.

It was not until after he was forty years old and had more than sufficient time for an intelligent curious person to have learned what happened when he finally contacted Hank.

Even then he admitted he was in close contact all his life with one of his aunts who knew Hank well, liked and held him in relatively high esteem.

At the time he contacted him, her son... Hank refers to him as *"her son"* for reasons stated below... told him many things about his mother, including one that showed what she was like and how little she really cared for the son she was so intent on preventing Hank from having any influence on. Also another he had a little sadistic chuckle over.

"Her son" told him; after he ceased coming to get him his mother moved away and left him with his grandparents, which adds credibility to the pregnancy rumor. Then, after two years, when he was almost five years old, she married one of the ones the sheriff warned Hank about and returned to take him to live with them.

Further, he said that husband demanded she lay out his blue collar clothes for him every morning, and she complied with this for years. Also, she worked as a beauty operator.

He said he did not think she had a great life, nor did he think highly of this stepfather.

Hank calls him *"her son"* because what he conveyed to him about his beliefs differentiated him dramatically from the way he would have raised him.

His expressed values were appalling to Hank. As his wife stated, he is definitely *"a product of nurturing, not nature."*

He believes Hindu are a cult, although he belongs to some unnamed Christian group; one of those where its followers gather in neighborhoods to create their own cultural environment in which to raise their children... probably to shield them from reality and the truth of the world, while teaching them the earth was created only six thousand years ago.

This was partially confirmed when he was offended Hank pointed out that, by definition, if Hindu are a cult, his group would also qualify as one.

His wife told Hank they *"believe the Bible is the only true written word and it is their obligation to go forth and spread the word."*

They were not very receptive when he pointed out *"that statement relegates every other written word to be false,"* and further, *"it would be best if everyone would believe what they want to believe and just let everyone else do the same... in peace."*

The fact *"her son,"* seemingly proudly, told Hank he went on his first blind date with this future wife wearing Bermuda shorts and flip flops, and she proudly informed Hank and his wife they did *"not use"* butter knives at their home, as she was digging into the ceramic butter dish with the knife she was using to cut the food on her plate, demonstrated a cultural divide that proved the truth of Hank's wife's comment.

"Her son" grew up in a culture and under such different, uneducated guidance from that he would have experienced with Hank that his genetic *"nature"* was subdued, even suppressed, by the tutelage of his mother, her family and a step father who was the product of "guidance" that resulted in his being *"known"* to law enforcement at an early age.

Whereas Hank's father always offered encouragement and advice that resulted in his having high self-esteem, *"her son"* told him his step father, for the obvious reason he was not his offspring, was always denigrating him and telling him how *"stupid"* he was.

That resulted in his lacking self-confidence he should have possessed, and would have had Hank not been deprived of participation in his *"nurturing."*

That cultural divide, demonstrated by his ex, her parents, "*her son*" and his wife is something Hank was incapable of perceiving in his youth. However, the religion, Masonic nonsense, resentment toward someone planning to better himself, the less than stellar use and comprehension of the English language... all these differences indicate it would have never worked out for him.

In addition to all this, the really depressing aspect for Hank of "*her son's*" value system was demonstrated when he told him he got rid of a little dog he had for four years because he got new carpet in his house.

Hank could not believe anyone could be so uncaring of one of man's best little friends. Then that's when it got worse.

"*Her son*" informed him that was O.K because "*God gave man dominion over the earth and all its creatures*" to do with as he desires.

That was it! He was from a different world Hank sincerely hopes is not broadly represented in this country.

CHAPTER 20
LIFE EXPANDS

During the balance of the difficult year 1961 Hank did his best to cope with a situation he never dreamed he would experience.

He continued to do freelance architectural work and work for the home improvement company for part of the year. During that time he had another important learning experience about women.

An attractive young housewife on whose little Fox and Jacobs tract house in North Dallas he was supervising the installation of a patio cover invited him in for coffee one morning wearing her non-concealing negligee and suggested he should come back to see her after they were finished and his crew was not around.

His principle thoughts about this at the time were sorrow for the husband and how the "Sexual Revolution" also had a dark side not conducive to matrimonial bliss. It also made him wonder about the many magazines he began receiving after his wife departed, and another rumor the guy she eventually married after moving to the town where he and his family lived was thought to have sold magazines door to door in Grand Prairie.

This caused him to think maybe the beauty salon owner was taken for a ride because it is better to have a successful businessman responsible for one's bastard child than an immature magazine salesman with a questionable background and no money.

But he did not dwell on any of this. He managed to develop a reasonably good social life, and spent some time with his high school friends Bill and Jim.

Bill was the really good dancer and Jim was not too bad either. He was probably the lightest on his feet of any heavy man Hank has ever seen. He also had an affinity for burlesque clubs.

He and Hank went out to clubs frequently… at the county line "Strip" in Arlington, which was the closest place since the Christians had their way with Grand Prairie in 1953.

They also occasionally went to Fort Worth. But for other than weekends, the Colonial Club at "the Strip" was it. It was a pretty nice place with live music every night by a good regular band. So it was not necessary to travel farther.

Because of its proximity to Grand Prairie, people Hank knew were usually there, including ex high school classmates most nights, as were some attractive ladies he got to know pretty well.

There was Norma who referred to his king size bed as a *"playground,"* obviously, and for other reasons was a favorite. One of these was her uniqueness and strong sexual desires.

Being with her when her desires were being satisfied was like being suddenly engulfed by a small tsunami of warmth.

Then were two who shared a large nice home. One was an accountant, the other a nurse. They liked to party and had parties at their home. The nurse was really attractive with a beautifully sculpted body covered with freckles, but her most prominent features were her perky breasts with erect nipples that pointed upward at a forty-five degree angle when she was vertical. There was also the nearby American Airlines Stewardess College that was like an offertory of pretty perky young ladies.

One night, a girl from High School, a year older than he, came into the club. Betsy had changed a lot... five ten, striking.

He could not recall they ever spoke in High School. But they got along really well that night, and for most of the time thereafter.

Until he left town she was a regular companion. She had the most beautiful, long legs which he has an affinity for, and were probably a big factor in her becoming a house model at Neiman Marcus in Dallas. They were unavoidably noticeable.

It was the second or third date when she sealed their fate, at least for a while.

When he went to pick her up one evening, she was not ready. Gave him something to drink and said she would be ready in a few minutes. But she must have already been *"ready,"* contrary to what she said.

A few minutes later she walked back into the living room stark naked holding a pillow in front of her with its bottom at the top of her legs, somewhere about three feet off the floor, and said... he never will forget it... *"There's no use in postponing the inevitable,"* as she turned around and headed back toward her bedroom leaving him watching those long, inviting legs and derrière moving seductively down the hall toward her bedroom.

They did not go out that night, or many others.

Another night in the club a really big guy who weighed at least two and a quarter moseyed over to the table where Hank was sitting. He didn't have a clue what he was doing, but it was a disquieting experience at the beginning because of his reputation.

He was rumored to be a hit man, which was believable since the club owner gave every indication of having "connections." It was also rumored when he was on army reserve duty a smart ass professional boxer determined to take him on to prove himself because of his size.

This one apparently confirmed Hank's belief boxers could not be very smart because he reportedly took one swing, after which this big one hit him once, sending him to the hospital with a concussion that resulted in his boxing career being over.

As he got to the table, he said to Hank, *"My wife thinks you are a really good dancer and she wants to dance with you."*

He thought something like, *"Oh shit, my life is over,"* and so young, too. But apparently the big guy could tell his concern because he followed up with, *"It's O.K. She really likes to dance, but I can't dance. So, I would like for you to dance with her."*

How could he refuse? As they walked back to the guy's table, he introduced himself. Then when they got to the table, he formally introduced Hank to his wife and told her, *"Hank would like to dance with you."*

"A gentleman and a killer," Hank thought.

She was an attractive Latina. What we would call *"stacked,"* moderate height. She was a very good dancer. Hank had seen her before. She was always well dressed in good quality, but tight fitting dresses and high heels. Her husband, the big guy, always wore a tie and sport coat... probably sport coat because it would have been difficult to buy suits for his body.

They danced a couple of times. He took her back to their table where her husband said, *"Have a seat,"* in a nice way. Asked him what he would like to drink. Bought a drink for him and thanked him for dancing with his wife. Also said he would appreciate his doing so whenever he had time. Seemed like a nice guy trying to keep his wife happy.

They were in the club a couple of times the next two weeks when Hank was there. He danced with the wife some each of those nights and had drinks with them. They were nice people. Even took him out for a late dinner one night, treated him like an honored guest. Then big guy asked him if he would do a favor for him. Of course, Hank said *"Yes."*

He then told Hank he was going to be out of town the following weekend on business and his wife couldn't go with him, so he wondered if he didn't have a date, whether he would take his wife to the club Friday and Saturday nights.

Hank could immediately determine this arrangement was fraught with danger.

What if she wanted something more than dancing and he refused, which he would because he valued his life.

Then if she told her husband he did what he didn't because he wouldn't he would be dead, anyway.

He didn't like the thought of this. It was a lose, lose proposition, but he was trapped. So he picked her up and took her to the club both nights. They danced, had drinks and talked for two or three hours. It was just like a normal date, even when they danced.

She danced more closely than when her husband was there... too close, and she got the normal reaction an attractive woman with a hot body should expect when she presses her body against her male dance partner.

It was beyond his control and obvious, causing him to think again he was dead, but she leaned back, smiled at him like she was toying with him, and did it on purpose to get the reaction.

No one dared ever ask her if she would like to dance, and Hank had a good time except for the few seconds she made him think he was going to be dead.

The relief he felt Saturday night when he left her at her door was not a total relief. He was still concerned what she might tell her husband, and whether he would still be alive the next day.

He was and when he saw them the following weekend the big guy hugged him as he shook his hand. Thanked him profusely for taking care of his wife. Told him she said he was a perfect gentleman, and would not let him buy a drink.

He danced with her a few times, but not to slow numbers. Then they insisted he have a late dinner with them again.

They went to dinner. Big guy paid. Hank's money wasn't any good, and when she went to the ladies room, he told Hank, *"I really like you. You are a good guy. You let me know if you ever have any problems. You know. If anybody is ever bothering you, you let me know. I'll take care of them for you."*

Hank admits this was tempting, but, no. He didn't think he could live with the results if he told big guy about a certain young lady, to use the term loosely, and her boyfriend, future husband and the misery they caused him.

But they will never know how close they came to being very sorry for the trouble, pain and emotional strain they caused him and what they did to his son.

He saw the big guy and his wife frequently before he left town, danced with her and had dinner with them. It was always pleasant.

They seemed a lonely couple without friends who cared about one another. She liked to dance. So they went out. Hank was happy for the experience and again, thankful to his father for spending all those hours teaching him to dance.

⟢ ⟣

He continued to date Betsy regularly. Occasionally went to a party at the house of the accountant and "perky" breasts, and went out with Bill and Jim. Had a few dates with some others. Notably, or not, with a stripper and a part time prostitute he knew from dancing with them at his favorite club.

Both were good looking, nice girls… just not the take home to mother kind, especially his mother, or ones to think long term about. But he wasn't thinking long term. He was just killing time. Trying to have a good time and stay safe… and alive, which was occasionally dicey.

Jim liked Jack Ruby's Carousel Club on the second floor of a building on the west end of Commerce Street near Union Station and Dealey Plaza. So they went there a few times.

It was not the typical strip joint. It was as close to "high class" for a burlesque club as it would have been possible to find at the time.

The girls were pretty and good dancers. No bump and grind... choreographed routines, negligees, slow and seductive. Ruby would sit at the table with you for a few minutes... smart club owner, not unlike Hank's father or the couple who owned Shakers in L.A. in his approach to generating repeat business.

He was never bored, stayed busy between work and social life. But he knew this was not what he wanted to do with his life.

Betsy was the only one he spent any time with he thought might fit into the kind of life he eventually wanted, but not at that time in his life. He did not want to get involved and end up in a situation he was afraid could end like the one he recently got out of. Nor did he want a ready-made family.

Betsy, like so many attractive young women married pre "Pill" had a child, a three year old son. The same age as Hank's.

His small world was closing in on him. He had to get out.

But even if he did get out he was made aware there was something he could never get away from. Though his taxes were prepared by an accountant, the I.R.S. decided he needed "servicing" the first year his earnings were above poverty level.

It was as if they were lying in wait for him to make a sufficient amount for them to get away with taking a little more, as if they viewed taking a couple of hundred dollars a year more from those who moved into taxpaying status would not be a problem... much like that later perennial government parasite Dick Cheney viewed the caged animals he was waiting to be released so he could shoot them the day he shot his friend while HUI, hunting under the influence.

This was Hank's first experience with being hunted down and "serviced," by the I.R.S., but it would be far from the last

CHAPTER 21

THE FINAL STRAW

1 **962.** New Year's Eve 1961, actually early New Year's Day 1962, put Hank over the precipice regarding leaving. It was time to go before he was driven to the point of cutting his metaphorical umbilical cord in a permanent way... or dying.

He and Betsy were going out to a club to celebrate and his father wanted them to come by so he could take photos of them dressed up for New Years before they went out.

They agreed to do that, but since Betsy had to take her son to a baby sitter they drove separately and met at his parents.'

When it was time for them to leave for the evening they decided it would be best if Betsy drove in case he drank too much of the Jack Daniels he developed a taste for recently to get rid of the "taste" of his ex in laws and his recent experiences with them.

So unaware the other really bad "taste" he had been dealing with for years longer than his ex in laws was about to become the equivalent of seriously bad acid reflux, they went in her car leaving Hank's pretty, hot red Oldsmobile Super 88 convertible there.

When they returned to his parent's home at 2:00 AM Hank could see, immediately, something had happened to his car. It was backed into the car port. Not where he left it.

He looked at it and was surprised to find the right rear caved in. The entire right side from the door to the rear of the fender was destroyed, and it was obvious the fender was pried away from the tire so the car could be moved. But since it was after 2:00 AM, he did not bother his parents until a reasonable time the next morning... then he went to find out what happened to this car.

His mother immediately started her usual protect *"Sunshine"* crap; *"It was an accident. He didn't mean to do it."* Yet he had taken Hank's car without his permission, which was strange because he would never let him drive his car, and his father would not let him drive anything.

He wouldn't even be sixteen for six months.

Hank demanded to know what happened.

The little S.O.B. didn't bother to say he was sorry.

Hank gave him credit for not lying about that because he wasn't sorry. But he wanted to know what happened to his car. So he kept pushing for answers, and finally found that *"Sunshine's"* friend David was with him when it happened.

He went to see David who told him the literal S.O.B. was deliberately spinning the wheels on ice to see how many miles per hour he could get the speedometer up to. He even showed Hank the embankment north of town he slid the car into while he was doing that, and said he laughed about wrecking it. He thought that was what he was trying to do.

Later in the day Hank got back with the information about what really happened. His mother, father and *"Sunshine"* were sitting at the dinner table. The little S.O.B. was facing him. His mother had her back to him and his father was sitting at the end of the table, sideways to Hank.

He told them what *"Sunshine"* did. Told them David showed the place to him where he wrecked the car. She said, *"I don't have any reason to believe David. He* ["Sunshine"] *told me what happened, and I believe him. He has no reason to lie to me about it."*

Hank's father sat there with his mouth shut. The little S.O.B. sat there grinning at Hank with his shitty little smirk Hank had seen so many times over the years. This time it said *"Ha, ha, I just destroyed your lovely car, and got away with it. Ha. Ha."*

All the while she was looking straight at him, fully aware of what happened... aware of his attitude, and that he was lying.

It was model airplanes and Chevy coupe all over again, eleven and eight years later. Only this time, it was something expensive Hank worked and paid for, and really liked that it would not have surprised him to find out she gave the keys to her *"Sunshine."* But he never did.

His father might have known, but kept his mouth shut because he did not want to be thrown out of the house again. Lovely f#&%ing family!

He said *"Fuck it!"* and left thinking; thankfully, his mother would be the one to eventually bear the full brunt of the damages and expense of what she created. Expenses that would exceed that cost to him and his property at that time by thousands of percent, as well as totally disrupt her life to an extent she could never have imagined.

The next weekend he went to Dallas and virtually gave his Oldsmobile away in trade for the '62 Impala. He was not happy. With the new car, yes; but he was not happy.

A few days later he went to a party at the girls' house in Arlington where the last he remembers was playing pool when a familiar, pretty girl came in with a bottle of Vodka and asked *"Would anyone like to help me with this"* as she thrust the bottle in front of her.

Hank thought: *"Why not? What the hell? Things couldn't get any worse."*

The next he remembers he was waking up to the sun coming up, lying on his back with water up to his neck.

He was close to the shore in Lake Arlington with the accountant holding his head above water to keep him from drowning while she was calling for someone to help get him out of the water.

No help responded, but someone hollered *"Let him drown,"* indicating they were not happy with him for some reason.

He doesn't remember how he got there or why some at the party were so unhappy with him. Nor does he remember how she got him out. But he does remember being so sick from alcohol poisoning for two days he thought he was going to die.

That was it. He had to *"get out"* before he died. He really needed to find out what was out there before being where he was killed him.

A few days later, having sold his little house to his high school friend next door neighbor, Hank put all his clothes into the trunk of the Impala, the $500 cash he had into his pocket, and just after sunset, drove north on 8th Street to the Dallas/Fort Worth Turnpike.

Just before the entrance to the Turnpike he pulled into the gravel parking lot of the veterinary clinic on the east side of the street, dug into his pocket, took out a quarter, flipped it, calling heads; west, tails; east, caught it in his right hand and slapped it down onto the back of his left.

As he uncovered it, he saw it came down with the heads, *"Go west, young man,"* side up.

That was how he ended up in California for the past year.

⟛ ⟛

Suddenly he was awakened from his two day mental review of his past to his current reality of May 1963 by the Texas spring aroma of freshly cut Johnson grass.

He was turning off of the Turnpike, southward onto 8th Street. The vet's clinic was on his left.

Just as he passed it, the street with the hill where the truck's broken axle almost dumped him into the lake turned off to the right, then the street entrance into the park where he had the picnic with the lovely young lady that summer day almost ten years before. Memories he was recalling the last two days.

Now, again, he had only memories of what he left behind... like the memory of the girl and that picnic in the park, about that short, fleeting relationship.

He wondered; *"Will that be all I will have left of Los Angeles... of Heidi, ten years from now... nothing but memories of a short, sweet relationship? Is that going to be my destiny? Will that be all there is to my life?"*

Grand Prairie was looming before him again as it had on his trip back the last two days. Some of it as it was from above in his childhood dreams. But now he thought maybe he should have looked at it, Grand Prairie and his time there, from a different perspective.

He thought; *"I did well in Los Angeles on the basis of what I learned and experienced in Grand Prairie, especially what I learned from father.*

"Maybe my problems were not so much Grand Prairie. Maybe it was family life, thanks to mother and ' sunshine,' or the way I handled my own life the two and one-half years prior to getting out... and the consequences of that.

"Maybe it was what I did to myself there after getting into the world on my own that soured me on Grand Prairie."

The bad memories were more prominent in his mind than the good ones because, like war versus peace, it is the bad experiences that are disruptive to our lives.

The good, peaceful experiences that enhance our lives are accepted without question as part of life's normal progression... but not the bad ones.

It is those that are frequently the result of something we have done to ourselves... being with the wrong people, being in the wrong place, or other bad decisions we should or should not have made... that leave us asking that perennial question that only merits asking about what we can control, that we should relegate only to what happens to ourselves; why? Why did I do this, or not do that, say that, why was I there... why me?

It is not unlike making decisions and choices. We never know whether we made the right, or best decision or choice. We are left to wonder about that. But the wrong ones always eventually become obvious.

Shouldn't be that way, but seems to be. Maybe future experiences would change that for Hank, if not for the world.

CHAPTER 22

INDUCTION

May 6. UNITED STATES ARMY RECRUITING STATION, Crane Bldg. 1200 Jackson St., Dallas, Texas.

The induction center was on the second floor of this building in the west end of downtown Dallas, a couple hundred feet east of Union Station and less than two hundred yards, if that, south of Dealey Plaza where railroad tracks cross over the continuation of Commerce, Main and Elm Streets. A block to the northeast was Jack Ruby's Carousel Club on Commerce Street.

All this was a familiar neighborhood to Hank for sixteen years because it was necessary to drive through this any time he went to downtown Dallas, the Farmer's Market, his grandfather's house, the suppliers of his father's earth moving equipment and the frequently needed replacement parts, as well as every time he went to the movies in the big movie theaters in downtown Dallas..

However, there was nothing familiar about the induction center. It was a big room with stations for examining, probing, prodding, squeezing, feeling and drawing blood.

It made him feel as though he could empathize with the cattle being run through the pre slaughter gauntlet at the meat packing plant about two miles to the north where his father took him years before to see how cattle were processed and killed.

He was being *"processed."* That's what they called it. But they avoided addressing the possible end result being the same as the cattle suffered.

Obviously, he didn't think he was going to be killed on Jackson Street by the government, right there in downtown Dallas. But he was being processed to be put on a course to potential death at the hands of the government that was definitely preparing him to be put into harm's way where getting killed carried a high probability.

He and the other inductees were being treated like herd animals; made to strip down to nothing but underwear then marched around from examining station to station where they were made to bend over while given a digital proctologic exam in full view of others. Ditto, while they had underwear pulled down, testicles squeezed and told to cough.

They were probed, poked, squeezed, and handled like meat, which seemed to be the way they were perceived by the government employees doing this who were, most likely, exempted from the potential end result because of these actions for their employer.

There were at least a hundred inductees, maybe more. Several from Hank's high school class of five years previous, only two of whom would accompany him later.

He wondered how long they had been doing this... inducting hundreds every day. If it had been going on for some time, all over the country, it meant there was a big military buildup. That had to be what they were doing, but why then?

It was almost two years since Kennedy requested the authority to enlarge the military in July 1961. But that request was because of the Berlin Crisis in June 1961 that was resolved five months later, in November 1961...eighteen months prior to this day.

But before it was resolved Kennedy scared the hell out of most of the population of the country. Not with the troop buildup, but by announcing the government was designating and stocking fallout shelters because this was, essentially, a statement by the President of the United States that he was preparing the country for nuclear war, not unlike the British Government building bomb shelters in London two years before Hitler invaded Poland.

Hank knew the country was scared because when the announcement was made he was working for the construction and home improvement company.

There was so much press and concern about the possibility of nuclear war that home fallout shelters were being discussed, and seeing a business opportunity he designed a home fallout shelter, got it approved as such by all the appropriate government agencies, his company advertised it in the Dallas newspapers, received many responses, and they sold and built several.

Many people spent a lot of money to create family fallout shelters in their backyards. This was happening throughout the country.

The Cuban Missile Crisis was resolved seven months before in October. But it served to further nuclear concerns that lasted for some time.

He and his father even discussed the possible outcomes of this more than once via phone in 1962 after he was in California.

They discussed whether there was anything they should be doing like whether they should be getting out of the Los Angeles and Dallas metropolitan areas. But they could not determine how that would help them.

If American cities were going to be made into nuclear waste zones, as Hiroshima and Nagasaki were at the end of WWII that would be the end of everything, anyway. No place to go. No place to hide.

The people were being put in a position to be worried about this, and could not understand being put into this position by those in their government?

Just as his father, uncles, almost every adult he heard talk about it while he was growing up was convinced of what has since been proven true: it was not necessary for "Fortress America" to get into WWII, and increased its magnitude dramatically by doing so.

There was no way, given the vastness of the country, its Atlantic and Pacific shore lines, its relatively large population and its power, that either Japan or Germany would have attacked the U.S. They could not afford to do it financially or politically. They did not have the manpower to conquer the U.S. They and Roosevelt knew that.

So, Roosevelt, as previously mentioned, deliberately got the U.S. into WWII to endeavor to solve economic problems of the Depression. Classified documentation released in recent years disclose this to be true, as well as the fact he deliberately permitted the attack on Pearl Harbor... sacrificed the lives of almost three thousand Americans... to get the U.S. into the war, against the desires of the vast majority of Americans. Proof of this has been disclosed in many writings.

The Roosevelt Administration was aware when the Japanese fleet headed toward Hawaii, and Roosevelt deliberately delayed communications to warn Pearl Harbor, but even prior to that the U.S. took actions attempting to provoke Japan into attacking the country.

Japan is a resource poor country. It does not produce oil, coal copper or other necessities. The Roosevelt Administration was doing everything within its power to deprive Japan of oil. But, without going into the history of this, there is one fact that should cause any doubters to accept the deviousness of Roosevelt and realize his actions were the ones that should have gone *"down in history"* as acts *"of infamy,"* and treason.

What vessel is the core of any U.S. naval fleet, the vessel that permits the U.S. to project its power around the world through its air power? That would be the aircraft carrier.

The vessels missing from Pearl Harbor when it was attacked were the two aircraft carriers Roosevelt dispatched away from the known attack zone the day he learned the Japanese fleet was headed for

Hawaii. He knew he would need them in the Pacific when the war he was so desirous of getting the U.S. into with Japan began.

⚓

At this time of Hank's induction the Cold War between the West... primarily the U.S... and the Soviets was a verbal and arms stalemate for eighteen years after the end of WWII in Europe when the Allies permitted the Russians to beat them into Berlin, then cut a deal to divide Germany just as they cut a deal to divide Korea at the 38th Parallel eight years later.

Both of these deals almost seem like prior planning for future military action when determined needed to anyone who would, rightly, think the people in control of the U.S... the only ones to ever cook a civilian population with a nuke... capable of such evilness.

But we shouldn't blame the Russians for wanting some control over Germany. The Germans invaded Russia at great loss of life to Russians, and their comeback just over only twenty years after they were defeated in WWI was dramatic. They were enemies for a very long time.

Who was to say the Germans would not do it again?

Had the U.S. been in Russia's position vis-à-vis Germany, it would be a good bet it would have done the same as the Russians.

But because Russians were communists, as were the Chinese, the U.S. Government decided all communist governments were the enemy. Never mind the Chinese Communists came to power partially as a result of U.S. support of the Soong Dynasty, and Chiang Kai-shek was a U.S. ally while he was looting China in the first half of the twentieth century, or the Russians were U.S. allies during WWII.

These two nations had combined populations at least six times greater than the U.S. Both were relatively resource rich - Russia with energy, China with people. Both had a history of being powerful nations. They were also enemies of one another. But that did not matter... same ideology. That made them the perfect foil for a continuation of the buildup of the U.S. Military/Industrial complex.

Ideology, or religion; either can be used to get the masses to support a government if it positions either as an enemy of the people... different religion, bad, different ideology, also bad. There was not a large enough unified religious enemy at the time. But there were a lot of communists. So they were it.

But, surely in spring of 1963 there was no thought of putting troops on the ground in Europe again with the objective of invading Russia. No one could be that stupid, hopefully.

Surely they heard of the outcome of that stupidity when Hitler and Napoleon tried it. The outcome would be the same for the next to engage in that doomed to fail mission.

The thought of putting more troops into Germany to drive the Russians out of East Germany made no sense. Both Berlin and Cuba had been resolved. Thus, any action along those lines would just be a return to another European ground war that was prevented nineteen years before by letting the Russians have what the Berlin squabble was about. That wouldn't make any sense.

No. None of it made any sense given the Cold War between the U.S. and Russia was presented to the American people as a nuclear standoff that had virtually zero to do with ground troops anywhere. So, what was up?

⇒⊹⊹⇐

After the hours of squeezing, poking, probing, drawing blood and asking a lot of questions, that part of the processing was over. The inductees were permitted to put their clothes back on. Then they were informed whether they were eligible to be in the Army.

Hank assumed just from observing them in only their undershorts that ninety-nine percent of the inductees were sufficiently healthy to be cannon fodder. But there were exceptions. One of his classmates was dismissed for a reason that rendered him incredulous He was excused from being cannon fodder because he had only one testicle.

What could being minus one testicle have to do with not qualifying as cannon fodder?

Now, we know it was the government; the same people who located a Naval Base in a landlocked position hundreds of miles from the ocean. But this is difficult to understand because it could only be because if he lost the other one, he could not father children.

Presumably this meant it was O.K. with the government if anyone took a bullet through the heart if he had two, and was thus rendered unable to produce more fodder. But it was not O.K. if someone had only one and got it shot off with the same negative effect on his procreative ability.

Two were O.K., but one. No. What sense did that make?

It should not have been a consideration given the stakes that were purportedly the reason for the increased draft numbers.

The President and others were supposedly concerned about two nuclear powers getting into something that, unless Americans were being lied to by their government, would result in those fallout shelters Kennedy was having stocked with supplies being filled with American citizens.

Surely, there was no thought those with two who qualified as cannon fodder would be of any benefit out in the open getting theirs roasted.

The U.S. had thousands of troops, an air base and a lot of equipment in West Germany just a stone's throw away from the publicized trouble spot of Berlin. The Asian communist situation was resolved ten years before in a militarized standoff with thirty-six thousand U.S. troops on the ground in Korea without mention of need for any more. None of this made any sense.

Troops were not needed in Germany or Korea. Kennedy had already bent his spear in Cuba. But that was also resolved. No troops needed there either. So what was really up?

Since the U.S. had gone through its worst post war recession two years prior to the 1961 troop expansion and fallout shelter announcement. Could those in the government, being "the best and brightest," have decided that was a warning about the future of the economy and begun positioning the military and country for another Roosevelt-like action to ensure the growth of the military/industrial complex and thus, growth of the economy?

Actions of the prior two years made it appear as though the U.S. was looking to start something, somewhere, and they were preparing the people for it. There were bad communists everywhere that had to be stamped out... eliminated as a threat to the people of America... before they could attack... or before the economy tanked.

The U.S. already had troops in Vietnam. They were there since WWII. They were engaged, since 1955, in "advising" U.S. puppet dictator Diem of South Vietnam in his civil war against North Vietnam communists and Viet Cong in the South. But it was not until February 1962 the U.S. quietly formed MACV, Military Assistance Command Vietnam.

In other words, a new military command and structure were already created for Vietnam under U.S. commanding general Westmorland just like they formed for the European theater under Eisenhower and the Pacific theater under MacArthur for WWII.

The U.S. had a management hierarchy in place for a war in Vietnam two years before the alleged Gulf of Tonkin incident. The only element missing was the troops to be commanded... the expendable cannon fodder.

Thus, the logical answer was Vietnam. But that was not mentioned as a reason for fallout shelters or expansion of the military.

Was the U.S. government lying to the American people as it was before WWII and about almost everything since? Yes.

Was Kennedy sucked into preparing for the invasion of Vietnam under the pretense a massive build-up of ground troops would be required in the dispute with the Russians over either Berlin or Cuba? Possibly.

He wasn't a geopolitical genius... or similar to most contemporary U.S. Presidents, any other kind of genius... and he seemed to be too "distracted" by "Hollywood" to spend much time learning what he needed to know to be effective as President.

Still, given Vietnam was the likely destination the government had in mind for Hank and the hundreds of thousands of other young Americans, it would be a troops-on-the-ground affair, not a nuclear holocaust. So one or two would not seem to make a difference.

However had they known about Vietnam, how it was going to turn out and about the one and you are out rule, there might have been a lot of young American males with one.

There is a crude male saying about something really desirable. *"I would give my right... or is it left... nut for that."* Whatever, Hank is pretty sure they would have.

Had they known what their government planned, many of the fifty-eight thousand young men who died and tens of thousands seriously wounded in Vietnam would have had a great enough desire to avoid death or serious, incapacitating injury to have gladly done exactly that. Consider; your life or a testicle. No choice.

After all the inductees were processed, they were given a choice of doing something other than being inducted into the Army, which likely meant being trained as an infantry, frontline soldier with a high probability of death or serious injury in combat.

They could "volunteer" for something else; the Air Force, or a better deal in the Army. Hank can't remember exactly how this worked since they hadn't been given any I.Q. tests or any tests that would indicate they were qualified for anything other than grunt riflemen.

So it didn't seem to him like there was really any upside. If you didn't qualify for something better, you would still be doing some kind of "grunt" work somewhere, if for no other reason than the act of volunteering demonstrated probable limited qualifications.

But there was a whole, hell-of-a-lot of downside. Inductees had a two year commitment. But whether they were dummies who walked into the nearest recruiting station and joined or "volunteered" that day, there was no difference. The commitment would be three years. Not two.

Three years? Not a consideration for Hank. But some saw it differently. One was the ex-friend classmate neighbor from around the corner on 14th St. who set Hank up to be initiated that night their sophomore year and molested the Mercury hood that afternoon the following year..

He went for three to get something better. He did not know, but he would be sorry. Also what he would find out a year later about this would serve to exacerbate whatever ill will he had for Hank that caused him to do what he did those two times in school..

After all of this was over and *"done"* with, all who qualified were sworn into the U.S. military, essentially giving up any rights they might have as human beings.

⚔

The orders read: "SPECIAL ORDER NUMBER 103 6 May 1063 1. TC 261. Following individuals are inducted this station   (4205-04) this date in the Army of the United States in the Grade of Private (E-1) for the active duty commitment of twenty-four months unless sooner discharged or extended by proper authority and assigned for processing and further assignment. Last meal furnished breakfast 7 May 1963. One Army meal ticket furnished. Travel by privately owned vehicle not authorized. Group travel directed. Travel as directed is necessary in the Military Services."

There it was. Hank was in the Army for twenty-four months unless the "proper authority," whatever that might be, decided to keep him longer and send him wherever it decided. This meant, as he assumed; he lost all rights to his person and his future. The government owned both. The words are clear in their specificity.

He also, noted he was "not authorized" to travel by "privately owned vehicle." He would learn later that, fortunately, after the Army owns you it is not so thorough.

All the inductees and "volunteers" were told to be back the next morning at an early time… as the orders state… for their "Last meal." Also, not to bring anything but the clothes they were wearing. No watches. No rings. No Wallets. Nada.

Next AM, after their "Last meal," they were literally herded onto buses.

It was frightening. It was the biggest change ever in the lives of those being treated this way, and it was clear the "proper authority" didn't give a damn. Rather, it was deliberate. It was as if "they," the government, wanted to scare them.

Unlike getting married, becoming a father, this was really frightening. Those happened in familiar surroundings around familiar people, but this? Strangers shipping him off like a head of cattle? Hank resolved one thing they did for him by treating him like that was; *"It will be a cold day in Hell before I will risk my life for the lying cowardly bastards in Washington or their little enablers who were treating me like I am not human."*

They expected to treat people like this and then have them be good little soldiers and put themselves into the line of fire, risking their lives for absolutely no reason but to line the pockets of lying fat cats and their cronies in Washington?

He had already lost his freedom to his government, but now the military of that government that planned to use him as cannon fodder was treating him this way?

He resolved his sole objective during his term of forced confinement would be *"nothing but to survive, nothing else,"* and there was no way in Hell they were going to train that out of him, no matter how hard they tried.

He didn't know how long he was on the bus. No watch. And because of having to get up early, he slept some during the trip. But he could tell it was late afternoon, early evening. So it must have been at least a ten hour bus ride.

━◁┼ ┼▷━

"US Army Reception Station (4057) Ft Polk, La."

They opened the door of the bus, and immediately a huge black man wearing a lot of Sergeant's insignia began screaming for them to get off *"faster, faster."*

The draftees could not have been fast enough to be treated like humans.

They were put into a line going into a building through one door. It didn't take long. Hank sat down in a barber's chair and a guy with clippers, zoomed them across his head just enough times to relieve him of all the hair thereon…took maybe one minute.

Then through another door they walked past a long counter on their left about chest high. There, behind that counter were some men in military fatigue uniforms tossing fatigue clothing onto the counter for them to pick up and take with them out the door at the other end of the room.

They were sorted and taken to various barracks, about fifty in each one. No one in Hank's he had seen anywhere before. He didn't know how they divided or sorted them out. But the guys in his barracks were mostly from Alabama, Mississippi and Louisiana.

Good that he spent so much time working out in California and packed on a good twenty pounds of muscle. This was the toughest, most rustic, bunch he was ever in close contact with, and a number of them wanted to show how tough they were, real intellectual giants. Everything was about how strong they were.

They kept challenging others in feats of strength. Hank had been doing many repetitions of sit ups across the parallel bars in Poinsettia park for almost a year, and had strengthened his stomach to where he could let his 115 pound cousin Donna stand on it. So to forestall any more challenges he challenged them to something he seriously doubted any of them could best him at.

He got up on a top bunk, had one of them hold his feet while he extended his entire body off the other side of the bed with only his legs across the mattress. Then with his entire body cantilevered into thin air parallel with the floor, holding his hands behind his head, he challenged any one of them to join him. None of them were willing to try that one.

After finding out how strong Hank's stomach was, to complement his arms and chest, which they could already see, they decided to play with the others.

His year of physical conditioning in L.A. paid off his first day in the Army. It would also pay dividends during the next year of strenuous physical training in three different programs, enabling him to easily outperform others and even get a choice assignment.

The next morning they were called to formation where they were formed into platoon groups with each of the barracks being a platoon. Then they were called to attention, which was not a problem for all but one of them, probably because they had seen enough movies to know what that meant. But for Hank it was a problem.

He… the only one… was unable to stand at attention. It was not his fault, but that did not spare his being called names and harassed unmercifully.

The problem was his added upper body muscle weight when he was at the counter where clothes were tossed to them. The one doing the sizing-up for clothing could see only their upper bodies.

He assumed Hank weighed two hundred pounds and tossed a pair of pants with at least a thirty-six inch waist to him. Since he wore thirty-two inch waist size pants, the ones given to him would not stay up unless he held them with one hand.

Therefore he was in formation at attention on only his left side with his right hand holding up his pants. However, when he told them this they didn't believe him. Demanded he get to attention. He did. His pants fell down.

After this, someone took him to Supply, or S 4. There, they cut a length of cotton rope long enough to go around his waist and be tied. This is the way he was dressed for the next six days he was in the "Reception Station."

During those days... about five hundred of them, best he could determine... they were given tests for hearing, vision, speech, I.Q., dexterity, math, English, etc., etc.

There were so many of them versus the limited number of testers and equipment, there was a lot of time for them to be kept busy while not being tested. Thus, they were alternatively cycled through testing and policing the grounds, which meant walking around bent over picking up cigarette butts. Six days of testing for the Army to determine what it was going to do with each of them, and conditioning to be good little automatons.

Hank was cautioned by his father and others to never volunteer for anything in the Army. Ignoring that, at formation the next morning, he volunteered.

There was a Sergeant in front of the formation asking if anyone had any carpentry experience. Before anyone else could respond, he quickly raised his hand. Really, how much more boring or demanding could something to do with carpentry be than walking around bent half over picking up cigarette butts?

The Sergeant was one of the older WWII veterans Hank would learn later comprised the majority of the NCOs, Non Commissioned Officers, at Fort Polk. He was given the job of replacing broken windows in the many buildings that were disused for years, but were now being readied to house all the new troops being prepared for action in Vietnam.

Volunteering worked out well for him. Rather than spending the non-testing time walking around picking up cigarette butts for the next five days, he spent the time helping the sergeant take broken pieces of glass out of windows, replace them with new panes and putty, or glaze them into place. But more importantly, while the others were having their time wasted, he was spending time working in close proximity to and talking with a military veteran of over twenty years, learning about what he could expect and what he should do during his time in the Army.

The last morning, May 13, in the "Reception" center, five or six of them were in a small room while everyone else was outside policing the grounds. There was another Sergeant with a lot of stripes at the front of the room. He asked if anyone had *"any questions?"*

Of course, Hank who discovered long before that morning that questioning was the premier way to learn, had a question. So he asked the sergeant *"Why are we stuck in this little room while all the others are still outside, having fun policing the grounds?"*

In a rather annoyed way, the sergeant responded, *"Because you are the only ones taking the Officer's Candidate Test. Any other smart-ass questions?"*

Hank, astutely and quickly ascertained that meant only one percent of the new troops being tested qualified for that test, and decided before the sergeant decided to put him outside with the other ninety-nine percent of the new recruits he should be quiet. So he responded, rather enthusiastically, *"No, Sergeant. Thank you."*

CHAPTER 23

TRAINING BEGINS

H EADQUARTERS U.S. ARMY RECEPTION STATION (4075) Fort Polk, Louisiana SPECIAL ORDERS NUMBER 93 10 May 1963 1. TC 254. RSG dir as indicated this sta. NTI. Asg to: Co M 1ˢᵗ Tng Regt (BCT) USATC(Inf) (4020). Rept date: 13 May 63. Gr / pay gr: PVT E1. ADC: 2yrs...

There was more, but this is the important part. What all of this said was; Hank was assigned to Company M 1ˢᵗ Training Regiment. The training was for the Infantry. He was to be there that day, May 13ᵗʰ, his rank was Private E1, the lowest rank, his pay grade was the same, and his Active Duty Commitment was 2 years.

These were the second orders he received in a week stating his commitment was "twenty-four months" or "2 yrs." He didn't know until almost two years later how important this and the first orders statement that he was "inducted" would be.

The pay grade information was also interesting. He learned only when he received his first pay that he was being paid $78.00 per month from which they took $2.83 FICA, $4.00 Income Tax and some other deductions, leaving him with a total net of $50.00 per month, $1.67 per day, plus room and board. He would be making $610.00 per year. Net.

There were twenty-five names on the order, including his; seven Latin names, ten with serial numbers beginning with "RA," meaning they volunteered... were not inducted.

There were four others. These were grade E2, their active duty commitment was "3yrs," but there was a big difference. Their Base Pay Entry Dates were from 1959 to 1961 and their pay ranged from $111.00 to $640.00 per month.

This meant these guys had previously served and, for whatever reason... one can only imagine... rejoined the Army and taken a cut in rank to go through Infantry Basic Training for six weeks again to become Infantry "grunts" for three more years.

It is obvious why they rejoined the Army. This was before the "Great Society" of Lyndon Johnson when welfare became widely available. The pay of the two at $630.00 and $640.00 per month, based on November 1959 and February 1960 Base Pay Entry Dates, was indicative of multiple dependents.

The military is not a meritorious system. It is like welfare in terms of compensation; the more dependents the higher the pay. There is no way these two went from $78.00 per month to over $600.00 in three years. They had higher pay to begin with because they had multiple dependents. They were both out of the Army for just under six months, and returned within time to retain some rank and benefits.

The proof of that is that one of the other two with a Base Pay Entry Date of September 1960 was earning only $111.10 per month. He did not have dependents. If he had, his pay would have been much higher.

Hank found it depressing that men could not find anything better in the U.S. economy to support their families than risking their lives in almost certain combat situations had to be "despair and disillusionment" of the highest degree.

Surely the U.S., at that time really the richest nation in the world, could do better than that. But that aside, he would learn the next day why there were four of them.

The first night in Company M all the troops were assembled in the Company Mess Hall for a welcoming talk by the West Point graduate Company Commander Captain.

Hank was stunned. He could not believe what he was hearing. The assumption must have been that all the new troops had I.Qs slightly above retarded, and had never been anywhere, seen anything, or studied any history or government, that they had not even attended high school… that they were total and complete dummies… which he would learn in a few days was a valid assumption for the majority of them.

He began to look around the room to see if anyone else might be as stunned as he, but was able to find only one pair of eyes with an incredulous *"you must be shitting me"* look on his face.

He could only imagine what the next six weeks of training and communal living was going to be like.

The next morning they were called to formation in the space behind their barracks. There were four barracks. Thus, four platoons made up the company.

There, in front of each of the platoons, was one of the four volunteer recycles, each with a blue arm band with three sergeant chevrons.

They were the acting platoon Sergeants, the ones who would be marching them around, ensuring the troops were where they were supposed to be, when they were supposed to be there, and in an orderly fashion. It was assumed because of their prior service experience they would be good at this.

The routine the rest of the training days began that first day; a morning run, breakfast, formation again, and off to training consisting of map reading, military organization, communications, fire and maneuver, hand to hand combat and bayonet training that would be beneficial for staying alive and protecting squad and platoon comrades.

Some days they also engaged in physical exercise like Army Drill One. Other days they were trucked off in appropriately named "Cattle Trucks" to firing ranges to practice, or in most cases, learn how to fire their weapons, which were WWII vintage, single firing, standard issue of the day, thirty-caliber rifles.

Hank's platoon's real Sergeant, not the "Acting Jack" with the blue armband, was very hard on him, continually haranguing him with comments like *"You run like you're on the rag"* during the morning run even though he was in much better condition than any of the others. Also, during the monkey bars that it was a requirement to complete before being permitted into the Mess Hall, he was on Hank's case. If a soldier failed to complete the bars he was sent back to the end of the line lessening his time to eat his meal.

Hank did not have a problem with either the run or the bars, but none of the other troops knew that because most could not see what he was doing when being harassed. They could only hear what the Sergeant was saying.

It was infuriating, but he had to take it until one morning at the after breakfast formation, less than two weeks into the six weeks of training, the Sergeant called Hank *"front and center."*

When he got to the front of the formation the Sergeant took the blue Acting Sergeant's armband off the "Acting Jack" and put it on Hank's arm, while directing the ex "Acting Jack" to go take his place in the formation. Then he told Hank to march the platoon to the place of training for that morning.

He could not understand why he, a total military neophyte, was given that responsibility even though he could tell the retread was intellectually challenged.

There were almost five dozen others he could have chosen. But he followed the order, called the platoon to *"attention, left face, forward march, column right,"* to the street, then *"column left,"* up the street to-ward the training site for the morning.

He did not make it a half block before some of the guys began acting up, making comments and being disruptive to the process of marching in step and formation.

He did not have to look to know who they would be. The young-sters, several who were black, were a problem, whether falling asleep during the day or staying up after lights out. They were just kids who should not have been there. They should have been given a chance to grow up.

Their inability to cope with order and discipline at their age could be expected, and they were likely afraid they could be facing death. Hank was. However, they had to be disciplined.

He immediately ordered *"Platoon halt. Left face. At ease."* Then he told them he didn't ask for the position, but that didn't matter. He was going to do the job, and they were going to help by conducting themselves properly and respecting whoever was in charge, which they would do from then on because if they did not they were all going to pay the price. Then he ordered *"Attention. Front leaning rest position, move."*

As they dropped to the pushup position on the asphalt street, he went down with them. Then, while in the position, he looked over the platoon and told those whose backs were not straight to get their butts down and as quickly as possible because the rest were waiting for them to assume the proper position to begin their pushups.

After a couple minutes, when some of them were already sagging, he began counting out the pushups. He knew he could do more than any of them because he could do fifty on the parallel bars before he left L.A. So he just kept doing pushups and counting as, one by one, they began to stop and drop. He did not stop until they were all down. Then he got up and ordered them up.

After ensuring all were in the proper *"attention"* position he ordered, *"At ease,"* and had a heart to heart chat with them in which he explained what they just experienced would be standard operating procedure every time he had a problem with them. Further, if they had a problem with that, he was not their problem, and they should have a chat with whomever they thought was their problem.

Thus, because he understood peer group pressure, and used it effectively that day, he did not have the problem again.

⚊⚔⚊

Because of the blue armband, he was entitled to the private room by the back door of the barracks. But that first night, he went to the recycled guy who was demoted in front of everyone and told him to keep his room, he earned it and apologized for the day.

He was sure the ex "Acting Jack" knew the demotion and promotion was a big surprise to both of them, that he had nothing to do with it and he certainly did not deserve the room of the guy who was earning only $111 after already serving two years.

He did not know at the time, but this decision and the experience would be one that would serve him well when he encountered a similar situation in business ten years later.

Training continued for the remaining four weeks. They did a lot of marching, running and P.T. that included training for the Physical Combat Proficiency Test that included hand grenade throwing and the forty yard low crawl for which they informed Hank he set the post record. All that upper body training in Los Angeles paid off.

The nature of the training proved he was correct about Vietnam. There was not any mountain or city combat training. It was all about jungle warfare, including movies they showed wherein troops were caught in river crossings and jungle situations to their demise. Then they took them into the field to train against making the mistakes portrayed in the films.

They played war in the field with blanks and camped out where the most challenging effort was eating mashed potatoes from the sectioned metal trays before rain washed them away, jumped into and out of foxholes and fired weapons on the firing ranges.

There was a day of in and out of foxholes full of water that caused their pants to fill with sand that made them miserable. That day culminated in a twenty-seven mile forced march with pack, sand filled clothing, weapon, steel helmet and full dress pistol belt.

He felt lucky to make it through the six weeks without any major problems. Most of it was difficult and strenuous, but not that challenging because of his year of physical training in Los Angeles. Just because of that dumb luck, he came through it very well.

Some of the others were not so lucky. One of the Mexican kids got drunk each of the few times they were permitted to go to the enlisted men's place they inappropriately called a "club" that sold cigarettes, beer, candy, snacks, and had a few benches and tables. He had a top bunk he would fall out of, hitting the floor hard enough to awaken everyone.

One went AWOL, absent without leave, was caught and put in the stockade. Another went completely bonkers one night, was in the communal shower threatening suicide. The Military Police came and took him away. They never saw him again.

These were depressing situations, but there was another that depressed him even more.

Several were just kids, eighteen year olds, just out of school. They demonstrated, when not in training, just how young and immature they were. Actually more immature than he remembered anyone he knew being at that age.

Maybe they were just compensating for what they knew their destiny to be. He didn't know, but thought they must have known.

He used a shampoo that came in soft plastic bottles that had flip up nozzles with a small hole that, if the bottle was squeezed hard, would squirt the fluid in the bottle in a stream.

When he emptied one of those bottles and threw it into the barracks trash, one of the kids found it before the trash was emptied. He and another used it as a water gun, playing with it like Hank could remember doing when he was pre-pubescent.

They were training during the day with real guns and bullets for real war and playing "shooting" at one another after training with a makeshift water gun, just as kids were doing all over the country. Yet, those in our government were perfectly willing to send these kids, and as many more as they could get their hands on, to die in some goddamned jungle halfway round the world, for no reason except monetary gain.

Hank did not want to go there. He was old enough to fear being sent into some jungle as a frontline, "grunt" rifleman. He just spent six weeks training to learn how dangerous that could be. But it did not take him the full six weeks to figure that out.

Before the end of training, he applied "*Bob's rule*" again, asking to be entered in training for Airborne and Special Forces.

He didn't want to jump out of good planes, or eat snakes in the jungle, but the six weeks of required Advanced Infantry Training and months of additional Airborne and Special Forces training would buy a few more months of deferment from being sent to Vietnam, which even though the American public was not informed, the numbers being inducted into the military, the refurbishing of Fort Polk, the training he just went through, the creation of MACV, all confirmed what was being done in Vietnam was going to be expanded into a larger war by those in the U.S. Government owned by the Military/Industrial complex that was a major component of the U.S. economy. Therefore, it was best to buy time any way possible to avoid Vietnam.

⤚⤙ ⤙⤚

After Basic Training Hank received a fourteen day leave. The orders were:

HEADQUARTERS FORT POLK Fort Polk, Louisiana SPECIAL ORDERS NUMBER 153 26 June 1963 96. TC 254. REASSIGNMENT directed as indic this sta. NTI. PVT E1 006.00 ADC: 2 YRS BPED: May 63 ETS: May 65 Asg to: Co E 3rd Tng Regt this sta Lv data: 14 DDALVAHP Rept date: 12 Jul 63 Sp instr: WP OA 12 Jul 63 For tng in MOS 111.00 Upon compl of AIT EM for Abn and Sp Forces Tng. (EM rel fr: Co M 1st Tng Regt UNOINDC)

He went back to Dallas to pick up his car, saw Betsy, and decided he should do something worthwhile with the time left before going back to Fort Polk for more Infantry Training and then off to Airborne and Special Forces Training, as the orders specified.

His friend and school classmate, Bill, agreed he would take a road trip with him, but they decided to go out the night before they were going to leave, as they did before Hank went to California.

They went to a club in the Trinity Industrial District west of downtown Dallas in the area where the "Sportatorium," other clubs and entertainment venues were located. Not a terribly bad area, but not one of the greatest.

The club was one in which he had seen entertainers like Ben E. King and others of the same caliber. It was small. The entertainers were close. Intimate. There was a dance floor. It was always a fun place. No trouble, until that night.

He was leaving the dance floor when he saw him approaching. John was a classmate for twelve years. He was always mean and crazy, a bully, six feet three inches... maybe four, way over two hundred pounds. The longest arms Hank has ever seen to this day. Not one you would like to meet, anywhere.

He made some comment about seeing Hank on the dance floor and, sarcastically, about how if he *were a little girl* he would like to get close to his body and all the action he saw when he was dancing. Hank knew this was not going in the right direction.

John and Bill had a stormy past, but they got along reasonably well... considering. Both were sort of juvenile delinquents. John was held back one year in school. Bill's father a Texas Ranger sent him to military academy one year. But that was insufficient. At eighteen, Bill was enlisted in the Navy by his father. He must have been twenty, with two years in the Navy, when they graduated while John was still in high school.

Although Hank had zero desire to be anywhere near John, somehow the three of them ended up in his car for a trip to another club. But for some reason John and Bill got into an argument and John was slapping at Bill.

Just to be safe, Hank pulled off the street into a parking lot. John and Bill got out. It appeared John was going to hit Bill who was only about five feet nine and weighed all of one hundred fifty pounds. Hank got out to prevent that, but shouldn't have. It turned out not to be a smart move.

He walked around the front of the car, stepped between them, facing perpendicular to them with arms outstretched, palms toward both in a "stop" position, and began talking to them, first to John, then... That's as far as he got. As soon as he turned his head toward Bill, John hit him as hard as he could on his left jaw, spun him around, laying him out across the hood of the car.

When he got up Bill was a good twenty feet away. He decided he did not want any of what Hank just got. He didn't want any more either. Thus, he did not reciprocate, which seemed the best approach, given who he was dealing with. That was the end of it.

He doesn't remember how they parted that evening. How they got back to the club in the same car to get rid of John. In fact, he doesn't remember much else except he could not eat anything but soup for an entire week, and Bill critiquing what happened.

He, now brave, said Hank should have hit John back. *"He was so stunned you got right back up, after the way he hit you, you could have taken him, you're big enough."*

He reminded Bill who he was talking about; John they had known for more than a dozen years, John who was crazy, who had been making his living for at least three years, since he either graduated or quit school, playing bumper pool for a hundred bucks a game, the same John who, when a guy who lost three hundred bucks to him in the Colonial Club at the "Strip" in Arlington pulled a forty-five on him, reached across the table, took the gun away from the guy and almost beat the poor guy to death with his own gun, that John? *"You wanted me to hit that John? What? You wanted me to die?"*

Bill reconsidered. Reckoned Hank was right and decided even if he had hit John and prevailed that night, he would have lost. John would have hunted him down until he found and killed him. That was the way he was.

Hank was glad he was doing the thinking for himself that night. If not, he probably would not be here today to recount this story. He never saw John again… thankfully… heard, years later, he was killed in prison, and has no reason to doubt that. He was one crazy mean son-of-a-bitch who was destined to end badly.

There were just some guys Hank went to school with it was best to stay as far away from as possible and hope to never see again. John was not the only one.

Another example was Les who when Hank was in the eleventh grade was one of three guys he was out with one night.

At the end of the evening, rather than wanting to go home Les asked to be taken to see his girlfriend, Linda, a sophomore he had been dating for a while who was the daughter of a preacher that knew Les well.

When he went into Linda's house that night she was already in bed, but her father, knowing Les well, told him it was O.K. for him to go in and talk with her, which was a mistake none of them would have ever guessed.

Les went into Linda's bedroom. But he did not talk with her. He shot and killed her.

Neither Hank nor the other two knew Les had a gun with him while he was with them that night. Hank heard about it the next day when one of the others phoned him about it.

⊷⊶

That post basic training night with Bill in June 1963 Hank was less than six months into his twenty-third year. At that time, given some of the people he had been around, plus the truck and auto accidents, he was lucky to have lived that long. But that was not the worst of it. More was yet to come.

He was barely able to eat because of his jaw, but otherwise O.K., and got underway on his trip with his brave friend Bill the next day.

They went northwest, as he had only fifteen months before on his trip to Los Angeles, up through Amarillo, then farther northwest across New Mexico to Eagle Nest in a beautiful valley with a large lake, and on to Taos that was quiet and beautiful then; before the influx of people and fast food restaurants, where they saw the oldest church in America.

Then they went north to Alamosa, Colorado, up through a big farming valley, and eventually to the Arkansas River, which they drove along back eastward to Canon City... a trip Hank would make many times years in the future.

Bill had to get out of the car and go down to the river to wade in the rapidly flowing water, which Hank advised against because of the current. He lost a shoe after putting only one foot into the water and got stickers in his foot that Hank removed.

They went to Colorado Springs, to the Broadmoor Hotel for dinner. The Smothers brothers who had a comedy TV show at the time were at the next table. Hank's conclusion after that experience was; there was still hope for him. If those two could do it, he could.

They went to the top of Pike's Peak where there is a great view he got with the wind up movie camera he bought in Los Angeles, along with some film of a deer drinking from a stream beside the road as they headed back down. Then they headed back toward Grand Prairie where Bill lived the rest of his life.

This return part of the trip is the most vivid memory of Bill for Hank because he was frightened into saying he was sure he was going to die there, that day, when late in the afternoon near Raton, New Mexico there was a roadside chair lift like those at ski resorts that went up the side of a mountain where it was promoted there was another great view Bill insisted they needed to see.

So, onto the lift and up the side of what appeared to be a mountain that was not "a" mountain because what they could not see from below was about halfway to the top they could see was a valley, the floor of which was hundreds of feet below their feet dangling from the chair lift seat.

He has never seen anyone as scared as Bill was for those few minutes they were hanging high above that abyss Bill was sure they were going to fall into and die except when he looks into a mirror when thinking about it.

He saw Bill once or twice after that, the last time almost twenty years later not long before he died of a heart attack in his mid-forties.

In the interim, he married one of their high school classmates, had a daughter and made his living for years as a Snap-On Tool franchisee.

Hank is glad he had this experience with Bill who he thinks also had a good time... except for the chair lift. He is also glad Bill had his time seeing the world during his short time in the Navy, even if it was forced upon him.

He got to spend time in one of the greatest cities in the world, of which he had great memories, Hong Kong, which he told Hank about, and he was able to confirm for himself many years later.

Hank and Bill had many more memorable good times together over a period of ten years prior to this trip. Bill was a good guy and a good friend. Too bad he went too young, as have too many of Hank's friends.

Life is tenuous, at its best.

CHAPTER 24

ADVANCED INFANTRY TRAINING

July 12, 1963, late afternoon, Fort Polk, Louisiana, there was a long line down the walkway parallel to the street in front of the Orderly Room of Company E 3rd Training Regiment when Hank parked the Chevy at the side of the street and got in line to await his turn to report for duty. He was near the end of the line… he never liked to be first, or early.

After quite a while, his turn to report came. He went into the Orderly Room and presented his orders to the First Sergeant who checked them out, welcomed him, gave his barracks assignment to him and told him to go to Supply to pick up bed linens.

At that time Hank said, *"Sergeant, what do I do with my car?"* The Sergeant replied, *"Car? What car?"* Hank said, *"The gold Chevrolet parked out front."*

The Sergeant pointed out that he was not supposed to have a car there. Hank corrected him, pointing out the fact that the orders said nothing about not having a vehicle, and, further, given his previous orders specifically directed travel by "privately owned vehicle" was "not authorized," and the current orders were silent on the issue, there did not seem to be a prohibition against his having a car, which, by the way, was the best means of transportation available for his return to Fort Polk that is in the middle of nowhere.

He told Hank to take a seat. He did.

After all the other new Company E members were signed in the Sergeant went into an adjacent room. After a few minutes, he stuck his head out the door and directed Hank to join him in the room.

It was the Company Commander's Office. He was the only one who got to meet the Company Commander upon reporting for duty. He doesn't usually perform that task. But, for Hank, that evening he made an exception.

All was resolved amicably. They decided to impound his vehicle in a nearby NCO parking lot and take the keys. After training was over in six weeks he could have the keys. Also, if there were passes granted, he might, possibly, be permitted to use the vehicle.

⇥⬩⬩⬩⬩⬩⬩⬩⬩⬩⬩⬩⬩⬩⬩⬩⬩⬩⬩⬩⬩⬩⬩⬩⬩⬩⬩⬩⬩⬩⬩⬩⬩⬩⬩⬩⬩⬩⇤

Training began normally, pretty much the same as Basic Training. Up early, formation, run or P.T., monkey bars and breakfast. Then off to training, which was a little different.

It was more about weapons. That is the reason it was referred to as training for MOS 111.00, or "Triple Stick" as it was called. It was heavy weapons for Infantry, or heavier than what he was exposed to in Basic Training.

No more map reading, or other subjects they must have assumed were adequately learned in Basic Training, or they didn't care. There was much time spent on the firing ranges that were farther away from the Company Area, so there was less marching. The troops were usually trucked to training in the "Cattle Trucks."

Then one Friday, not much more than a week after training began. The company was out on a firing range. A jeep drove up to the range. The driver got out and went to the NCO in charge.

After a few words, the NCO called Hank to him and told him to go with the driver.

When in the Jeep, he asked the driver where they were going. He said the First Sergeant wanted Hank back at the Company. Then, when they got back he told Hank the *"Top,"* or First Sergeant, was waiting for him in the Mess Hall. So that's where he went.

The Sergeant was sitting at one of the tables drinking coffee, reading a paper and eating some cake. Rather than telling him to sit down, he said, *"Cooky just made some cake. Go tell him to give you a piece and get some coffee, if you want some."*

He went to the cook. Got a big, warm piece of Chocolate cake and a cup of coffee, and returned to the Sergeant's table where he then told Hank to have a seat, go ahead and eat the cake, asked him if it was good and made brief conversation about the training.

Then he slid Hank's car keys across the table and tossed a small piece of paper to him with them as he said, *"Here is a weekend pass. I want you to take Specialist Fourth Class Smith to Alexandria for the weekend. His father died and the funeral is tomorrow. Have a good time. See you Monday morning."*

The Specialist was a member of the Training Regiment staff who worked in the kitchen. The sergeant spent a lot of time in the Mess Hall during the day, reading, drinking coffee and taking care of his paperwork of which there seemed to be a lot. He had gotten to know the Specialist and liked him. That was good for Hank because he had a vehicle.

Alexandria, Louisiana is a good sized city about sixty miles east of Fort Polk where England Air Force Base is located. Unlike the town near Fort Polk, Leesville, or *"Fleasville"* as the troops called it after having been there on a pass, it is a real city with a lot to do. He had a good, unexpected weekend. Thanks to the Impala, again.

He was back in training a few days the next week when the Jeep arrived on the range again. The First Sergeant wanted him back at the Company again. Same deal as before. Get some coffee and cake. Have a seat. But this time he wanted to talk.

He informed Hank he was looking at his file, was curious about his architectural/construction background, and how much building experience he had, which they discussed for some time.

Then he addressed his good physical condition, and asked if he thought he could score in the ninety percentile range on the PCPT if he did not train as much as the rest of the company, to which he replied, "*Yes. That would not be a problem.*"

He then asked Hank if he was excused from most of the training, except weapons qualifying, would he be O.K. with putting in extra training time if he did not qualify satisfactorily. Hank had no idea where he was going with this, but, of course, he agreed.

They finished their cake and coffee, The Sergeant said, "*Let's go.*"

They got into his Jeep and he drove to the base hospital. There he introduced Hank to the Bird Colonel in charge of the hospital.

He was more doctor than Colonel. Based on his conduct, Hank assumed he was probably a reserve officer who had the misfortune to be "called up" because of the expanding military needs. He preferred doctor to Colonel.

From the beginning of the meeting, it was obvious Top had spoken with him about Hank at length prior to the visit, which meant it was also before their little chat in the Mess Hall. The Colonel got right into explaining what he had in mind.

Like the rest of Fort Polk, the hospital was not used for years... probably since WWII, certainly not since the Korean conflict a decade previous. The Colonel was obviously aware of the magnitude of the planned troop buildup and thus, the needs of the hospital.

He already had rough plans for what he wanted. What he need-ed was someone to do final plans and supervise construction of the changes and improvements.

Based on Hank's previous understanding with the First Sergeant, it was agreed he would take on responsibility of the plans and su-pervision of construction for rebuilding the interior of the hospital under the supervision of the Colonel.

Two and one-half months after his induction into Uncle Sam's Army, he was being driven to work, had a desk and drafting table at the hos-pital, was out of "Grunt" training and reporting directly to… actually working with… a Bird Colonel. Not bad. Fast Track.

In reality, he was no longer taking orders and reacting to them as in Basic Training, and as everyone else who reported for AIT Training with him two weeks previously was still doing, and would be for an-other month. He had a desk and a job with at least two dozen soldiers reporting to him. He also had some time to do things for himself.

Even though he had a sweet deal in terms of his job, he was still living in the Barracks in the big, open bay with more than twenty oth-ers who were aware he was receiving some kind of special treatment. They didn't know what it was, but they were aware he was missing from most of the training they were doing every day.

As was usual, one night after lights out, the blacks on the floor were gathered in the far corner from his bunk, making noise, pre-venting him from sleeping. He hollered something like, *"Shut up! Go to sleep."*

Then, shortly afterward, he heard someone coming up behind him as someone else yelled *"He has a knife."*

He was on a top bunk. There was a bay of tall metal lockers be-tween his bunk and the next one. He had his back to the lockers. Whoever was coming up behind him was between his bunk and the lockers. He rolled over and hit him hard in the face as he rolled. Whoever it was went backward into the lockers, making a hell of a commotion.

Either the next day or the following, he was standing in the line to the Mess Hall talking with the guy in front of him. He did not see it coming. The biggest, most muscular black guy in the company walked by, and as he did swung his steel helmet he was holding by its chin strap up and hard, hitting Hank in the mouth.

He instantly began spitting out parts of broken teeth and blood. The bastard broke his two upper front teeth. One was broken off diagonally from the gum on one side downward to halfway down on the other side. The other was badly cracked.

⚊⚊⚊

Hank swears he has known, and even been helped by some very nice black people in his life, including his summer workmates seven years before, but to be honest, he also swears many of the ones he lived with in the Army were undisciplined, belligerent bastards. And some of the people he knew with experience in Vietnam, including a high school classmate spoke of them with great disdain. He guessed they didn't like being there any more than he did.

Given what he received as a military fix for his broken teeth was a lot of gold showing in the front of his mouth, he could empathize with that position, at least for the balance of his time as an enlisted soldier because he was reminded every day, every time he looked in the mirror.

But he continued his hospital project, qualified with the standard issue, infantry semi-automatic M-14 rifle, as he had in Basic Training. Got experience firing and qualified as necessary with the M-60 machinegun... his second favorite after the Browning Automatic Rifle he also qualified with, as well as the Carbine, 45 pistol and two shoulder fired anti-tank weapons, the old WWII Bazooka and the newer

Recoilless Rifle, so-called because, unlike the Bazooka, it was rifled, causing the projectile to spin and be more accurate.

He received training in setting and disarming land mines, and throwing live grenades into target foxholes. He also scored better than he agreed with the Sergeant on the Physical Combat Proficiency Test for which the Sergeant commended him.

He also graduated Advanced Infantry Training with the MOS 111.00 on or about August 24th with everyone else in Company E 3rd Training Regiment, but he did not receive orders for his next duty, as he had upon completion of Basic Training, and as had all other members of Company E. Nor did he leave when the other trainees in the company left.

He was to have received orders to move on to Airborne and Special Forces training as shown in his original orders for AIT, but did not. He stayed and continued the architectural and construction work at the hospital.

He guessed they determined what he was doing for the war effort was more important than getting to Airborne and Special Forces training… what must be called another dumb luck deferral from Vietnam, and something that would happen to him twice again; eleven and eighteen months later.

The only paper placed in his Records Jacket at the end of AIT Training was a "CERTIFICATE OF CLEARANCE AND/OR SECURITY DETERMINATION UNDER EO 10450" that showed a classification of "SECRET," which it indicated as the second highest classification after the highest, "Top Secret."

That paper dated "19 August 1963," which was during the last week of training, indicated "DATE INVESTIGATION COMPLETED 31 July 1963," the end of the second week of AIT training when he began the hospital work, was signed by a "Captain, AIS (Army Intelligence Service), Security Officer, G2" on 19 August 1963.

He didn't have a clue what this was about.

Then a week after the AIT course ended, the First Sergeant called him in for another chat in which he addressed the fact he was perusing his personnel file again and noted he took the Officer's Candidate Test at the "Reception Center." Then informed him of something he was not aware: he passed the test.

The Sergeant asked him if he might like to be an officer to which, of course, he responded in the affirmative. Then he suggested he might consider flight training and being a Warrant Officer, not a Lieutenant, pointing out the advantages of learning to fly at the government's expense, and told him both fixed and rotary wing schools were available.

Hank told him he never had a desire to be a pilot, and would prefer to be a Lieutenant.

The Sergeant said he would get the application form. He did, and during the next week Hank got the required documents together, and the Sergeant had the application typed.

To complete the form, he asked which OCS School Hank preferred, Engineers, Artillery, or Infantry. He said that would be his order of priority.

＝＜＋＋＞＝

When he received his pay for August he noted it was still $78.00 per month with the same deductions, and he was still netting $50.00 but he was able to see information he did not recall on his previous paperwork. He was making more than he thought.

The other deduction of $18.75 was for a Savings Bond he doesn't remember whether was an elective, or it was an automatic contribution to the war effort to which he was opposed. But the important part was the Army was paying his child support of $55.00.

That meant he was not making just $610 per year. He was making $124.58 per month, or over $1,500 per year, although he was still netting only $50 per month in his pocket.

He was making $163 per year more than the E2 he replaced as "Acting Jack" in Basic Training who had three years of active duty.

This information also proved he was correct in his assessment of why the other recycles rejoined the Army.

Given his pay with one dependent at a court fixed rate, his guess was their pay at over $600 per month indicated each of them had three or four dependents.

He really felt sorry for those poor guys. He thought having to rejoin the military to support a family, as we would say today; "*sucked.*"

⋙＋⋘

The "APPLICATION FOR APPOINTMENT" to "OFFICER CANDIDATE SCHOOL" was completed September 6, 1963. The Top Sergeant called Hank in to sign it, and informed him there was a slight hitch regarding what they discussed about schools.

Engineer School was not available. So they scratched that out and inked in Artillery and Infantry as number one and two choices, in that order.

Hank had applied "*Bob's rule*" again, big time, and went back to his construction supervisory job to await news about the application.

A few days later the Sergeant called him in again. His application was accepted contingent upon going before a Board of Officers who made final decision about acceptance or rejection.

There were three Field Grade Officers. Put him "*At Ease*" and began questioning. The last question was, "*You are in a combat situation. Two of your men jump up and begin running to the rear. What do you do, private?*"

Hank responded, "*I would shoot them, Sir.*"

"*Attention, dismissed.*"

As he was leaving, he thought "*Oh crap. I am sure that was the right answer.*" But he was so abruptly dismissed he was sure it was over.

When he got back to the company Orderly Room, the First Sergeant asked him, *"Well. How did you do?"*

He told him he thought he screwed up. He was standing in front of his desk. The Sergeant said, *"Just a minute,"* picked up his phone, called someone he obviously knew, had a brief conversation, asked if Hank passed the board, got up, walked around his desk to where Hank was standing, stuck out his hand and said, *"Congratulations, Lieutenant."*

⊨⊣ ⊢⊨

He went back to work at the hospital again to await orders for OCS. But before the end of September, the First Sergeant called him to the Orderly Room again.

When he got there, the Captain wanted to see him. So he and the Sergeant went into his office where they discussed the state of his work at the hospital and, since it was winding down after two and one-half months, they had a way he could be of more help to them even if he needed to continue at the hospital a while longer.

His platoon Sergeant during AIT was another WWII veteran. He was in his mid-forties, pretty heavy, big gut. He put himself to sleep every night with a six pack just killing time until he had sufficient time to retire reasonably well.

The Captain informed Hank they had a RA platoon coming into the next AIT class that would be going to Airborne Ranger and Special Forces training after AIT as a requirement of their obligation. Problem was; they would have to pass stringent physical requirements before entering Airborne training, and the company did not have anyone who could handle that training job. They thought he could. He agreed. Thus, as he would another time, Hank would train soldiers destined for airborne although he was not airborne trained.

The suggestion was, since he would be upgraded to Rank E5, or Sergeant, upon entry to OCS, they would go ahead and upgrade his rank status to Sergeant E5, without the pay increase, but he would have all the duties and rights of the rank, including the three permanent Sergeant's Chevrons on his sleeves, shiny helmet liner with Sergeant insignia, private room, access to his car at all times and NCO club rights.

⊷⊶

COMPANY E 1ST BATTALION 3D TRAINING REGIMENT (AIT) Fort Polk, Louisiana UNIT ORDERS NUMBER 27 10 October 1963 1. TC 315. UP par 12 AR 624-200 fol indiv APPOINTED to TEMP ACT NCO GR indic. TO BE ACTING SERGEANT (E5): PVT E-2 Co E 1st Bn Tng Regt (AIT)

Thus, five months and four days after induction into the Army, Hank completed two Infantry training programs, helped remodel a military hospital, received an appointment to Officer's Candidate School, had a private room, was a member of the Advanced Infantry Training staff, was walking around wearing a uniform it usually took three years to earn and had NCO club privileges. Fast track? Vietnam was getting farther and further away.

Although he had not received orders indicating the change, he noticed on these TEMP ACTING NCO orders his rank as of the end of September was upgraded from E1 to E2, and his September MILITARY PAY VOUCHER also indicated this rank change included a pay increase from $78 to $84.50, a whole $6.50 for a one pay grade move up.

There was something else on the PAY VOUCHER that appeared again on his October VOUCHER. There was a notation in the "remarks" section of both stating: "Transfer to 504 AG Co ADMIN APO 326 NY, NY," an overseas military address for Europe that indicated a high probability he was to be assigned to Germany.

This was never explained to him, so he doesn't know how it happened, but it indicated that after AIT he was headed to Europe - not Airborne training, and certainly not Vietnam.

He never found out about this or the "SECRET" security clearance either, but this one was important. It meant he was not going to be sent to Vietnam, and the Army had, for some unknown reason, decided not to send him to Airborne training, as he requested, and was the only reason he was in AIT. More dumb luck or...

Someone... a person, an individual he did not know and who could not have known him... intervened and decided, or more likely, was ordered to stop him, a lowly draftee, from training to jump out of airplanes, as he requested, and save him from Vietnam by redirecting him to Europe. And it was obvious this person and/or whoever ordered this was way above Hank's immediate command, as they were seemingly unaware he was accepted to OCS because his orders for OCS were not cut at the time.

Now the Army works in mysterious ways, but this was beyond mysterious, and caused him to reflect on Heidi's parting comments about his being sent to Germany.

Did she, her family or those she could have been working with, or for, actually have contacts within the U.S. Government or its military that could reach this far down within its structure and accomplish this? If so, Hank would be eternally grateful, but there were serious implications for him and every other American as well, especially if she and/or her family, contacts or whoever could pull this off were connected with those in Brazil, Germany and the U.S. who had not given up on totalitarian world domination.

⊷≺╀ ╀≻⊶

The RA, Regular Army, group arrived shortly after Hank's enhanced status to Sergeant. He began getting them out for early morning two mile runs, Physical Training in Army Drill One and dealing with them and all their problems as his platoon Sergeants had with him and his mates in Basic and AIT Training. The only difference being, he did not harass any of them, as his platoon Sergeant did him in Basic Training. But he was not planning to promote any of them.

He didn't think there was one of them worth promoting. They seemed fairly normal. Just a little slower than he was accustomed to, even in the construction business where he worked with laborers and low wage personnel. These young men did not seem like they were the sharpest butter knives in the military drawer. So he decided to find out what he was working with.

After the first week, he went to the Orderly Room and pulled their personnel files, got their Army G T scores that correlate to civilian I.Q. test scores, wrote them in a column, added them up and divided by the number of them. The result was another of those "despair and disillusionment" moments.

Here was a large group of young men who voluntarily joined the U.S. Army for training and deployment as Airborne Rangers for a period of three years whose scores equated them, relative to the population at large, as having an average I.Q. six percent below the low end of what could be called "normal."

No wonder he was having a little trouble with them... at times, more than a little. They seemed to have as much trouble getting along with one another as he was having with them. He did not know his room at the rear of the barracks would qualify him as the equivalent of domestic violence officer.

This bunch was much less, shall we say "sociable" than the two groups he lived with in the previous few months. The reason for that was the intelligence "thing" that no one wants to acknowledge. Whereas the prior two groups contained a majority of draftees, representative of the general population, these were all volunteers.

Hank insists based upon experience and common sense, he can assure anyone who doubts it that most... not all, but most... who volunteer for the military are not people who expect to excel in the private sector... then or today, keeping in mind there are exceptions.

It is not politically correct to talk about it, but the majority of people are not intellectually equipped, nor properly schooled, to effectively cope with our increasingly complex and demanding society, or with sudden radical change such as that experienced in moving from the freedom of private life to the totally controlled and highly... at least in 1963... disciplined military life. It is just too big a change for easy adjustment for some.

That and the deterioration, if not complete collapse, of societal norms are the primary reasons for the breakdown of discipline and personnel problems in the military, including suicides and rapes, and increasing societal dysfunction we are witnessing.

Coping is intellectual, as is, in most cases, the difference between failure and success.

One evening, two of these recruits got so upset with Hank for intervening in their confrontation they decided to take whatever their problem was out on him instead of one another.

This was another time his physical appearance rescued him, as it would in another situation he would experience in his Army career.

He went to the back door of the barracks, opened it and invited them outside, one at a time. They demurred.

This was not his only experience in the Army... not just the one of that evening, but the total experience of dealing with people like these... that solidly confirmed in his mind there was no way in hell he would want to be in a life or death situation with most of the product the Army was attracting as volunteers and pumping out of training. No way!

The six weeks with this group could not end soon enough. It also informed Hank that being a training Sergeant rank E5 at a base pay of $145.24 per month was probably not the best deal the U.S. Army had to offer.

CHAPTER 25

THE DAY "AMERICA" DIED

HEADQUARTERS FORT POLK Fort Polk, Louisiana 71446 SPECIAL ORDERS NUMBER 284 19 November 1963 2. TC 221. Fol reassignment dir. WP TDN 2142010 01 1461 1462 1463 1464 1465 P1513 S99-599 PVT E2 111.10 Co E 3d Tng Regt USATC (4020) Asg to: US Army Artillery and Missile Sch, Ft Sill, Okla Rept date: NLT 1 Dec 63 Lv data: 9 DDALV WP OA: 22 Nov 63 Auth: Ltr, HQ 4th US Armr, AKA DC-B SUBJECT, Selected Applicant for Army Officer Candidate Sch, dtd 15 Nov 63 ADC: 2 yrs BPED: 6 May 63 ETS: 5 May 65 EDCSA: 1 Dec 63

November 22, 1963. Having decided to take his nine days leave before OCS, Hank said his goodbyes in the morning, got into the Impala and headed toward Dallas to have a little R&R, rest and recreation, he thought was deserved after his recent six week ordeal and prior to his coming six months of the unknown.

The Army paid $30.96 in travel pay for the trip from Fort Polk, Louisiana to Fort Sill, Oklahoma. That was six cents per mile for the five hundred sixteen miles the Army calculated the distance to be, which wasn't bad given the cost of gasoline in 1963 was no more than two cents per mile. In fact, six cents per mile was about what travel cost then.

He did a lot of highway travel in the 1960s, and the average cost per day was twenty dollars. Ten dollars for food and a night in a Holiday Inn, plus five hundred miles at two cents per equals twenty dollars for gas, food and lodging for a five hundred mile day.

The portion of the trip to Dallas was about one hundred ninety miles. So he was going to spend almost twelve dollars of his travel pay on the seven hour trip.

He burned through less than six dollars a few miles west of Shreveport on Highway 80 when it came on the news: *"President John Kennedy has been shot in Dallas."*

He spent the rest of the trip listening to the coverage of this on the radio. What unfolded was unbelievable... still is today.

The story was that a guy named Oswald shot Kennedy through the head at about 12:30 PM as his limousine was going downhill around the curve on Elm Street in Dealey Plaza toward the railroad underpass that would take him westward out of downtown Dallas... and he did it from the 5th story window of a building in Dealey Plaza at the top of the hill.

Hank spent a lot of time on firing ranges during the prior six months with a number of different weapons. He was also familiar with the location of the shooting, having traveled though that very spot probably hundreds of times during the last seventeen years.

He remembers thinking; *"That Oswald guy must be one hell of a shot, hitting something the size of a human head at that range is damned good, but doing it when it is moving away, downhill and around a curve at over twenty miles per hour? Well............"*

After he supposedly killed Kennedy, Oswald managed to get to the Texas Theater on Jefferson Boulevard in Oak Cliff, a theater where Hank went to movies after high school.

He could not fathom why he would have gone there because to get there he would have to cross the area where Kennedy was shot and all that was going on there, unless he went east, then south and back to the west to take the Zangs viaduct, bridge, that is the only other route to Oak Cliff from that part of Dallas. This did not make any sense to him.

If Oswald shot Kennedy and was trying to get away it would have made much more sense to keep going either east or north to get away and avoid capture. To double back, he would have to be not very bright, or something else was going on with this.

There was a lot more going on with this.

The previous June 4th Kennedy signed Executive Order 11110 authorizing the government treasury to again begin issuing silver certificates, U.S. currency backed by the nation's silver reserves, essentially curtailing Federal Reserve control of the money supply, thereby potentially limiting the expansion of government and its activities like unnecessary wars to the availability of silver in the reserves or what the economy could afford.

This one act could have sealed the President's fate, but he had also recently taken action to begin getting the few troops there out of Vietnam and stop the building nonsense of invading that country. But it was obvious to Hank from his recent experience; anything but that was happening. The troop build-up was accelerating and the training was definitely for Vietnam.

All most could do in November 1963 and for some time after, was wonder why, or question who killed Kennedy. However, in the intervening years that question has been answered for anyone intelligent enough not to choose to believe the lies of the Warren Commission of which Gerald Ford was a member, and accept reality.

Anyone with the intelligence to connect simple dots can go on line, Google the Kennedy Assassination, click the site "Secret Service ordered to stand down," watch the video and question why the head of the Secret Service detail with the duty to protect the President ordered the Secret Service Agents on the steps at the back of the President's Limousine to abandon it a few minutes prior to his being killed.

If you do this, watch the agent who would have been between Kennedy and Oswald on the right rear of the limo ordered off the car shrugging his shoulders and holding his arms out asking why in total incredulity.

This video, more than anything, demonstrates who killed John Kennedy and covered it up, especially given the Zapruder home movie that shows the shot that killed Kennedy came from his right front, the direction of the "grassy knoll," not from behind, as confirmed by six dozen forensic investigators over the years since.

Multiple writings and research behind them indicate the warmongering powers within and behind the U.S. Government did both the assassination and the cover up.

According to the book "*JFK And the Unspeakable*" by James Douglas, in addition to probably stopping the Vietnam War, Kennedy was at odds with the C.I.A. over Cuba and the Joint Chiefs of Staff over their plans for false flag events and their desire to attack the Soviet Union while they thought the U.S. had the advantage.

Of course, as the removal of the agent from the back of the limo to eliminate the possibility of questions about how Oswald could have made the shot around the agent shows, the Secret Service was also involved.

This was a vast conspiracy, contrary to what the naïve '*It can't happen here*" American public choose to believe.

Had he remained alive as President, JFK would likely have stopped the invasion of Vietnam and the following twelve years of useless war costing fifty-eight thousand American lives, tens of thousands of seriously wounded and hundreds of thousands of Vietnamese lives, as well as the death of the "America" that was… the America of promise and prosperity that has also since been further brutalized by more unnecessary war and unbridled expansion of the government permitted by inflation of the monetary base through Federal Reserve issued fiat currency not backed by silver or anything else.

That day Kennedy was killed, November 22, 1963, was the day the real America died. That day was the zenith of the American dream, and the death of it and the concept of "America" that existed since 1776. But it was also the day those who have willfully been destroying America for decades for personal gain began to seize a firm grip on the tiller of the United States ship of state prevailed over the dream, the concept and the people of "America."

Shortly after taking office, Johnson supported Federal Reserve currency issuance... money out of thin air that carries an interest cost payable to it by the government, but is not redeemable for gold or silver from the government reserves, i.e., free money that permits tremendous unaffordable government expansion without cost except to the people thru interest payments and denigration of their purchasing power, and impoverishment through inflation... eventually reversing JFK's Executive Order and beginning removal of Silver Certificates from circulation.

Johnson also expedited the buildup for the Vietnam invasion, then he and others in the government created the Gulf of Tonkin false flag event, lied to the American people and United Nations, and officially began that conflict in earnest.

By the time he left office in January 1969, following in FDR's footsteps, he was responsible for tremendous unnecessary war costs in lives and money, massive government expansion through his "Great Society" welfare programs and spending more than all previous Presidents combined, beginning a seemingly unstoppable spending spree of continuing destruction.

In the intervening fifty years between JFK's death and 2014 the United States was at war on a preemptive basis over twenty-four years, almost fifty percent of the time, in countries that posed no threat to the security of the United States.

The U.S. military has been greatly expanded into occupations in more than one hundred and twenty countries. The "defense" industry has experienced phenomenal growth, as has the wealth of those involved in it.

The government has greatly expanded control over the population, and President Bush began to deemphasize the title of Chief Executive Officer of the United States, favoring Commander-in-Chief of the United States Military... clearly demonstrating the priorities of those in control of the government Barrack Obama has studiously followed... nay, greatly expanded.

One of those priorities is taking as much money as possible from every productive citizen to continue to fund the out of control government, especially the Commander-in-Chief's preemptive military being utilized in pursuit of world hegemony, as was re-emphasized for Hank during his first seven months in the military..."re-emphasized" because of his first encounter only two years before when in 1961 the collection arm of the government, the I.R.S., just had to take a little more from him.

Although he was involuntarily serving in the U.S. military in 1963, the I.R.S. was still determined to squeeze more out of him... improperly, which has in his experience been their consistent *modus operandi*.

Even with his meager military pay, they decided there was an impossible "deficiency" of $120 in his tax payment for the year. They would do exactly the same the next year of 1964 when he served the full year, which seemed strange to Hank causing him to wonder if they could be taking back $120 each year from those who were serving. Or maybe it was only those who entered taxpaying status prior to induction.

Doubtful they would do that to the poor unfortunates who volunteered because they would not have volunteered if they were making enough to have to pay taxes.

The United States of America, Ronald Reagan's *"shining city on a hill,"* has been dragged down off that hill and into the gutter among the worst states the world has known... those so many Americans died to ostensibly bring about a cessation of their evil deeds.

Anyone who chooses not to believe this will inherit his just rewards. But anyone who desires to be informed about the reality of what his country has become since it has been under control of the evil shepherding it into the waste bin of history amid the company of those failed states that took similar courses the United States is on, need read only two books, in addition to *"JFK And the Unspeakable"*: Jesse Ventura's book, *"63 Documents the Government Doesn't Want You to Read"* and *"Family of Secrets"* by Russ Baker about the Bush family.

The fact people within the government and military of the United States produced official documents, including plans and details of operation for assassinating leaders of countries in the same way Kennedy was killed, killing people whose only "crime" is to disagree with those in control of the government, planning to kill American citizens by flying a commercial airliner into a building in this country and blaming it on a foreign country to enable the U.S. to start a war against that country, and many other criminal acts, should be sufficient evidence to cause any decent law abiding citizen to desire to distance himself and his country from these people by whatever means within his power.

This written evidence of the moral and ethical decay wrought on their country from the top down is more than sufficient for the removal of these people, and seeking the ultimate penalty for those who were also key participants in the assassination of President Kennedy.

The evil disclosed in these books, which continues, is like an operating manual not only for the assassination of Kennedy but of the "America" that was for almost 190 years Reagan's *"shining city on a hill,"* an assassination of the beacon for the entire world... the killing of a bright future for all of us.

The day John F. Kennedy was assassinated was the day the real "America," the "America" of yore that was the shining light, the beacon of freedom and hope, died.

CHAPTER 26

OCS PART 1: SURVIVAL

H EADQUARTERS U. S. ARMY ARTILLERY AND MISSILE CENTER Fort Sill, Oklahoma 73504 SPECIAL ORDERS NUMBER 282 2 December 1963 5. TC 310. UP par 11 AR 624-200 the fol indiv APPOINTED TO TEMP GR indic. TO BE SERGEANT (E5)

After that on these orders were listed seventy-six names of which all but three had serial numbers beginning with "RA," meaning they joined the Army voluntarily. Of those, seventeen had rank of E3 to E5, indicating they were in the Army longer than the other fifty nine. That meant fifty six joined with the specific understanding they would enter Officer Candidate School even though they had no guarantee they would graduate, and if they did not, they would still have a three to four year commitment to remain in the Army as enlisted personnel.

There were additional orders for another thirty-three Candidates to join the class under the same conditions. Thus, the total class was one hundred and nine candidates of which over one hundred had at least a three year commitment whether they graduated, or not.

This seemed like a risky bet for them. But, on the other hand, it made Hank question; *"Why me? All of my orders specified 'ADC,' Active Duty Commitment, of either "twenty four months" or '2 yrs' with an 'ETS,' Estimated Time of Separation, of '5 May 1965."*

Given he had only seventeen months of commitment remaining and six months of it would be spent in OCS training that was rumored to cost the Army fifty thousand 1963 dollars, almost five hundred thousand 2013 dollars per candidate, with an extremely high failure to complete rate, Hank didn't think he seemed a good investment for the Army.

After reading the congratulatory letter from the school Commandant for being *"selected to attend the U.S. Army Artillery and Missile Officer Candidate School,"* he had second thoughts about whether it was a good investment for him either. The specter of Vietnam was the only reason he concluded it would, as the Commandant said, *"prove worthwhile."*

But, rather than endeavor to explain the cause of his "second thoughts," let's permit the words of the Commandant, exactly as they were written, underline and all, explain what Hank had gotten himself into:

U.S. ARMY ARTILLERY AND MISSILE OFFICER CANDIDATE SCHOOL
OFFICE OF THE COMMANDANT
FORT SILL, OKLAHOMA

SUBJECT: U. S. Army Artillery and Missile Officer Candidate Course
TO: Selected U. S. Army Artillery and Missile Officer Candidate School Applicants

"I wish to congratulate you on having been selected to attend the U. S. Army Artillery and Missile Officer Candidate School. Your period will prove worthwhile and interesting and I wish you success in attaining your goal of becoming a commissioned officer in the United States Army.

"The mission of this Officer Candidate School is to produce junior officers who have the professional knowledge, character, and capabilities for practical leadership required to lead Artillery elements successfully in combat.

"In undertaking officer candidate training you should consider carefully what will be expected of you. <u>You will not be afforded the opportunity to resign from OCS unless you are to be turned back because of sub-course failure or have a valid compassionate reason for separating.</u> You must pass all of the academic sub courses and you must meet the exceptionally high standards of leadership which have been established. You will be subjected to rigorous mental and physical pressure throughout a twenty-three week period. You will be expected to perform a variety of tasks in an exemplary manner, using the least time possible. You must be prepared to face strict discipline, vigorous physical training, and exceptionally high standards of soldierliness.

"With regard to the vigorous physical training program, I wish to forewarn you that the physical conditioning program conducted at OCS is of a considerably higher caliber than most programs being conducted in other units and is conducted under extreme weather conditions….. Be prepared upon your arrival to become rapidly acclimated to the Fort Sill area which is very hot in summer and very cold in winter.

"You must apply yourself diligently to the accomplishment of each task in order to complete the course successfully.

"The daily schedule is so confining that you will have little free time. During the first five weeks candidates are restricted to the immediate OCS area and are not allowed to have visitors...... As you advance in the course you will acquire more freedom, provided your academic and leadership grades are sufficiently high and you are not restricted for disciplinary reasons.

"Each candidate is required to pass satisfactorily such academic subjects as Artillery Transport, Gunnery, Target Acquisition, Communications, Materiel, and Tactics and Combined Arms. The grades from these subjects comprise 65% of your overall grade and are on a college level in degree of difficulty. A working knowledge of basic mathematics, logarithms, and trigonometry is required of each candidate in order to complete successfully the Gunnery and Target Acquisition sub courses. Speed and accuracy are stressed, and few and far between are the candidates who maintain passing grades without serious and regular study. The remaining 35% of your grade is based on your leadership performance.

"The OCS Program is designed to graduate second lieutenants who have a military academic proficiency plus demonstrated leadership ability. It is traditional that we turn out top-flight lieutenants of Artillery. I hope that you will meet the high standards of this school and that you successfully complete the course. GOOD LUCK!"

C.A. Christian Jr.
Colonel, Artillery
Commandant

Completing the U. S. Army Artillery and Missile Officer Candidate Course was anything but "LUCK!" Luck had nothing to do with it. To finish this course required suppression of one's desire to kill everyone who was a member of the training cadre, in addition to successfully completing the academic program and the extreme physical requirements while being starved into a physically weakened state and functioning under extreme mental and physical duress.

It was not until the movie based on the novel by Aleksander Solzhenitsyn about life in the Soviet forced labor prison camp system, the gulag, that Hank saw or heard about anything to compare with what he was subjected to at Fort Sill.

The movie, *"One Day in the Life of Ivan Denisovich,"* released in 1971, is a fictional presentation of daily life and death struggles wherein the prisoners were, literally, worked to death under extremely harsh conditions in the Soviet Siberian prison camps.

Of course, OCS candidates were not being worked to death. They would have been thrown out if they were thought to be going to die because neither the Army nor the school wanted that blemish on their reputation. But Hank is absolutely certain the conditions the candidates were subjected to relative to civilian life in the United States at that time was as severe as the prisoners in the gulag experienced relative to civilian life in the Soviet Union at the time of their incarceration.

A day in the lives OCS candidates began with the scratching of the needle on the recording of Reveille at 5:30 AM in the winter months... 5:00 AM summer... and the following mad scramble to get dressed, out the door and into formation for a two mile run.

⊷⊷

1964. One morning early in the program he awoke to a change that had a depressing, negative mental effect on him. His cube mate... the quarters were divided with waist high partitions forming "cubes" of space for two candidates... was gone... disappeared.

His bunk was in the stockade state. The mattress was folded at the end of the bunk and all the bed linens were gone. Everything of his was gone. It was as if he was never there, although he was there a short time he was there long enough to experience a physical metamorphic change from skinny to a sculpted, muscular physique.

Hank did not know what happened to him. He was just gone. He could have died. He could have been failing the academic part of the program, although he seemed to be knowledgeable about the courses and doing well. He could have been turned into hamburger and served to the candidates for dinner that evening. He did not know.

This abrupt, disappearance without warning or explanation was a SOP, standard operating procedure, part of the program. Half of the candidates would experience this during the twenty-three weeks of their incarceration… and training.

These expulsions from the program were deliberately handled in this manner to create added mental strain on those left behind. The plan was to eliminate half the class before graduation. They wanted to get rid of those who could not function well when mentally distracted… under fire, so to speak. But they wanted to do it in a way that would result in further eliminations through mental stress and strain. It worked on many. Their commentary indicated when the uncertainty of these disappearing acts and other deliberate attacks on mental stability were getting to them.

Before they were permitted to begin the morning run they were inspected. Demerits were handed out for hanging threads, referred to as lanyards, which were the cords yanked to fire a 105 Howitzer. For boots and brass that were not adequately shined. For not being satisfactorily clean shaven, for a smile or a frown, perceived or real, for whatever reason a member of the cadre could conceive to ensure each candidate had a sufficient number of demerits to be subjected to the Saturday morning "Jarks."

Some mornings they went on a normal two mile jog in platoon formation. Other mornings they did the run and calisthenics in the form of Army Drill One or Two, each of which consisted of ten repetitions of twelve fairly strenuous exercises. Then there were a few special mornings when they added a twist to the program.

One cold, windy morning with snow on the ground and the thermometer hovering around twenty degrees, cadre had the candidates break from formation, run into their "houses"… didn't call them the barracks they were… and return to formation with their foot lockers.

Then after instructed *"Right shoulder foot lockers,"* they did the morning run *w*ith footlockers on their shoulders.

Hank factiously guessed it was so cold they thought the added workout would warm him and the others up. But that was not it. When he returned he found what was planned. It was a footlocker inspection structured to create more demerits. They were told *"Footlocker inspection, three minutes."*

There was a standard layout for footlockers wherein everyone had to have his socks, toothbrush, razor, toothpaste, soap dish, shoe polish, extra belt buckle, hat… everything placed just so. Position and spacing had to be perfect. It took quite a while to get it right. So candidates were careful to keep their lockers "right."

Whenever something was removed, they carefully replaced it. To do all of it from scratch and get it right took fifteen minutes, minimum. A lot of demerits were handed out that morning, as they were another special morning, again compliments of the cadre.

Upon returning from the morning run the candidates found all their clothes, equipment and footlocker contents… everything… in one huge pile in the middle of the floor. They had been what they called *"nuked,"* which was bad because like footlockers, the cubical area had specified places for everything.

Hanging clothes had to be in a certain order with specified distances between hangers. The items on the two shelves allowed were specified, as were their order and spacing. The floor under bunks was the same. Shoes, boots, helmet, canteen and other items had a specific place with distances between each specified.

Hank can't remember how long it took to get it all back together. But this time, since the damage was so great, cadre let the candidates leave the mess until after classes, and permitted some time before they came in and handed out demerits.

There was also special treatment for individuals whenever the cadre decided one needed it. It might have been because of demonstrated endurance and they wanted to see how far they could push everyone, or it could have been because they perceived one might have been pushed to the breaking point and just needed a little extra shove over the edge. None of the candidates ever knew except those among the disappeared.

A few mornings he was given a rough time about the lack of cleanliness of his shave. He was accused of not having shaved. He explained that was incorrect. He shaved every night like everyone else, as they were well aware since one of them monitored even the evening showers. The problem was his heavier than average, dark beard and fair complexion.

In civilian life he always shaved in the mornings, not at night. But OCS candidates were not afforded that opportunity. At OCS there was a mandatory shower and shave time in the evenings, and by morning his beard had grown out sufficiently to cause him to appear less well shaven than the others. They didn't buy his excuses.

For a week he was made to shave in the mornings, outside in plus or minus twenty degree weather. But that was not the worst of it. He had to dry shave. No water, no shaving cream, just the cold weather and a razor dragged across his face to scrape off the stubble.

In his opinion, that would have been more than sufficient punishment, or whatever it was that motivated this, but no. He had to do this while wearing steel helmet, heavy field jacket and gloves. And, he had to perform this task while in a front leaning rest position... the position one must assume to do pushups.

This resulted in him scraping his face with a sharp razor in the cold weather encumbered by his helmet and gloves while holding himself up on one arm. When shaving the right of his face his body was being held up by his left hand. Then, he had to change hands for the other side.

Before he could get up, he was inspected. If the inspector found, or wanted to find, a missed spot, as was usually the case, he had to redo that side... frequently both sides.

Only when the member of the cadre inspecting him approved the shave, or saw a sufficient amount of blood, was he permitted to get up, stand at attention and thank the nice officer for approving his shave. Only then was he dismissed.

While he was being put through this ordeal of butchering his face in the freezing cold for no reason he could discern, he wondered *"What the Hell am I doing here? What would I be doing had I just let my young military career run the course the government predetermined for me? Where would I be and what would I be doing had I been sent to whatever post 504 AG Co Admin APO 306 NY NY was that the Army thought important enough to provide a "SECRET" security clearance to me and divert me from Airborne and Special Forces Training?*

Could it have been a posting in Germany that only six months after their parting in Los Angles, would have put him in close proximity to Heidi? Could she have something to do with it? Was she involved somehow, as he speculated before?

She was either very mature, well-traveled and worldly for her age, or she was older, but all he knows is he never believed in Predestination. He prefers to have a say in the direction of his life. But could his meddling in the direction of his military career have diverted him from a course that would have dramatically changed his life?

It's possible.

❧

After the morning ordeals, candidates were marched to the Mess Hall for another daily ordeal… endeavoring to consume enough fuel to keep themselves strong enough to deal with what they were being subjected to every day.

They could not sit down at the table until ordered to sit. Each table had a Table Commander. When he told them to sit down they had to be careful not to sit on more than the front six inches of the chair. They also had to be careful during the course of the meal.

They had to sit up straight with hands in laps unless they were endeavoring to cut or pick food out of plates and get it to their mouths. If utensils were utilized properly, they could get a bite to their mouths. Then if utensils were properly replaced on the table they could chew and swallow the bite they got into their mouth.

But this was difficult to do. The job of the table commander was to minimize intake of food under the pretense of conditioning to always display proper eating habits and table manners. He accomplished this by making it impossible to consume the meager portions on plates by harassing the hell out of candidates during the entire meal, and if he decided; stopping them from eating by having them stand behind their chair at attention until the meal was ended.

They were not permitted to speak while at the table without asking for and receiving permission. They were not permitted to swallow food they managed to get into their starving mouths if they began chewing before the utensils were returned to the table.

Eating was like the rest of the "training." It was pure Hell. And as in religion wherein depravation is considered one of the courses to a better afterlife; they were also deprived.

Absolutely zero condiments were permitted on the tables. No sugar. No salt. No pepper. No sauces. No spices, also no jellies, preserves or butter, and no stimulants. No coffee. No tea. And it was obvious from the taste. No salt, pepper or spices were utilized in the preparation of the food. Deprivation of taste bud utilization was also part of the "training."

Hank wondered if those planning the meals were Mormons. Or, maybe the meals were from recipe books used in prisons before some degree of humanity was included in the lives of prisoners. He didn't know. But he was certain he was religiously being prepared for some afterlife, if he could survive the current one to be promoted into it.

Whatever the intent of the program, its effect was to weaken. Hank had hardly any fat on his body prior to entering OCS. Yet within two months he lost ten pounds, and when before OCS he could do fifty pushups, after two months, he could barely get past twenty-five.

The table commanders were candidates who, only a couple of months previously, endured what they were subjecting others to. Thus, they had no sympathy. In fact, what they were doing was part of the training for both. They were being monitored and graded on "leadership" while participating in this "training" of others.

Some demonstrated they were just mean bastards who, when given the opportunity, enjoyed the role of bully because they were probably bullies in school. Hank took great pleasure in the fact some of them were to enter the ranks of the disappeared.

He thought these did not deserve to be Commissioned Officers responsible for the well-being of other humans, especially under life or death circumstances. These were people who would be among those who would be the running ones he was asked about at his OCS Board, and whom he would have been happy to dispatch to their future "post."

This eating training was enabled by there being overlapping classes present in the school at the same time. The course was divided into three levels. The first two months candidates were the equivalent of Basic Training "grunts." The second two months they were elevated to the level of non-commissioned officers, or Sergeants, filling the slots normally occupied by them in the real Army. The last two months, they filled the slots occupied by Commissioned Officers.

After breakfast it was back to their houses for whatever was needed for training that day. Then they marched to buses to be taken to the training venue of the day.

Most days were the "college level" classes the Commandant referred to in his welcoming letter. These classes were held in buildings and classrooms like would be found at any public college. Also, as would be found at any college, there were different classes and courses of study, and different groups of students.

Because of this, the facilities were not geared to only the rules, restrictions and requirements of the OCS program. The normal amenities expected in a facility like those were available. They had vending machines. Vending machines full of candy.

Candidates were warned to ignore the vending machines. Use of them was strictly forbidden. Should they be found utilizing the machines or with a product from one of them, there were penalties the extent of which varied, but the minimum was demerits and there was the possibility of disciplinary action. But they were not concerned about that because they were hungry.

Several even had informal meetings about approaching cadre officers about the fact of being hungry and feeling weak, but decided that a waste of time. They were trying to break them down physically and mentally. Thus, they were not going to get any satisfaction there. They resolved to take matters into their own hands.

At the risk of relatively severe penalties, most decided the Payday and Snickers candy bars were too tempting to pass up. Hank did and he knew a few others broke the no vending machine rule... with great satisfaction.

Candidates did not tuck bottoms of their fatigue pants into the tops of their boots. They used blousing rubbers that were twisted fabric coated rubbers with hooks as on a necklace that permitted them to form a circle when the hooks were connected after they were placed around their legs. Then when around the legs, the bottoms of the pants were folded up under them and placed where they would be two or three inches below the tops of boots.

The fit was snug. It had to be. Candidates weren't allowed to use pockets on their uniforms because the little bulges of stuff in pockets would detract from their appearance.

In fact, most of the pockets on uniforms were sewn shut. Therefore, after they had boots on and pants legs positioned snugly around the tops of boots, before buttoning up and latching belts, whatever needed to be carried was dropped down pants' legs where it was easily accessible when the blousing rubber was stretched. Thus, after getting coins needed for the vending machine out of the little coin purse used to avoid rattle, they simply undid their fly and dropped it back down the pant leg.

Quickly downing a Payday or Snickers or two in a toilet stall, as frequently as possible, was risky. But all those extra calories occasionally helped, made Hank feel better, anyway.

CHAPTER 27

OCS PART 2: "LEADERSHIP"

Hank did not find the "college level" academic program as challenging as the Commandant's letter indicated in stating a "working knowledge of basic mathematics, logarithms and trigonometry" was required.

He had four years of high school math, including algebra, geometry and trigonometry, plus college algebra and trig. After a short period, he was reasonably certain he could pull through with a B or a gentleman's C, as usual, without breaking his neck studying, or unduly worrying about it.

After all, he made it through high school with a heavier academic load than most without studying much, working and helping in his father's business, and suffering the stress and strain caused by his mother. Also, during the one year of college he carried a heavy load. Eight to five three days a week. Eight to three two days a week. Eight to noon on Saturdays, and made it through satisfactorily under the stress of getting married and knowing he was not going to be able to continue after the first year, but was going to have to go to work to support himself and two others.

Although the information was the academic portion was sixty-five percent of the grade, one could be brilliant and ace it, but still flunk out if he failed the leadership portion that was only thirty-five percent because to graduate required satisfactory completion of both.

In fact, since all in the class except Hank, and possibly one or two others who had prior military experience, were college graduates, he concluded it was failure in the leadership part of the program that would earn membership in the disappeared group.

It would not have been possible for anyone to have gained entry into Artillery OCS without having studied trigonometry. Thus, it was doubtful any of those college graduates who studied trig would have failed this part of the program unless it was the pressure of the leadership part of the program that got to them. Thus, the sixty-five, thirty-five was probably deliberately misleading... a red herring.

"Leadership" is ambiguous.

When one's ability to be a leader is being determined by others it has to be at least partially subjective, and those determining whether someone has the qualities and characteristics required to satisfy the requirements of the leadership position for which he is being evaluated cannot do this in a vacuum. It must be done within the environment in which the evaluator and the one being evaluated are living and functioning.

The evaluating cadre did not go to class with candidates or look at their academic grades. They were just watching and listening as candidates interacted with them and classmates, and when responding to the stress and strain it was the cadre's job to continuously heap upon them to make life as intolerable as possible. Thus, it was these people who determined whether a candidate graduated and became a Lieutenant... not the academics.

The situation was not unlike domestic life where one can be doing brilliantly at his job, but if he is not taking care of business at home, or is screwing up in some way, he is not likely to be successful there. And if he is not, he is likely to be out. That was the situation at OCS; either get along with, impress, or satisfy the cadre, or you were out.

After all those years with his mother Hank knew he could tolerate whatever they could throw at him to endeavor to "stress" him out of the program. Also, he already determined he possessed a good portion of the characteristics the Army was looking for in terms of leadership when he was promoted into a leadership position within two weeks of induction and was given the training Sergeant position after only four months of military experience.

But there was still one factor of concern.

He never did anything to cause his mother to mistreat him, but she did it anyway. Meanwhile, she did not mistreat his brother... well not intentionally. Although the effect of her treatment of him in terms of the way he dealt with his own life amounted to her mistreating him... actually sacrificing him for her own subjective reasons.

There it was. His mother did not dislike him for anything he did to her or his brother. She disliked and treated him as she did for subjective reasons. The fact of his doing reasonably well in school had zero bearing on her treatment of him. Therefore, subjectivity was of much more concern to Hank than academics.

Dealing with a group of different individuals successfully is much more difficult than dealing with a bunch of numbers. There are many more people who can do difficult math successfully than who can successfully motivate, impress and lead other people. And one who is good at this can hire all the math whizzes he needs, but if he needs others to provide leadership throughout his organization he will find these people difficult to find.

Hank's focus was on getting along, not irritating, or alienating anyone in any way, and coping with the overall stressful situation in ways that would show he was difficult to rattle... that it would be difficult to cause him to fail to function well under fire, additionally, to be the neatest, most squared away in terms of appearance, the condition of his space, footgear, brass, to minimize the number of demerits received. Not to do anything to detract from his already proven leadership characteristics.

He managed this quite well, based on the number of demerits he received… or did not receive. He did fewer Jarks than anyone else in his house. He also received official verbal recognition of this from the cadre staff.

Toward the end of the program, he was called to the office of Lieutenant Gatehouse, which made him think, *"Oh, no! This can't be good for me."* But he was wrong.

Gatehouse was the one who was hardest on him. He was also the most disliked of the cadre by all candidates. He was what they called a *"little prick."*

He did not seem to like anyone. But he seemed to hold a special place in that regard for Hank. So he could not anticipate being called to his office to be a pleasant experience.

And that's the way it began. When he walked in and reported, Gatehouse seemed his usual self, corrected him about something he said. Then he got to what he wanted to see him about when he said, *"You are not the smartest guy in the class, but we* [cadre staff] *think you have the coolest head we have ever seen. For that, we have rated you, number two in the class."*

Now, it should be noted: Hank was not number two in the overall class, including academics where he ranked a good B, as was his target. But this assessment by the cadre of the subjective part he was concerned about because he determined it was more important meant more than the overall grade.

Also, it was one of the few aspects of his life to which he could attribute his success to his mother. It was not her intent, but she was the only one he could give full credit for his *"coolest head"* ranking.

"Leadership," as they classified it in Officer Candidate School academic classes, which included problem solving and military subjects was his third highest grade.

Surprisingly, Communication & Electronics and Target Acquisition, which were pretty important since ultimately that's what it was all about, were his two best grades. And, not surprisingly, math-heavy Gunnery was his lowest… right after another of his least favorite things, Artillery Transport that was about trucks.

⚔ ⚔

The days they were not in the "college" classes, the candidates went to the field for participation in problem solving, other graded leadership tasks, and familiarization and work with the actual functioning of an artillery battery.

They spent time working in the fire direction center where fire missions are received, calculated and passed on to the gun batteries where soldiers adjust the guns and fire them according to the instructions given to them by the Battery Commander based on instructions sent to him from the fire direction center.

Time was also spent as members of an actual artillery battery, loading, adjusting the guns for the missions received and firing them.

In the course of the training, candidates filled every position in a gun battery from the ones loading the powder charges into the shell casings, adjusting the settings on projectiles that determine when the round explodes relative to its proximity to the ground, manning the guns, adjusting settings for elevation and deflection, putting the ammunition into the gun, pulling the lanyard to fire it and functioning as Battery Commander.

They did field surveying just like surveying in construction and engineering. Not one of Hank's favorite things, especially on cold January and February mornings with nothing between Oklahoma and the North Pole from where it seemed the icy wind that cut through their field jackets, heavy wool shirts and pants and long handle underwear originated.

Spent time becoming familiar with various artillery pieces, 105 Howitzer - the work horse of Artillery, 155 Howitzer - the most accurate Artillery piece ever. 175 Howitzer, a long barreled piece, so long it appeared to be drooping, capable of putting a round into an oil drum from twenty miles away, down range over the city of Lawton. Self-propelled eight inch artillery that demonstrated advanced technology in which the military was at least two decades ahead of civilian technology endeavors at the time when it received a fire mission as it was cruising down the road at thirty miles per hour.

Basically a tank with an Artillery piece on it for hitting long range targets, whereas a regular tank is designed for war against other tanks, or close-in targets, it was just an artillery piece with its own armored transportation that when it received a fire mission stopped quickly, front and rear dozer-like blades stuck into the ground, the turret began turning as the gun barrel adjusted up or down, and, Bang! It fired within seconds, hitting a target somewhere in the unseen distance decades before civilians had advanced computers or Global Positioning Systems.

The most time in the field was spent in Target Acquisition and directing fire, which was the most critical part of the entire Artillery task of laying fire on a target. This was also the most enjoyable part of the entire OCS experience… the equivalent of firing the M 60 machine gun in AIT… but it was what he learned about this almost four months into the OSC program that prompted him to employ *"Bob's rule,"* again.

For this part of the training, candidates sat in folding chairs on top of a hill with maps of the surrounding area they could see for miles around. An Artillery Officer was in charge. He was not a member of the OCS Cadre. He was on the staff of the Artillery School.

In the distance, there were many old disused tanks and automobiles. The officer would select a candidate to take a chair out in front of the rest. Then he would identify a target such as an old tank or car by color and direction from where they were.

They would look at their maps and determine the coordinates, longitude and latitude, of the target the officer identified. After determining the coordinates, the one in the hot seat would give his determined coordinates to the officer and call for adjusting fire.

A few seconds later the sound of the artillery round passing overhead would be heard. At that point everyone would put field glasses, binoculars, to their eyes and the one in the hot seat would determine where the round hit relative to the coordinates he provided.

After that he would give instructions like, *"Add 100, right 100,"* which meant the target was 100 yards beyond and 100 yards to the right of where the round he called for hit the ground. If he was sure his instructions would put the fire on the target, he would so indicate by calling, *"Fire for effect."*

Seconds later the sound of eighteen artillery rounds passing overhead would be heard. But if he was not sure his instructions were on target, he would call for another single adjusting round.

Grading was on how quickly the candidate could get it right... the rounds on target, which was important because the more adjusting rounds called for, the more time the enemy would have to determine where the observer directing fire on him was located and do the same to him. This was always going to be a high spot... church steeple, hill top... a place with a view of the area. So, if you were not quickly correct, you would be dead.

Having eighteen 105 Howitzers, the fire direction center, all the personnel behind this training and the cost of the ammunition being fired was pretty expensive.

One day, a candidate who was a Kansas State football player and knew he was not going to Vietnam because he had a deal to play football for an Army football team called *"Fire for effect."* As he got up, picked up his chair and headed back to join the rest because his time in the hot seat was over, the eighteen rounds passed overhead. At that time, he said, *"Damn. This is really a rich man's sport."*

That was true in the context in which it was said. But truth is; it would never be a rich man's sport unless the "rich man" was a politician or executive at a "defense" company participating vicariously.

Few rich men were ever going to be forward observers. No. Forward observer was the entry level position for the Officer Corps in the Artillery. Neither rich men, nor their sons, ever enter any enterprise in the entry level position, especially not this "enterprise."

As the candidate said, *"This is a rich man's sport."* But the rich men engaged in it were never going to be sitting on hills, or church steeples in Vietnam directing artillery fire onto poor, hapless Vietnamese citizens in the sweltering heat and humidity of Vietnam.

They were going to be in their big, cushy chairs in tall office buildings reviewing the profit reports on sales of artillery weapons, artillery shells, fire direction center equipment and the other implements of war used and consumed in the unnecessary invasion and attack on that small country almost a half a world away from the comforts of Washington, D.C. where the other rich men responsible for it were sitting, reviewing the body count reports sent to them by their "management" team at MACV.

However, Hank did agree with the comment in the context in which it was stated. This was entertainment for candidates, entertainment in a world otherwise full of only stress, strain, depravation, abuse and fear.

What guy doesn't like blowing up stuff and enjoying the noise and sparks? Sort of like a movie on Saturday or football game on Sunday, a diversion from the rest of his week.

Hank was certain the cadre and the "management" of the Artillery School were also aware of the entertainment aspect of this. But it was purposeful.

The reason so much time was spent on this was; it was the meat of the course. This was what it was all about. The rest would be of benefit to the military only to the degree it was retained in the heads of those who survived their assignments as forward observers.

The candidates were there to become proficient at locating a target, conveying the correct coordinates to the fire direction center and blowing the hell out of whatever or whoever was the target... nothing else. No "leadership" required.

That the government was willing to spend the equivalent of five hundred thousand 2013 dollars on each candidate selected from what seemed to be the top one percent of its Army in terms of intellect and education to be trained only for this function with the expectation he would last an average of three minutes in combat that was not necessary informs us a lot about the nature of those in control of our future for the last four decades: it was worth this expenditure in money and human life just to "kill" one target.

Given that war is about money, especially unnecessary war, it must have been determined that one successful mission would generate a sufficiently larger expansion of the conflict to generate a satisfactory return on investment in the shells used in the "kill."

The human element? The highly trained, fairly intelligent, Commissioned Officer? Not a consideration. Not a problem. Just another example of what the U.S. Government and its military call *"collateral damage,"* today.

It could be called this because it was the result of killing the enemy that could not have been killed without the firing and resulting explosion that could result in the enemy sending back some kind of explosion causing his death. Ergo: *"collateral damage."*

The other training in the "college" level classes was mostly of benefit to the Army or the trainee to the extent it included map reading, enhancing proficiency and speed in acquiring a target and getting fire on it. The rest of this training would have only a small, residual value to the extent forward observers survived and were able to progress to fire direction center supervision or Battery Commander positions and above in the Artillery.

"Leadership" training and grading was a misnomer.

The concern by the Army about its future forward observers was not about potential to lead other men in combat. The concern was whether they could be depended upon in critical combat situations to do the job of the forward observer.

It did not require "leadership" to keep one's head cool in a combat situation and not be distracted from completing the task at hand if he was alone on high ground, in a tree, or in a tall structure. The concern was whether he could do the forward observer job under severe stress and strain. That was it.

"Leadership" would only be of value in the officers who survived the entry level job.

—◄—►—

Given all this, it would seem the disappeared ones were the lucky ones and those who were to graduate were the unlucky ones.

Those who failed to complete the course successfully and receive their commissions in the Artillery were sent off to complete their time as enlisted men in mostly non high profile positions with a much longer life expectancy than three minutes.

Since halfway through the course indications were Hank had a fairly high probability of graduating, receiving a commission and becoming a forward observer, it was the three minute life expectancy part that caught his attention.

This definitely did not comport with his sole objective of survival. And, as he vowed, they had not trained that objective out of him. But options seemed non extant. Was there a way out?

How about *"Bob"?*

BATTERY E
U. S. ARMY ARTILLERY AND MISSILE OFFICER CANDIDATE SCHOOL
Fort Sill, Oklahoma

24 March 1964

SUBJECT: Request for Commission in the Corps of Engineers
TO: Commandant
                   U. S. Army Artillery and Missile
                   Officer Candidate School
                   Fort Sill, Oklahoma

1. I request Commission in the Corps of Engineers upon completion of Officer Candidate School.

2. The following is submitted for consideration:

a. I have had considerable experience in the construction business. Working in all phases of the business, I have experience in estimating, contract negotiations, purchasing and direct supervision in the field. In the past I have been concerned with the excavating and paving business, but as of the last two (2) years my primary interest has been in industrial and commercial fabricated steel buildings. In dealing with steel buildings, I also did some designing and worked in close relation with our Architect and Engineer.

b. I have completed 33 hours of Architectural Engineering at Arlington State College. I have also completed two years of drafting, as well as math courses including College Trig. and Engineering Algebra. I have designed and built residences and several fallout shelters in the Dallas area.

3. Since my primary interests, capabilities, and experience are closely allied to the Engineers field and its components, it is felt that a Commission in the Corps of Engineers would best serve the interests of the services through full utilization of my education, experience and potential.

Henry Thread
SergeantE5
Battery E, USAA&MOCS

What? It was worth a try. What were they going to do... demote him?

⟫╫ ╫⟪

After classes activities varied, dependent upon the training that day. Some days they dressed and marched in a parade or just practiced on the parade grounds. Other days were spent doing extra cleaning in their houses, polishing brass, boots and shoes. Some days it was extra physical training.

Whatever, it was terminated in time for another formation and opportunity for more demerits then marching off to the Mess for another joyful experience at the dining table.

After dinner, back to their "houses" for three hours of study, a communal shower and shave, and getting ready for the next day until lights out at ten P.M.

Candidates were not to attempt to study or do anything other than sleep until the scratching of the needle on the record seven or seven and one-half hours later signaled the beginning of another fun filled day.

After lights out, it was customary for cadre or those who attained the third level of training to quietly sneak into the houses endeavoring to catch candidates trying to get in a little extra studying with a light under their covers. This would accomplish nothing but extra demerits... best not to try it.

So it went Monday through Friday, and sometimes Saturday mornings. But for the most part, Saturdays were reserved for the famous Jark March. This was named for the general who supposedly devised this particular torture as payment for accumulated demerits.

It was four point two miles from the OCS area parking lot to the top of a little hill called NB4 and back. The hill had a concrete block house on its peak.

The uniform for this sport was fatigues, combat boots, steel helmet, full dress pistol belt with full canteen and standard issue combat rifle, weighing nine and one-half pounds, held at port arms, which was at chest height with the left hand palm up under the stock and the right hand palm down behind the trigger guard.

Candidates were formed into platoons of columns ten or twelve men long, with...just to make it interesting... the tallest men with the longest legs at the front of the columns. Then there was a quick march in formation to the base of the hill where they could break formation to get to the top and back down as quickly as they could. Back at the bottom they were formed into platoons again for the trip back to the OCS area parking lot.

This had to be completed in less than forty-two minutes to remove the number of demerits that required the Jark. If it was not completed within forty-two minutes or less, they were given a fifteen minute rest and another go at it. Also, if one had enough demerits for two Jarks, they would be done back to back fifteen minutes apart, but no problem. For physical emergencies, an ambulance was always following. During the hot season, it was needed a few times.

One could not graduate, no matter what his academic grades or leadership ranking, until all his accumulated Jarks were "marched" off. Thus, toward the end of the course, there was a lot of Jarking off of demerits.

Halfway through the course, life at OCS became a little less demanding either because it really was, or because of acclimation to it. But it was probably real in some ways.

Candidates were no longer "grunt" equivalents. Relative to the other candidates at the school, they were the equivalent of NCOs with some of that traditional responsibility for keeping things operating in good military fashion.

Because of these added responsibilities, cadre had to give a little slack for candidates to perform them. But there was no slack in the amount of time fully engaged in the demanding nature of the program. Also, attrition continued, as it would almost right up to the end. The only difference being in the way the disappearing ones were treated.

Rather than becoming hamburger, there were indications some, having made it into the third trimester of the program without having been made disappear, were given a second chance.

They were set back to the last two months of the class behind. Then if they corrected whatever got them into trouble, and they performed satisfactorily during the second go at the last two months, they could graduate with the next class.

The last two months were noticeably less demanding in the stress department, in some ways. There was still stress. But not abuse. The physical program continued. But, given the prior four months of running and exercise, everyone who remained was in excellent physical condition. So the physical part of the program was "no sweat," except the Jarks.

CHAPTER 28
OCS PART 3: SUCCESS

This third trimester was lighter on mental harassment in the petty ways it was previously dealt out. It was more intellectual. Candidates had responsibilities. They were cycled through the various Officers positions that existed in a real Artillery Battery, and wore identifying insignia that made them fair game for any member of the cadre.

They had to know the numbers and details of their unit of responsibility. If they were stopped by a member of the cadre, he could ask questions about anything he desired, including questions about their temporary faux command.

If they did not answer correctly, they received demerits. They were constantly being graded. It was still evaluation of performance under stressful conditions... just a different kind of stress.

One week Hank was Unit Information Officer. In this position he had to pick an international subject of interest to those in the military, research it, write a brief and make a Saturday morning oral presentation to candidates and cadre who could also ask questions.

He chose the ongoing religious differences between the Turkish Muslim and Greek Christian populations on the Mediterranean island of Cyprus that had recently boiled over into serious, physical conflict, again. He must have done O.K. because he was not disappeared or recycled after his presentation.

By the middle of the program, candidates began to have time off occasionally on weekends if they did not have a Jark or were not restricted due to disciplinary action, which Hank never was. So since he missed out on the Jark fun some weekends he was able to go into Lawton overnight two or three times.

This time off was enhanced by having the car he drove to his post again, and the Impala was waiting in the parking lot for the times he could use it.

He could afford a hotel room for overnighters those two or three times he had an overnight pass because his pay grade was upped to E5 upon entry to OCS, increasing to $145.24 per month, which increased his net to over a $100.00 per month.

Betsy came to visit one weekend when he had a pass. That was a really pleasant break from the OCS world. He thought it too bad he could not take her back to the OCS area where she would have been a big hit. She probably would have been recognized because her photo was around, in public, for most of the four prior four months.

During these first four months of the program, candidates carried clipboards when going to the "college" classes. During the remaining two months, they carried little black notebooks almost all the time because they were needed to keep the information regarding their Officer's duties with them at all times, except during physical training.

When carrying the clipboards they were allowed to put whatever they wanted, within reason, on the back of them for decoration. On Hank's he placed an eight by ten glossy photo of Betsy in a one piece bathing suit she sent to him for that purpose.

Given the confined nature of the OCS program the first four months and the twenty-something males being confined, he could not have attracted more attention if he had the Playmate centerfold on his clipboard. In person, those widely viewed, long legs would have been a really big hit.

In addition to completing their Jarks and other prerequisites for graduation, candidates also had to satisfactorily complete an Escape and Evasion course.

This was an event where they were dismissed from a location with only a map just after sunset, and had to traverse several miles of enemy territory on foot to a point indicated on the map before sunrise without being captured.

During his time in the military Hank had to complete other E & E courses, including another similar to this one in distance and time. But this being OCS, just completing an E & E course would not have been sufficiently difficult.

Early in the day they were taken into the field near a decent size river, in terms of its width and flow. There was a cliff that was at least sixty feet in height on one side of it they spent several hours engaged in going up and rappelling down. Finally, they departed this venue by making their way across the river by pulling themselves across with their arms, on a very long, sagging cable, while hanging by the backs of their knees.

He wondered if this was training for the future in case the high ground he was occupying as forward observer had to be evacuated suddenly. Or maybe they were going to have need for this in the E & E course that night?

Since they were up at 5:00 AM that morning and would be up until that time the next morning, they were either going to need this training for the evening event or it was just to tire them out before the E&E to make it more challenging. He managed to finish the course without encountering a river or a cliff.

During the event, if they were captured prior to reaching their destination they were returned to the point of origin, and from there were permitted to start over. But, as with everything else in the OCS program, it was not that simple.

For starters, it was obviously best not to get captured. But if one was captured, it was best to have it happen early. The farther through the course when captured, the greater the time required and total distance to be traversed to the finish because of having to cover the already traversed distance again.

Unfortunately, he was captured, as were most. But fortunately, he was, as were many, captured early... within a mile or so of the starting point. This was obviously for a reason.

When captured they were not returned to the point of origin just to be turned loose to have another go at it. They were held there for a while to lessen the time remaining, which should have been a sufficient delay to add to the degree of difficulty in completing the course, but oh no, not for OCS Cadre.

The starting point was beside a running stream that was about twenty feet wide and two feet deep. In the middle of it was a containment area made of three rolls of concertina wire.

Captured prisoners were placed inside that area and left to stand in the flowing water long enough for boots, socks and feet to be thoroughly soaked, water logged. This could be half an hour... more or less... whatever cadre running the event decided.

Additionally, if someone was a bit troublesome when he was captured, he was subjected to a much greater degree of stress before being permitted to start over.

Standing in the middle of the stream outside the containment area was one of those six feet tall metal lockers like the ones in locker rooms that are large enough for someone to stand inside. The difficult prisoner was placed inside this cramped space for the time the others were held in the containment area. If he complained or did anything other than quietly suffer through this, they kicked and beat on the outside of the locker subjecting the one in it, in Hank's opinion, to a mild form of torture. He avoided that. Only got his feet wet, but he did witness one candidate subjected to the locker torture.

Although he finished within the time required, his night did not have a happy ending.

Sometime after midnight, he was standing at the rear of a three-quarter ton vehicle, which is much like a large pickup truck, but in the usual, military squared off form.

This vehicle was one of many in a multi vehicle convoy that was to take them back to the OCS area after everyone finished the course and was accounted for.

The place on the road where the convoy was parked had a slight downhill slope in the direction in which the convoy was headed. The three quarter ton had a pickup-like tailgate that was down. This tailgate was between the top of Hank's legs and waist in height off the ground where he was standing.

Suddenly, someone hollered *"Watch out!"* loudly and close enough for Hank to realize it was intended for him. He turned just in time to see the headlights of the duce and a half, a truck over three times the size of the one he was standing behind, that was parked about ten feet behind it, coming toward him.

It was too close for him to get out of the way. He instinctively jumped up, as if to get into the back of the three quarter ton while putting his right hand down, as anyone would normally, to protect against the truck coming toward him.

His thighs and right hand were pinned between the large steel bumper of the duce and a half and the edge of the three quarter ton tailgate that was only about an inch and a half thick. His feet were over a foot off the ground.

At the hospital, when the accident was described to the examining doctor he told Hank he didn't know how lucky he was. In his opinion, had he not jumped, his pelvis would have been crushed and he would have been a paraplegic the rest of his life. But because of his jump, the muscle tissue of his thighs was compressed around the femurs, and because his hand was also pressed into that soft tissue, none of the bones in his hand were broken.

Lucky indeed. He survived so many truck related accidents his remaining cat life count was beginning to run really low. If our count is correct, this was the fifth and he had only four to go, but should the other vehicle accident be included in the count he had used six. Twenty-four years old and only three of nine lives left.

Over the next few days, a foot long section of both thighs and his right hand went through all the color stages of serious bruising, and he had difficulty walking. It was painful. But what was very disconcerting, actually frightening, was when all that bruised tissue was almost black it looked as if his legs and hand were going to rot off.

The Saturday after the accident, he had accumulated a sufficient number of demerits for a Jark, which he endeavored to do, but couldn't keep up and fell out of formation.

The OCS Artillery Officer Commandant he had the interview with as a result of his letter requesting a commission in the Corps of Engineers, rather than the Artillery, drove up and offered him a ride in his car. He thanked him and refused. The Commandant responded he "*knew*" he wouldn't accept and wished him "*luck*," something he was inclined to do. Something about that bothered Hank. But he finished that Jark.

Although it took him a lot longer than forty-two minutes, they gave him credit for it, permitting him to finish something else.

HEADQUARTERS

U. S. ARMY ARTILLARY AND MISSILE CNNTER

Fort Sill, Oklahoma 73504

SPECIAL ORDERS

NUMBER   111   11 May 1964

24. TC 416. By order SA fol indiv DISCHARGED from enlisted status eff on EDSCA FPUR EAD as commissioned officer.

Type disch: Honorable - DD Form 256A

EDSCA: 25 May 64

HEADQUARTERS

U. S. ARMY ARTILLERY AND MISSILE CENTER

Fort Sill, Oklahoma 73504

SPECIAL ORDERS   14 May 1964

NUMBER   114

53. TC 220. Fol reassignment dir.

2D LT ENGR USAR P1331 HQ & HQ Btry USAAMOCS Ft Sill Okla TDPFO

TDY enr to: Ft Belvoir, Va

Rept date (TDY): 6 Jun 64

Pd (TDY) Approx 9 weeks

Crs: Engr Basic Off Crs (5-A-C20)

Asg to: 168th Engr Bn (Cbt) Ft Polk La

Rept date: 3 Sept 64

Secty clnc: SECRET

HEADQUARTERS
U. S. ARMY ARTILLERY AND MISSILE SCHOOL
Fort Sill, Oklahoma 73504

AKPSIOC   26 May 1964

SUBJECT: Appointment as a reserve Commissioned Officer in the Army Under Title 10 United States Code, Section 591 and Section 593

A: **Engr**
B: **1331**
C: **AR 350-50**

1. By direction of the President you are appointed a Reserve Commissioned officer in the Army, effective upon your acceptance, in the grade and with the service number shown above. Your branch and component assignment are shown after A, above.

2. This appointment is for an indefinite term.

What all of these orders meant was; on May 25, 1964 Hank was to be given an Honorable Discharge as an enlisted man. The next day, May 26, 1964, he was going to graduate from Artillery OCS and be appointed a commissioned officer in the Corps of Engineers only one year and three weeks after he was inducted into the U.S. Army.

After receiving the commission, his first assignment was to report to Fort Belvoir, Virginia on June 6, 1964 for nine weeks of Engineer Basic Officer Course.

During that time he was going to receive extra, Temporary Duty Pay. After that he was to report to the 168th Combat Engineer Battalion at Fort Polk, Louisiana on September 3, 1964, and, oh yes; the Army would own him for "an indefinite term."

This was pretty astounding for an inductee with only one year of college that could not have happened had not the OCS Commandant provided a positive recommendation for a commission in the Corps as a result of the personal interview he conducted with Hank after receipt of his "request" letter.

This was not the first, nor the last, time he received a position, recommendation, promotion or acceptance to something for which he was sorely lacking formal qualifications on the basis of a personal interview.

It all seemed so easy. Did he just give good interviews, or was there something else going on? Will he or we ever know?

⟞⟤ ⟝⟣

From Hank's point of view this meant he was almost thirteen months into his 24 month obligation, he experienced a hell of a lot and again succeeded in ways he could never have dreamed.

His time in the army was definitely fast track… seemed almost like inside track for some reason unknown to him.

He was promoted twice without asking, and got everything he asked for. Very un-Army-like from what he has been told by everyone he has spoken with about this, including career Army Officers. But it was not over. He would be promoted again without asking. Was he really lucky?

He successfully completed the most physically and mentally demanding training course in the entire U.S. Military, other than Navy Seal training. Learned more about himself than he could have ever thought possible and gone from slick sleeve private E1 inductee with only one year of college to a commissioned Second Lieutenant in the branch of the Army with the highest average education level of any branch of the U.S. military services… all in only thirteen months… and was going to another nine weeks of training before being sent back to Fort Polk where he began his Army career thirteen months previously.

"*Bob's rule*" came through again, big time.

Had he not asked, he would not have been accepted and completed six months of OCS, would not have been commissioned in the Corps of Engineers and would not be assigned to another nine weeks of training.

On the most base level, we must agree what Hank received as a result of applying "*Bob's rule*"... the added respect and prestige of Gold Bars on his collars, a five hundred eighty percent increase in net compensation from $50.00 per month to $290.00, including allowances, and an added eight months deferral from the possibility of assignment to Vietnam... was a much better deal than just getting laid for one night.

However, the Commandant's congratulations letter of welcome to OCS six months earlier did not come even remotely close to describing the amount and level of "rigorous mental and physical pressure... strict discipline, vigorous physical training... extreme weather conditions" candidates were subjected to.

The vernacular of those who endured it is much closer to the reality of it: "*It was a Bitch!*"

It was such a "*Bitch*" only fifty-one of the one hundred and nine candidates who began the program in Hank's class completed it and were commissioned Officers.

Thus, only 46.8 percent of those who began the course finished it. That amounts to an attrition rate of over fifty-three percent... an unheard of percentage of failure in any course, anywhere.

It was something he wanted so badly to get out of so many times during those twenty-three weeks he doesn't think he could be paid enough to repeat it. But it was the experience of a lifetime. It was the one that contributed most to everything he has done since.

It was the proving ground for his understanding of his abilities and lack of limitations... how much physically and mentally he is able to deal with without being adversely affected.

It created a high pain threshold for both. Not just for Hank, but for all who completed it.

They have to be a tough, smart bunch of sons of a *"Bitch"* you could trust with your life.

To be continued...

IN PART II

Stay with Hank as he continues post Officer Candidate School ... to the Officer Corps and a continuation of his endeavor to avoid being sent to die needlessly in a jungle half way around the world just because those in charge of his government decided to start an unnecessary war there.

ABOUT THE AUTHOR

A college dropout with a Master's Degree from Harvard University, he spent the past sixty, plus years experiencing the world in a diversity of ways, some by choice, some not.

He worked construction, was an enlisted man, Non-Commissioned and Commissioned Officer and staff member of a prestigious U.S. military school, small business owner, held multiple executive management positions, including Chief Operating Officer and board member of a NYSE company at the age of thirty-four, conducted business in North America, Australia where he started a company, Europe where he also lived, and Asia, including the Philippines, Japan, Taiwan and the People's Republic of China.

These adventures, plus experience and successes in consulting, management and investment in marketing, real estate, finance and the entertainment industry, and a little fun along the way, resulted in his experiencing the world as most Americans never do.

www.ingramcontent.com/pod-product-compliance
Lightning Source LLC
LaVergne TN
LVHW011216080426
835509LV00005B/149